STREAK

Joe DiMaggio
and the Summer of '41

Michael Seidel

With a new afterword by the author

INDEXES BY SKIP McAFEE OF THE
SOCIETY OF AMERICAN BASEBALL RESEARCH

UNIVERSITY OF NEBRASKA PRESS
LINCOLN AND LONDON

Library of Congress Cataloging-in-Publication Data
Seidel, Michael, 1943–
Streak: Joe DiMaggio and the summer of '41 / Michael Seidel; with a
new afterword by the author; indexes by Skip McAfee.
p.   cm.
Originally published: New York: McGraw-Hill, c1988.
Includes indexes.
ISBN 0-8032-9293-7 (pbk.: alk. paper)
1. DiMaggio, Joe, 1914–99   2. Baseball players—United States—
Biography.   I. Title.
GV865.D5 S45   2002
796.357′092—dc21
[B]
2001052238

To the Memory of Jack Seidel

for whom Joe DiMaggio was as great a source
of admiration and wonder
as he has always been for me

CONTENTS

It's amazing the hold he has on people after all these years. You would think a whole new generation of baseball fans had grown up who didn't know him, but they know him just as well as their fathers did.

—Lefty Gomez

PREFACE

Great streaks in baseball are idealized versions of the game it-self. They combine absolutes of concentration and duration; they exhibit on a continuous basis what one normally expects inter-mittently; their pace is glacial, and their crucial moments are lightning-quick. The very days of a streak generate all the cap-tivating rhythms associated with baseball: its anticipatory poten-tial, its tensions, its attenuations, its gratifications. And the individual effort required for a personal hitting streak is com-parable to what heroic legend calls the *aristeia*, whereby great en-ergies are gathered for a day, dispensed, and then regenerated for yet another day in an epic wonder of consistency.

No other sustained performance in the history of baseball builds with the drama and explodes with the energy of Joe DiMaggio's 56-game consecutive hitting streak launched on a hazy Thursday afternoon in New York on May 15, 1941, and grounded on a damp summer night in Cleveland on July 17. Surely, none is more mem-orable. The following pages, in prose and pictures, focus on 56 base-ball games and on the unforgettable days of a spring and summer in America. There are other books that chronicle the whole DiMag-gio saga, including the private marital obsessions that have contrib-uted to Joe DiMaggio's place in the order of things through the 1950s and 1960s. I am not charting the biography of a man but the rhythms of a legendary sequence, perhaps the most admired se-quence in sports history. To be legendary is to be worthy of written record—that is what legendary means. My intent is to inscribe DiMaggio's great streak in a context worthy of the memories it evokes.

In a recent film version of Raymond Chandler's *Farewell, My Lovely,* set in the spring and summer of 1941, Robert Mitchum, playing Philip Marlowe, follows the magical course of DiMaggio's 56-game streak in counterpoint to his own experiences in the sleazy night world of murderers, frauds, freaks, hookers, and addicts. The daytime world of baseball, sunshine, and energy is antithetical to Marlowe's misadventures and somehow restorative after them. But in a larger sense, even beyond Marlowe's immediate comprehension, the tracking of DiMaggio's streak in the movie is deeply nostalgic. Marlowe imagines through DiMaggio's presence the heroic best of a land in its last summer glory before the wartime winter of its discontent.

DiMaggio began hitting during the spring thaw of Hitler's ruination machine in Europe, and he continued during a time of massive preparation in America for a war at once anticipated and dreaded. The days of the streak record the energies in a land preoccupied by war but as yet untested and unscarred by it. Early in 1941 America was excited by heroic prospects and frightened by bleak realities; fascinated by air power as a symbol of the frontier of modern adventure and horrified by the beginnings of saturation bombing in Europe; rallied by the concerted effort, especially in the media, to generate new reserves of heroic mythology and depressed by the Nazi threat casting an indecent pall over the western world; thrilled by the arming of democracy and spellbound by powerful isolationist voices such as that of the greatest American hero of all, Charles Lindbergh.

On the day DiMaggio's streak began, headlines the world over bannered the bizarre solo flight and parachute jump of Rudolf Hess into Scotland a few days earlier. A few days later, in silence and in secret, a crack division of Hitler's paratroopers were poised on Athenian shores for an innovative and daring aerial attack on the oldest civilized island in the history of the world, Crete. Before DiMaggio's streak was over the nation and the world would bear witness to the absorbing and climactic tracking of the huge German battleship *Bismarck;* the mysterious saga of the American merchant ship *Robin Moor* and the lifeboat odyssey of its passengers; the largest military campaign ever in world history, Hitler's monumental invasion of his nominal Russian ally along a 1,300-mile front on June 22, 1941; and the martial posturing in America culminating in midsummer with the hullaballoo over the first dispatch of American troops to a war zone, Iceland and its crucial Atlantic trade lanes.

Just three days after DiMaggio's streak ended in July, a secret project in England reporting on new weapons concluded that the Allies had the capacity to produce the atomic bomb before Hitler's Germany. The British began work immediately, and so would America. That legacy of the war we have borne ever since. It is the cusplike quality of 1941, before any real recognition of the outrages then in embryo—the total Holocaust in Europe and the dawn of the atomic age—that helps account for the nostalgic strength of the year's appeal today.

The events, sagas, and personal histories crosscutting those fabled days include the names of some of the greatest statesmen and henchmen the world has ever known as well as the names of other men, women, and a few beasts still very much alive in memory if not in flesh: Roosevelt, Churchill, de Gaulle, Stalin, Hitler, Mussolini, Hess, and Pétain, along with Charles Lindbergh, Henry Ford, John D. Rockefeller, Ronald Reagan, Gary Cooper, Humphrey Bogart, Tallulah Bankhead, Hope and Crosby, Abbott and Costello, Gene Tierney, Orson Welles, Veronica Lake, Rita Hayworth, Noël Coward, George Bernard Shaw, Fritz Kreisler, Lillian Hellman, Ernest Hemingway, Harry Truman, Claude Pepper, Lyndon Johnson, Joe and Jack Kennedy, Fiorello La Guardia, Lou Gehrig, Joe Louis, Billy Conn, Max Schmeling, Sugar Ray Robinson, Craig Wood, Bobby Riggs, and Whirlaway.

What follows is a journal of DiMaggio's streak and its games, of the players who played in them and remember them, of what actually occurred in them, of what made up the texture of life in America and in the world surrounding them. Baseball offered the land a good deal to remember in 1941: the drive of Ted Williams toward the .400 barrier, the approach of the immortal Lefty Grove toward his 300th victory, the Yankees' team consecutive-game home-run record enfolded so neatly within DiMaggio's streak, the dramatic and scorching race between the Dodgers and the Cardinals for the National League pennant, and, finally, a moment of infamy in October—Mickey Owen's passed ball in the fourth game of the '41 World Series. But DiMaggio's legendary 56-game streak will always remain the season's crowning achievement.

Once the streak was picked up by the press and the fans in 1941, its daily rhythm became part of a national myth in a sport calling itself the national pastime. As an emblem of consistency under mounting pressure, the streak surely touched a responsive chord in prewar America and was recognized to have done so immediately by those excited enough to speculate about its significance. To tell the story of the streak is to tell many interweaving stories of the year, to enrich a legend with details that make its best moments truly epochal. These are famous games and cherished times, and the Streak Journal records them. While there are games within the sequence that shed familiar light on baseball recollections, there are also forgotten games that shed new light, clearing up some distortions that add little luster to a legend that shines more brightly without them.

When I spoke to some of the key players from the 1941 Yankees and around the league about the days of DiMaggio's streak, they had forgotten much and distorted some, but they also had particular reasons for recalling streak games that otherwise might be lost to an account of the record and, in several instances, that led to significant revisions of streak lore. For example, the young Yankee Johnny Sturm, who played for only one year, 1941, before he was injured in the war, recollects the opening games of DiMaggio's streak as no other player at the time could or would. Here's why. The Yankees were slumping badly, and their manager, Joe McCarthy, had just rearranged the lineup. Sturm was inserted at first base, and he caught fire for a couple of weeks, logging a brief streak of his own near the beginning of DiMaggio's. Moreover, Yankee catcher Bill Dickey was in the middle of a 17-game hitting streak and Frankie Crosetti, back in the lineup with Sturm after displacing the rookie Phil Rizzuto at short, also was hitting on a daily basis. Sturm has vivid memories of these veterans all sustaining streaks, Dickey and DiMaggio ahead of him and Crosetti a game behind. He literally began as a regular swinging with the stars.

Recall is by its nature selective and oddly associational. A red-hot Johnny Sturm, remembering his debut and playing out a little private drama in which he matched Dickey, DiMaggio, and Crosetti in a four-way hitting streak, has those May days deeply etched in his mind. Furthermore, Sturm remembers another legendary ballplayer, Lou Gehrig, desperately ill and not even near the diamond then, whose very presence in New York City added to the impression these games made upon him. The New York baseball writers were keeping daily tabs on Sturm when he took over at first because they thought him a poor fit for the powerful Yanks and treated his insertion into the lineup as a desperation move on Joe McCarthy's part. Half mockingly, the writers matched Sturm's performance with that of Lou Gehrig's rookie year. The Yankees' collapse in 1940 and their miseries early in 1941 were still vocally and volubly attributed to the loss of Gehrig. One writer was involved in litigation initiated earlier by Gehrig because of what Gehrig regarded as slurs about his illness infecting the other Yankees in proximity to him on the road and in the dugout. This was no joke; Sturm says the whole clubhouse was unsettled when depositions were taken from Bill Dickey and Lefty Gomez well into 1941.

To talk with Sturm now is to realize that Gehrig exercised a more powerful hold on him in regard to the memory of the early DiMaggio streak games than the writers could have imagined. Earlier, in the spring training of 1940, a weak and weary Gehrig often spoke to Sturm in German, the language of their families. This meant more than Sturm could measure considering that speaking German in America in the year of Dunkirk and the battle of Britain had a certain edge to it. Now, May 16, 1941, the day after DiMaggio's streak began, McCarthy put Sturm into a revised Yankee lineup that included the veteran members of the Gehrig-dominated infield of the late '30s: Dickey, Rolfe, Crosetti, and Gordon. McCarthy had just benched his rookies, Jerry Priddy and Phil Rizzuto, and Sturm was all alone. He was Gehrig's ghost on the field a matter of weeks before Gehrig, only 37 years old, was to die at home.

Sturm felt the pressure, thought about it, and played through it: a rookie inserted into a legendary lineup. While the writers insisted he would hit neither for average nor for power, he matched streak games with the likes of Joe DiMaggio. One can still hear pride and a kind of quizzical resentment in Sturm's voice that make otherwise obscure games come alive. DiMaggio himself told me he had largely forgotten the earlier games of his streak which Sturm remembers: "I hit pretty good, and all the writers were keeping tabs. They noticed as soon as I started. But DiMaggio already had a head start and no one sensed it—not even him. Pretty soon I stopped and Joe kept going."

One writer, the respected Dan Daniel of the *New York World-Telegram,* tracked Sturm's streak at 4 games, then 5, 6...9, 10, 11. When Sturm reached 11 on May 28, Daniel mentioned in passing that Crosetti had hit in 10 straight and DiMaggio in 13. Jack Smith of the *Daily News,* perhaps tracking Daniel, picked up DiMaggio the next day at 14. Getting in, as it were, at the beginning of DiMaggio's streak via the attention paid to the wrong streak by the right writers helps dispel a story that every chronicler of DiMaggio's record has repeated for years: No one recognized the streak until the *Herald Tribune* in New York picked it up at game 18. This is simply not the case.

By paying attention to Sturm—and remembering along with him—we also come to a forgotten moment, the first really crucial one in DiMaggio's young streak. There was a game in Washington, D.C., on May 29 played in sweltering and near-cloudburst conditions. In the sixth the Yanks got a bundle of runs; Sturm smashed a single, and so did DiMaggio, a rip as clean as a whistle. But the rains came. The game reverted to the fifth inning score, a 2–2 tie; the Yankee sixth was wiped out, and with it Sturm's streak hit. So was DiMaggio's clean single, but Sturm recalls the image of another play in the fourth inning, when DiMaggio topped the ball and bounced it high off home plate. It came down finally, but "Joe just beat the throw to first. He kept the streak alive by a hair. Me? I lost my only hit in the rain. You know, DiMag was a little bit lucky that day." The great are always a little bit lucky.

No one has ever described this play before because no one aside from Sturm ever had reason to remember its context. Both in a taped interview now housed at the Hall of Fame and in a recent telephone conversation, DiMaggio mentioned a rained-out game so dim in his memory that he couldn't place it and a base hit so lost that neither the record books nor recall could get it back. He wasn't able for the life of him to unravel the details.

Unlike Sturm, he didn't lose a streak that day, and the one he sustained was not yet significant enough to worry over. Sturm's memories, for discernible reasons, produce a different kind of pressure and recover a moment muddied for DiMaggio, who so gropingly tried to recapture it.

If memories can sustain a legend, they can also betray one. Roger Angell, to my mind the greatest writer on baseball of any generation, insists that the great memorial power of baseball is sometimes awkwardly rooted in the very timelessness of the game. Isolated and suspended moments mythify the details of particular plays or sequences. Memory is transformed into something greater than or different from the occurrence that stimulated it. There is one stunning example of invented recall within the great arc of DiMaggio's hitting streak that is still perpetuated today. It begins with a famous description of a circus catch made at a climactic moment in game 45, when DiMaggio was trying to break Wee Willie Keeler's all-time streak record of 44. DiMaggio himself describes the catch in his *Lucky to Be a Yankee,* detailing how his brother, Dominic DiMaggio, playing center field for the Red Sox, ran back deep at Yankee Stadium to haul in a drive fated for streak destiny. Almost everyone, including chroniclers of the streak, believed in the drama of this great catch for years. There was, however, one small problem: Dominic DiMaggio never made it. The only ball Joe hit that day snagged by an outfielder was a long drive to Stan Spence in right center, backed up of course by Dominic, who had taken off at the crack of his brother's bat.

A bizarre sequence of fragmented memories are at work. In a long phone conversation Dom DiMaggio said he recalled little of his brother's streak, but he mentioned his supposed catch as one of the few incidents he could describe; he reminisced about it with wit. "Dick Newsome was pitching. Joe hit one a mile to center. I had to run a long, long way to get it. Maybe I just should have stopped short and let it fall. Joe and I talked about it later, but you know, we always wanted to beat the Yankees, especially in New York. I had to go after that ball. I went after them all. Another time I robbed Joe of two sure triples in a game in New York and Toots Shor called up and broke a dinner date on Joe's behalf that evening. Joe wanted those hits. I have to try to make the catches."

With a bit of close scrutiny one can figure out what probably happened. The memories of both DiMaggios and of several writers who concur in the story are actually a curious amalgam of another play that did occur during the streak, a ball driven deep to center by Joe DiMaggio in Yankee Stadium over a month before, on May 24. After misjudging the ball and then readjusting, Dom caught up with the drive and had it trickle out of his glove. The distortions of memory are accountable—a tense game, the same location where Dominic DiMaggio was in the vicinity of a long drive, a wished-for result that had in fact occurred before—and a wonderful but inaccurate mythic bit emerges as truth. To record the streak day by day is not only to reconstruct how Joe DiMaggio did it but to explain how on some occasions he didn't do it the way he and others remember it. Mythological variants write themselves into the legendary record.

Many other stories within the streak are composed of fragments of memory rather than memorial wholes. DiMaggio told me that he began thinking about the streak seriously around game 33, and that in large part may be so. But something intriguing occurred earlier, perhaps lost in the streak's jumble of internal and external memories. Ken Keltner, the great third baseman whose two superb plays helped hand DiMaggio the collar for the first time in 57 games on July 17 in Cleveland, told reporters right after the streak stopper that a month and a half earlier DiMaggio had hit a ground ball by him just like the ones he speared that night. He was absolutely correct: On June 1, in the eighth inning of the second game of a doubleheader, DiMaggio hit a bullet off Mel Harder just to Keltner's right. Keltner got a glove on it, but the drive shot by him behind third base. That was DiMaggio's only hit of the game. When the inning ended and Keltner moved toward the dugout, he remembered DiMaggio saying something—neither hostile nor argumentative—but he couldn't hear it above the noise of the crowd.

Keltner told reporters that the incident had struck him as odd at the time. He still thought it was odd when I asked him about it in a recent exchange of letters: "DiMaggio rarely uttered a word on the field. He was very quiet." Keltner went on to tell reporters on the night of July 17 that he recalled the June 1 incident precisely because the players that day first began to hear inklings of DiMaggio's streak at game 18, even though the *New York World-Telegram* and *New York Daily News* had, without much fuss, picked it up a few games earlier. Johnny Sturm has a vague memory of Joe DiMaggio's brother Vince mentioning the streak—perhaps by phone—to a Cleveland reporter he knew. In any case, Sturm knew the story was alive during the doubleheader in Cleveland because he remembers talking about it on the field and in the clubhouse.

DiMaggio draws a blank on game 18 and on his one-way conversation with Keltner. But Keltner heard something on the day the streak became general news, and maybe DiMaggio muttered, "Another inch, Kenny, and I start all over," as he passed Keltner on the foul line. Maybe he didn't. The incident stays buried within the confines of the legend. Keltner at the time had another reason for telling this story. He said that the recollection of a hard ground ball skidding past him and a remark by DiMaggio he didn't quite hear made him especially eager 39 games later, on the night of July 17, to play slightly deeper at third and guard the line. To recover what is recoverable of this incident is to provide a full effect for half a cause. And that effected happens to be the end of the streak.

Talking with and writing to the ballplayers who had something to do with Joe DiMaggio's streak in 1941 was a pleasure for me, and their help was instrumental in shaping this book. For example, in the same conversation with Dom DiMaggio in which I heard of the phantom catch that never was, DiMaggio began by saying he remembered almost nothing of those times so long ago. But when we began talking about his earlier days in minor league ball in San Francisco, Lefty O'Doul's name came up, Dom's manager with the Seals. O'Doul's name triggered for me a story I had just read in a May 1941 issue of the *Sporting News* regarding an incident that occurred a few days before Joe DiMaggio's streak began. O'Doul was with his Seals in Los Angeles to play the Hollywood Stars, and after the game Lefty got into a barroom scuffle with a fan about the relative merits or demerits of his ball club. O'Doul ended up hospitalized with severe lacerations that required delicate surgery after the fan smashed a cocktail glass in his face.

Dom DiMaggio recalled the incident very well because he was

on the east coast when he finally heard what happened and wanted to call O'Doul in the hospital. He got in touch around the middle of May. O'Doul told him about the piles of letters he had received, about the ballplayers who had called, about his version of the entire incident, and about the nature of the fight and injuries, including details not reported in the news stories. Lefty said the damage had been done after he thought the squabble was over—"Aw, the hell with it, this is silly"—and when he walked over to see if he could soften the bad feelings, he caught a glass full in the face.

That the O'Doul episode took place at the time of his brother's streak—a sequence he had thought about over the years with much more frequency than Lefty O'Doul's brawl in a Hollywood bar—surprised Dominic DiMaggio: "Was O'Doul in the hospital then? My gosh. I remember that so well—exactly after all these years." Something akin to the surge I heard in Dominic DiMaggio's voice about a connection that is both coincidental and memorial attracted me to writing the record of the streak and the time that surrounds it. The O'Doul affair and its conjunction with Joe DiMaggio's streak—events totally unconnected in Dom DiMaggio's mind—had the effect of stimulating other memories. DiMaggio began to get interested or reinterested in the year. An hour later—we were on the phone—he said humbly, "Gee, I don't know if I have been of any help to you." The fact is, he had been of tremendous help not only about his brother's 1941 major league record streak but about a younger Joe DiMaggio's record 61-game streak in 1933 while Joe was playing for the San Francisco Seals, about the Red Sox in 1941, about ballplayers and the war, about Ted Williams's run at hitting .400 that year. He was so much help that I didn't have the heart to disabuse him about the great catch he supposedly made on the day his brother went beyond Keeler's major league record. On the other hand, the details of the catch that never was helped me piece together the sequence that led to its invention.

This is the way I have tried to recall these legendary 56 games: by reconstructing their details, by drawing on the recollections of others, by placing the entire sequence in the context of memories shared in various ways by all. I owe debts to those who have helped me do so, especially to the dozens of ballplayers willing to share their memories with me, primarily Joe DiMaggio himself, Ted Williams, Bob Feller, Dom DiMaggio, Ken Keltner, Charlie Keller, and Johnny Sturm. In preparing materials, I had a great deal of help from the professional staff at the Hall of Fame Library in Cooperstown. Their knowledge, courtesy, and enthusiasm are resources that complement the library's extensive holdings. A great deal of assistance was also provided by the New York Yankees, especially by David Szen and Ann Mileo in the front office. For additional research help I thank Alan Kifferstein, Aaron Schneider, Meryl Altman, Jillisa Brittan, and James Van Dyck Card. And for the sort of endless baseball talk on which fans and fanatics thrive, I owe much to Elizabeth Wheeler, David Quint, David Bromwich, Ron Levao, Paul Fry, Alfred MacAdam, Gerald Finch, Steven Marcus, Rick Wright, and even Edward Mendelson, who knows little about baseball but so much about everything else. As for my young boys, Daniel and Matthew, their endless baseball questions encouraged me to supply, after my fashion, endless answers. And whatever energy and effort went into the writing of this book was all repaid for me by the visible delight in my son Daniel's eyes when he picked up the phone one day and heard Joe DiMaggio's voice on the other end.

Books are not only written; they are produced. I had early help in shaping this venture from a good friend, Catherine Schreiber, and from Jack Artenstein and Angela Hynes of RGA Publications. And I have had continuous help in readying it from my editor, Tom Quinn, at McGraw-Hill. His deftness and his tact are remarkable. I also thank others at McGraw-Hill for their efforts, especially Lori Glazer, Sue Raffman, Eric Lowenkron, and Richard Adelson. It was a pleasure to work with them all.

PROLOGUE

I. A Hero's Time

The special distinction of the heroic is something that is nurtured over time. Heroes, or those perceived as such, possess a quality that strikes a primitive chord in millions who are simply aware of them, who seem to know them, who seem to miss them. A hero's name becomes talismanic; it stands for something bigger, something better. Simon and Garfunkel surely understood as much about DiMaggio's name in their bittersweet balladic refrain for the 1960s: "Where have you gone Joe DiMaggio? A nation turns its lonely eyes to you."

America in the '40s had a more immediate and distinct sense of what resources might be expected from its heroes. At the tail end of the depression and just before World War II, the land distrusted the self-aggrandizing bluster of the roaring twenties and the heroic figure whose demeanor suggested the flamboyance of something already done and not the steely anticipation of something yet to be encountered. Quieter and subtler reserves of strength and potential had greater attraction for the 1940s. Whether in sports, the movies, or the armed services, the image of accomplishment in the uncertain months before war drew on the intense but not the hysterical, the skillful but not the boastful, the graceful but not the mannered.

Tall, silent, to a notable extent shy, figures of consistency, endurance, and understated style—those represented, say, by the mild-mannered Clark Kent or portrayed by Gary Cooper and Jimmy Stewart in the movies—touched the land's spirit before World War II and kept that spirit alive while the war raged. A *Newsweek* story on DiMaggio during the streak encapsulated the style of the epoch: "Close-mouthed, confident, steel-nerved." Such a description could well apply to others, including the great current heavyweight champion, Joe Louis, who was already a national symbol for efficiently dispatching the German idol, Max Schmeling, in their 1938 title fight and who in June 1941 responded to the prefight publicity surrounding Billy Conn by muttering, "He talks too much."

In what amounts to a tour de force monologue on DiMaggio, the colorful Toots Shor, at whose restaurant and watering hole DiMaggio spent most of his bachelor hours and a good deal of his married ones, remembers his friend during the 1940s. Maury Allen records Toots talking:

> There never was a guy like DiMaggio in baseball. The way people admired him, the way they admire him now. Everybody wanted to meet Joe, to touch him, to be around him—the big guys too. I'm not just talking about fans coming into the joint. Joe was a hero, a real legitimate hero. I don't know what it takes to be a real hero like Joe. You can't manufacture a hero like that. It just has to be there, the way he plays, the way he works, the way he is.

Nothing is more eloquent than Shor's simple "the way he is." DiMaggio himself remembers something about the way he was in the 1940s. He recalls attending a game in Yankee Stadium one summer day in 1945, after the war but before he rejoined the team. He entered the park with his 4-year-old son, Joe, Jr., when someone in the crowd recognized them heading for their mezzanine seats. There were a few shouts of greeting—"Hey, Joe. Hiya, Joe"—and then a chorus of cheers and screams until the whole stadium was charged with excitement. The reaction spoke for more than 4 years of war; it spoke for an entire generation and a single ballplayer whose presence embodied prewar memory and postwar relief. The ovation and the chants—"Joe, Joe DiMaggio, DiMaggio"—moved the great Yankee center fielder to the quick. When DiMaggio tells the story he does so as much from the perspective of a father as from that of a hero. He remembers looking at his young boy, another Joe DiMaggio, and the tot saying, "See, Daddy—everybody knows me."

Everybody knows the name borne by father and by son. Dan Daniel, a baseball writer and official scorer for many Yankee home games during the streak, wrote with an intentionally archaic turn in 1941, as if none other were quite adequate: "DiMaggio is the hero of the populace." Perhaps at a time when such a Roman tag had passed to the likes of Mussolini and Hitler, Daniel wished to reappropriate it for the proper modesty of a sports-loving republic. He surely was on the qui vive throughout the streak for those resonances which made it at once a symbol of its time and a heroic antidote to the times surrounding it.

The great American poet Wallace Stevens knew from a more sustained vision what Dan Daniel sensed from a more limited one. Heroism adjusts its dimension to the imminent, especially when the imminent is war. Early in the 1940s he wrote in the prose statement accompanying his poem "Examination of the Hero in a Time of War" that the consciousness of war is "a consciousness of heroic fact, of fact on such a scale that the mere consciousness of it affects the scale of one's thinking and constitutes a participating in the heroic." Stevens went on to write that wartime crisis wills fact into heroic shape: "In war the desire to move in the direction of fact as we want it to be and to move quickly is overwhelming."

Amid the turmoil of world war and the preparation for our undetermined role in its conduct, the attention paid to DiMaggio's streak and to that other legendary sequence of the summer, Ted Williams's run at the .400 barrier, provided a heroic, factual focus for a land whose imagination seemed primed for increments of power. This is not to make either DiMaggio's or Williams's accomplishments overtly allegorical, which would destroy the uniqueness of their interest; rather, the streak and the assault on .400 were special achievements in a land receptive to the rhythms of their effort.

Baseball could not and did not escape the wartime consciousness. No matter how seriously or frivolously one takes analogies between public affairs and American sports, one thing is certain: In 1941 the analogies were more unabashedly and urgently proffered than usual, perhaps in the face of or perhaps because of the gravity of the global scene. A huge front page illustration in a February issue of the *Sporting News* depicted the entire Yankee team trying to steam across the Atlantic as a freighter in the face of enemy torpedoes. The caption read "Battered Yankee Raider Being Rearmed for Flag Fight" with the goal of making "craft 'Terror of the Seas' again." Later in the spring the *Sporting News* varied its own theme, offering a piece on the relief pitching corps of the major league teams with the header "Convoys for Starters." The tallies of downed planes in dogfights over the industrial Ruhr Valley in Germany would appear in the newspapers of spring and summer under the rubric "Daily Box Scores." In any of a hundred other ways the baseball season could not be separated from the experience of world war around it. *Baseball* magazine cut through the small pretense of metaphor and began the year in January with an article titled "Baseball and War—An Analogy" by James M. Gould.

But more interesting than all the predictable terminological twists on offense, defense, strategies, reserves, corps, and the like was an article in the *Sporting News* (April 4, 1941) by the indefatigable Dan Daniel, that omnipresent commentator on the mood of the country in the spring and summer of 1941. He wrote on the magnitude of things in wartime; he had a much more global sense of the year than did any other sportswriter; and he saw very early that the way a nation thinks about itself is manifested on its playing fields. Daniel's vision of sports and politics embraced the patriotic and flirted with the jingoistic, but he was not unintelligent. He recognized the time as confused and confusing, though he very much wanted to locate in American sports an attitude toward world events that was substantive in spirit even if preserved in innocence. Daniel wrote of the season's opener in Washington, D.C., between the Yankees and the Senators.

"Frivolous," snorts Hitler. "Ridiculous," gutturals Mussolini. "Marvelous," says the American as he sees behind the curtain, as he grasps the things connoted by Mr. Roosevelt's throwing out the first ball and remaining to watch the fight to its decision. Let all the men in baseball get wise to the fact that the Washington preview is not just a local happening; that the President does not come out to inaugurate a local season. He opens the American campaign.

What did Hitler and Mussolini have to do with the opening of the baseball season, and what did Roosevelt's remaining for the entire game have to do with the war? Nothing, really. But to understand the connection in Daniel's mind is to understand something of the tone and temper of 1941: its commitment to endurance as the most timely heroic virtue. From the first pitch to the ninth inning, America, represented by its President, would be there for the duration. Daniel's phrase "watch the fight to its decision" was equivocal enough in April 1941 to include even the isolationists who wished to do only that—watch—but following through to the end ultimately meant a commitment to the war against the Nazis. Baseball as an "American campaign" is in one sense an American League opener, in another a campaign that gripped the entire world.

Daniel kept the connection between his version of the national game and world events at the forefront of his writing as DiMaggio's streak steadily made its way into baseball history. In one *Sporting News* column (May 29, 1941) he commented on the pregame national anthem line by line as its sound wafted up to him in the press box. The reporting here is the kind of patriotic reverie that H. L. Mencken of the *Baltimore Sun* would have treated with savage scorn, but Daniel echoes the strains as he hears them in wartime.

> ..."whose broad stripes and bright stars"....You think back to that line....The stars are blacked out over there, and the broad stripes are lash-marks on the backs of men in Poland. Starvation stalks and children die where the waltzes of Strauss used to be the theme song of *gemüttlichkeit* which has fled the world.... "And the home of the brave"....The Yankees take the field and the first batter comes to the plate. They are dropping bombs again over London...."Protect us by thy might, great god, our King".... "Play Ball!"

Baseball is played in counterpoint. And the bottom line is war: courage to face it, readiness to prepare for it. The lend-lease program initiated in March of that year was the most dramatic symbol of a nation gearing itself to massive increases in the production of arms and war matériel in part to replace the over 350,000 tons a month that German raiders and U-boats were sending to the bottom of the Atlantic. For an economy still moribund from the great depression, the business of the country was now war production. America would become Roosevelt's "arsenal of Democracy." *Fortune* magazine ran a springtime feature on nationwide construction of military installations for a draft army of well over a million that made the pharaohs' public works projects in ancient Egypt look like sand castles. *Life* ran its "Defense Issue" during DiMaggio's streak, charting with numbing precision the rate of increase in production for virtually every rivet in every airplane, every trigger on every gun, every decoration on every uniform. The spread was emblematic—it looked like a division on parade.

Not only were there special defense issues and features in the print media, almost every daily newspaper pictorial supplement in city after city across the land offered rotogravure images of a nation readying for war: overhead shots of armored divisions, hundreds of production line and assembly views, mute but awful photos of stockpiled armaments. All was number, increase, accumulation in the spring and summer of 1941. The newspapers recorded the daily fetish and the pace of the count: draft lotteries; the largest series of defense outlays in the country's history, supplying everything from pontoon bridges to pile drivers; huge tax increases projected to support the war effort; thousands upon thousands of new planes, tanks, and weapons pouring off production lines. Whatever question didn't begin with "how much" in early 1941 began with "how long." How long before we must enter the war? How long before England falters? How long can China hold out? How long until Hitler invades Russia? How long before Japan moves in the Pacific?

At a time when the preparation for war could not be severed from the threat of falling just short, the performance of Joe DiMaggio on the ball field helped buoy a nation forging a new and necessary myth of its own potential. On the very day that DiMaggio's challenge to George Sisler's modern-day streak record of 41 games straight made front page news in *The Washington Post*, a parallel headline boasted that American airplane production would soon be outstripping the Nazi production of 2,000 planes a month. In double columns, side by side, DiMaggio eased by Sisler as the United States prepared to ease by Germany.

Once the media began characterizing DiMaggio's streak as part of a larger myth of iteration, many began to view him as marking time for a year whose finale, like the streak itself, would be even greater than the sum of its parts. *Time* magazine ran a profile on DiMaggio that heightened the land's fascination with the streak, almost rivaling its concern with the war abroad: "In 102 years of baseball, few feats have caused such nationwide to-do. Joe's hits have been the biggest news in U.S. sport. Radio programs were interrupted for DiMaggio bulletins."

In the best piece of writing so far on the streak, an article for *Sports Illustrated* in 1961, Dave Anderson talked about the pre-war tension that marked America in 1941 and the way the hitting streak provided partial release for many. Individual games tested DiMaggio's endurance and fascinated a nervous land: "For the fans there was no escape from the magnetic force that drew them to their radios to hear the news announcer report the grim but still dreamlike news of the war in Europe and then, at some point in the program, add, 'and Joe DiMaggio got his hit today to extend....'" Dan Daniel in 1941 even hinted that there was a lesson in the streak for our barbarian enemies: "The eyes of the fans of the nation—yes, of the civilized world and some uncivilized parts, as well—were turned on the Yankee Clipper." And the Alan Courtney lyric—composed on a napkin in an upstate New York motel the night of the day DiMaggio broke Wee Willie Keeler's record at 45—implied more than baseball in its refrain when it asked for DiMaggio's presence, as it were, on the winning side.

From Coast to Coast, that's all you hear
Of Joe the One-Man Show.
He's glorified the horsehide sphere,
Joltin' Joe DiMaggio.
Joe...Joe...DiMaggio...we
Want you on our side.

He'll live in baseball's Hall of Fame
He got there blow-by-blow
Our kids will tell their kids his name,
Joltin' Joe DiMaggio.

II. Springtime with Hitler

Baseball, like the spring training that initiates it, is seasonally liberating. Its reappearance in the east and north once the season begins in mid-April enjoys the same implicit relation to the prime of the year as does daylight savings time. But even in February baseball starts to edge football memories and hockey scores to the rear of the local sports pages. At best, Frank Leahy, rookie Notre Dame coach for the upcoming season, hawked Keds tennis shoes in ads that promised a free book on the fundamentals of football. The 1940 Heisman Award winner, Tommy Harmon, posed in his letterman's sweater at the University of Michigan, enrolling for a last semester before the pomp and circumstance of a June graduation. A few football fans still chuckled over Sammy Baugh's response to a reporter's question after the Redskins 73–0 shellacking at the hands of the Chicago Bears in the 1940 championship game: "Would it have made any difference if Charlie Malone held on to that touchdown pass early in the game?" "Yeah," said Baugh, "the score would have been 73–7."

When baseball went south in the spring of 1941, Hitler cranked up his war machine in Yugoslavia and Greece. The Italians continued fouling the peripheries of the Nazi onslaught, stalling in east Africa in the spring of 1941 the way they had stalled the year before in Greece. In the far east, the situation was brutal and macabre. Chinese armies under Chiang Kai-shek held out against the Japanese in the highlands but were powerless in the flatlands and in China's bomb-ravaged cities. Meanwhile, the German Luftwaffe bombarded England while Nazi U-boats and raiders terrorized the shipping lanes of the northern Atlantic. Through the huge lend-lease program, America was in the war by proxy and seemed to suffer its indignities on the same terms; a local news story in March related how a Pittsburgh tavern owner dropped dead of a heart attack when a customer looked up at him wearing a Hitler mask.

Baseball felt the pressures of the year early. A few weeks into spring training, players and fans alike sensed that this was the last year of normality before the lottery draft, already 500,000 strong, would create a kind of wartime diaspora. Early in the year the *Sporting News*, after requesting that all ballplayers in the armed services send in a picture, began a feature, "From the Army Front," posting the whereabouts of minor league (and a few major league) ballplayers scattered throughout much of the country and some of the world. Bobby Feller of the Cleveland Indians, Cecil Travis of the Washington Senators, and Johnny Rigney of the Chicago White Sox all held early draft call-up numbers. The great slugger Hank Greenberg would soon take his name off the Detroit Tiger roster and sign on the dotted line for Uncle Sam's draft army. On May 6, shortly after the season began, Greenberg hit home runs off Yankee pitchers Ernie Bonham and Atley Donald in the Tigers' 7–4 win. On May 7 he prepared to wake up to the call of the bugle at Camp Custer, Michigan, giving up the highest salary in the majors for the pathetic wages of a buck private. "I'm not crying about being dropped from $55,000 a year to $21 a month," said Greenberg. The contrast carries as much meaning as the sentiment.

Larry MacPhail of the Brooklyn Dodgers' front office harangued any federal official who would listen that the staggered draft call-up was a disaster for baseball. A late summer number would involve the loss of a ballplayer's services for two seasons. Like many others, MacPhail had no inkling of Pearl Harbor and the interlude that would extend through the bulk of the decade. The Yankees' president, Ed Barrow, was more militant on the subject of the draft than on the outrages of world war. He argued that the European hostilities were holding baseball hostage. When Joe DiMaggio sat out part of spring training angling for an extra $5,000 to edge his salary even with that of Cleveland's Bobby Feller at $40,000 a year, Barrow complained that if the war heated up with the pennant races in August, the military draft would deplete every major league roster. All the high-priced stars in the league would be wearing the same uniform: battle fatigues. Why should he cough up for DiMaggio, who would only spend the money buying clothes he wouldn't need? John Lardner in a spring training issue of *Newsweek* had just reported that DiMaggio had been named among the best-dressed athletes of the nation: "That DiMaggio is a poem." Indeed, why should Barrow shell out high salaries for anyone if during the heat of the pennant race major league rosters would consist of only the blind and the lame? Woody Allen would later parody a similar notion in a wonderful bit on baseball from his film *Radio Days*.

The concern in 1941 was for the most part premature, since all major league teams stayed virtually intact. DiMaggio had a marriage exemption and would play through 1942, though in that year his Italian father, never having applied for U.S. citizenship, would be classified a wartime alien and would be barred from his shipping boat in San Francisco harbor. Ted Williams held a late call-up number and, according to his own recollection, was so absorbed by the thing he did best in 1941—hit a baseball—that he had little idea that a significant war was raging in the world until the bombs actually fell on Pearl Harbor. Of course, Mr. Barrow of the Yankees was still at it in 1942. He tried to use the war, on this occasion an impending wartime wage freeze, to keep DiMaggio and six other stars on his World Series championship team from seeking raises. Barrow understood more than most that players on the field appear as if they are managed but are treated in the front office as if they are owned.

Another baseball issue festered in the spring of 1941, tangentially related to the war but more centrally focused on team revenues: night baseball. Dan Daniel, mixing vexing and perplexing metaphors, wrote in a spring issue of the *Sporting News* that "night ball is the most vexing source of perplexity confronting the major leagues." The question turned on whether to increase each team's home allotment of night games beyond the seven then allowed. President Roosevelt wanted the number of night games doubled to help the war effort by discouraging the sneaky but traditional escape to the ball park during afternoon work hours. When war finally broke out, he put this request into writing to baseball's commissioner, Judge Kenesaw Mountain Landis.

For their part, most of the owners who within the past two years had purchased lights for their privately owned parks enjoyed the potential extra cash on the barrelhead from night ball: The 77 night games played in 1941 would draw over a million and a half customers, average over 20,000 a game, and fill parks like Cleveland's huge Municipal Stadium with over 67,000 fans on the night DiMaggio tried to take his streak to 57 games. But among those in 1941 who grew apoplectic at the very thought of night baseball, Yankee president Ed Barrow again found himself in the forefront. Barrow might have remembered the time he managed at Paterson, New Jersey, near the turn of the century, when, in a night game played with the aid of candlelight, his great shortstop and personal discovery, Honus Wagner, had a firecracker thrown at him by the opposing pitcher. The incident literally ignited a full-scale riot.

What would Barrow have thought of domed stadiums and artificial turf? Actually, in the spring of 1941 a whimsically named writer for *Esquire*, Felix Mendelssohn, Jr., predicted that in several years most major league ball in America would be played indoors, with temperature automatically controlled and lighting artificially produced. Mendelssohn didn't worry about—or even contemplate—replacing grass with an artificial carpet. So much the better. Only by the license of metaphor can a carpet represent grass in the first place.

Despite the strain of the draft and the controversy over night ball, baseball came as a relief in spring of 1941, some of it comic. Along with the art deco shots of palm-lined Florida streets, the *Sporting News* ran a full-page ad taken out by Al Schacht, "the Clown Prince of Baseball": "Dear Club Owner: Increase your attendance anywhere from 100% to 500%—I sincerely believe my record for the past four years on tour established these facts beyond a shadow of a doubt.... Time is flying. Write, wire, or phone today." While Schacht hustled up business, the Yankees in St. Petersburg hoped to avenge their miserable midseason plummet in 1940 that had allowed Detroit to grab the pennant. If only they could beef up an at once aging and infant pitching staff and fill a first base spot vacant in body and spirit since the disheartening illness of Lou Gehrig, they could make it back.

With rumors of Gehrig lying so ill in New York that he couldn't lift a cigarette, the Yankees began by wiping the slate clean and selling their resident first baseman, Babe Dahlgren, to the Boston Braves in the first week of spring training. Manager Joe McCarthy had the notion of moving Joe Gordon to first and starting his rookie double play combination up from Kansas City, Phil Rizzuto and Jerry Priddy. When Dahlgren left camp, McCarthy remarked that "his arms are too short to play first." Babe was hurt: "What's he think I'm a freak or something?" Dahlgren posed for pictures in the papers measuring his arms against those which happened to be hanging around the Braves' training camp. Later in the year Babe got revenge of sorts when a poll in the *Sporting News* selected him as the most obvious candidate among active ballplayers to play the part of Lou Gehrig in Sam Goldwyn's movie *The Pride of the Yankees*. Goldwyn had other ideas.

Meanwhile, in the National League in spring 1941, the Brooklyn Dodgers, with a team literally purchased by Larry MacPhail in 3 years of wheeling and dealing, set their sights on displacing the world champion Cincinnati Reds, whose ace right-hander, Bucky Walters, was at the top of his game. Little did they know that it would be the Cardinals, not the Reds, with whom they would be gripped in a death-lock pennant struggle for all 154 games of a thrilling season. Would the Dodgers cry uncle yet again?

A feature story in *The New York Times Magazine*, "Why Is a Dodger a Fan," considered the Dodgers' chances in terms of the team's zany history and wondered at the mysterious and compelling nature of rooting for the Dodgers, which, "like all great loves, is born out of suffering." The article offered a nostalgic review of great moments in Dodger absurdity: Hack Wilson getting hit on the head by a fly because he was busy arguing with a fan in the stands; Babe Herman's pants catching on fire when he absentmindedly put a lit cigar in his back pocket; three Dodgers in a Mack Sennett moment sliding into the same base at the same time.

Miraculously, the Dodgers would make it through the season only to face another agonizing moment in their history: Mickey Owen's passed ball in game 4 of the World Series with the Yankees. For now they played the Yanks in spring in a game that had a different sort of historic resonance. On April 8, at Durham, North Carolina, Larry MacPhail made all his Dodgers wear an experimental contraption, a protective lining inside their hats that MacPhail himself had patented after getting the idea from jockey skullcaps. MacPhail offered his patented invention to any major league team for the asking. No one asked until midseason, when Cleveland's Roy Weatherly got badly beaned and the Indian front office decided to take MacPhail up on his offer. Most players, however, shunned the device.

MacPhail had been a busy man inside and outside of baseball for many years. He not only brought lights and night ball to Crosley Field and Cincinnati in 1935 and the pennant to Ebbets Field and Brooklyn in 1941, but in 1918 he participated in a wild scheme to kidnap Germany's Kaiser Wilhelm after the cease-fire ending World War I. MacPhail and his cadre wanted to hold the kaiser hostage for favorable treaty negotiations. The raiding party got as far as Wilhelm's temporary Belgian residence, whereupon MacPhail stole an ashtray as a memento of the crazy escapade.

Around the leagues in 1941 other great teams and players shed winter fat and loosened springtime muscles at the balmy resorts of Florida: Luke Appling, Lou Boudreau, Joe Cronin, Jimmie Foxx, Charlie Gehringer, Lefty Gomez, Hank Greenberg, Lefty Grove, Gabby Hartnett, Carl Hubbell, Joe Medwick, Mel Ott, Red Ruffing, Ted Lyons, Paul Waner. Many of these players, whose names now grace the Hall of Fame, could not and did not survive the hiatus of the war years. To get an idea of the talent in the majors in 1941, the *Sporting News* profiled players by position. One feature looked simply at shortstops, singling out among others Appling of the White Sox, Boudreau of the Indians, Cronin of the Red Sox, Reese of the Dodgers, Rizzuto of the Yanks, Travis of the Senators, and Vaughan of the Pirates. This incredible suite of players combined to hit just under .300 (.299) in 1941 and, in a marvel of consistency, .297 for their combined careers, over 110 years in all at short.

Hope springs eternal in Florida: Alexander Pope sprung the phrase, Ponce de Leon the concept. In 1941 the *Sporting News* ran the usual stories on the year's most promising rookies, the most notable of whom—including rookie umps Jocko Conlon in the National League and Art Passarella in the American—were Pete Reiser, center fielder for the Dodgers, and Phil Rizzuto, shortstop for the Yankees. Reiser was only technically a rookie in that he had played in 58 games for the 1940 Dodgers, hit .293, and almost had the at bats to qualify for his sophomore season. But Rizzuto was raw, charged up, and innocent. In the midst of a long interview, the veteran writer J. G. Taylor Spink asked Rizzuto about his springtime love life. "How are you in the cupid league?" Rizzuto responded, "Cupid League? I never played in that circuit. I broke in with Bassetts in the Bi-State League, then went to Norfolk in the Piedmont, then Kansas City in the American Association, and then the American League." For the young at heart, baseball is all-absorbing.

The most highly touted prospect still in the minors early in spring training was a young man named Buddy Blattner playing for the Sacramento Solons of the Pacific Coast League. Pepper Martin, his manager, claimed Blattner was the new Frankie Frisch, but despite a couple of decent years after the war, he is best remembered as Dizzy Dean's sidekick and "podner" on the NBC television game of the week. Other minor leaguers were playing in obscurity when the season began but would be heard of one way or another before it ended. In April the *Sporting News* ran a piece on a phenom playing for Springfield of the Western Association who worked as a grocery clerk in Donora, Pennsylvania, during the off-season. He had just demolished St. Joseph with seven hits in a three-game series, including three home runs and a double. The youngster would briefly be called up to the Cards when the rosters expanded in September and would get in a few licks. It's a fine trivia question: What famous left-handed batter outhit Ted Williams in 1941? Answer: Stan Musial, who batted .426 for the Cardinals in 12 games.

Whatever else marked the year—Grove's 300th win, Ott's 400th home run—the 1941 baseball season would belong to a 22-year-old in his third year with the Red Sox and a 26-year-old in his sixth year with the Yankees. During spring training, Joe McCarthy heard some minor leaguers working at the Yankee camp talking about hitters. One youngster ventured, "Everybody's got a weakness somewhere—I've just got to figure out where." "There are two fellows in the bigs who don't," said McCarthy, "DiMaggio and Ted Williams. They hit anything. You can't get them out."

In 1941 the best pitcher in baseball, Bob Feller, told the *Sporting News* in the spring how he would pitch to DiMaggio and Williams, though he admitted that thinking about getting them out was not the same as actually doing it: "Keep them in and hard on DiMaggio; throw Williams as much breaking stuff down and away as possible." Feller said that DiMaggio approached the plate all business whereas Williams appeared jaunty and gladdened at the prospect of taking his cuts. He even smiled at the plate, which some pitchers might find either a bit daunting or a bit depressing.

Recently, I asked Feller if facing DiMaggio and Williams after the war changed his mind about anything he had said before it. He responded that even though DiMaggio continued to hit him well for average, he liked his chances pitching to him: "Well, you know, he was a right-handed hitter, and I always thought I had a good chance facing righties. It seemed to be I could get him out by keeping it tight and belt-high. Get it up and he sees it too well. Get it out and that big swing kills it. I tended not to throw low strikes because it took the jump off my fastball. So I jammed DiMaggio all the time at the belt, but he'd hit it somewhere. When I turned around, the ball squeaked by an infielder or dropped in front of an outfielder. DiMaggio always got his hits off me." And Williams? "Well, no one could ever throw the ball past Williams anywhere in the strike zone. Especially coming at him from the right side. Yeah, he was loose up there. Other guys don't move a muscle—faces like a Prussian general. DiMaggio was like that."

When I asked Ted Williams about Feller's assessment made in the spring of 1941 and repeated nearly half a century later, his response was interesting. Everyone threw him curves, if they could throw them at all well. "It got to the point where I didn't even key for the fastball because of the breaking pitches, and pitchers consistently tried to throw them low and outside." But what Williams remembers most about Feller was the hard stuff. "Guys who knew their fastball was their best pitch tried to challenge me with it. So did Feller. Don't think I could hit every one— I couldn't. Sometimes the background was tough; sometimes a pitcher just had too much stuff that day. Did I smile at the plate? I don't know, I guess I looked pretty lackadaisical. It was my build more than anything that made me seem that way—I was a loose and skinny kid back then. But if someone threw at me there was no smile, that's for sure. I got extremely angry, and I knew I was a better hitter after that. Oh, by the way, one more thing about Bobby Feller: He was the greatest pitcher I ever saw."

Williams even had something to say about Feller's comments on DiMaggio: "Bobby was pretty much echoing the book on DiMaggio, though I hated to see Boston's pitchers throwing him up and in, because when they made a mistake it was right down his alley." Since Williams played left and DiMaggio was a dead pull hitter, he saw the result of those mistakes often enough: "DiMaggio was an absolutely superb hitter—by far the best right-handed hitter I ever saw." Williams thinks of DiMaggio only in comparison with "Jimmie Foxx, who was in the same league as a hitter, though I only saw him in his last three seasons." DiMaggio and Foxx ended up with identical .325 lifetime batting averages. "Right-handed" is, of course, the operative phrase in Williams's remarks, and one senses from listening to him talk about hitting that a loose and skinny kid for the Red Sox was the best left-handed hitter he ever saw.

The very presence in the mind's eye of DiMaggio and Williams registers not only the thought of what they *could* do but the image of it being done: the width of a famous stance, the power of a famous grip, and the arc of a famous swing. Dominic DiMaggio recalls a time with the San Francisco Seals in the late '30s when his manager, Lefty O'Doul, coaxed Joe DiMaggio, then a big leaguer visiting his younger brother, into a filming session. Dominic was lunging at the ball, and O'Doul thought he could correct the problem if he had an image of Joe and Dom taking alternating cuts at the plate. The home movie camera ran while the brothers stepped in and out of the batter's box.

To this day Dom remembers the results. Joe DiMaggio's stance and swing were the image of what they would be for his whole career: feet far apart, stride a matter of inches, swing wide but whipped and powerful, head motionless and dead level. Dom could see the difference right in front of him. While his head and shoulders moved forward and down as he lunged at the ball, his brother's stayed parallel to the ground. With the wide stance, short stride, and level head, Joe DiMaggio's eyes were riveted on the approaching ball. He could put wood to it almost at will, which was one secret of the long streak, according to Dominic. Joe could—and did during the hitting streak—go games on end without striking out. In fact, he fanned a grand total of 5 times during the streak and a mere 13 times for the entire season in 1941, a statistic that remains absolutely remarkable. Perhaps even more remarkable, from June 10 to July 25, 1941, DiMaggio played in 41 games, came to the plate 166 times, connected for 70 hits, and never struck out once. If a power swing opens up the far reaches of the ball park for a hitter, habitual contact puts the ball in play, where that other law of averages—luck—gets a time at bat.

As for Williams, the key lay elsewhere. When Babe Ruth saw him play early in the 1941 season, he told Boston reporters that just watching the kid swing told him that Williams had a shot at

.400. "A baseball comes at you too fast to begin thinking about it only after it leaves the pitcher's hand. Most hitters cheat by timing a backswing to pick up the rhythm of the pitcher's motion." The reason, Ruth went on, "that my own number 3 was so visible on my back, even directly from center field, was that I exaggerated my backswing before the pitcher's release. But Williams waits much longer. The strength of his wrists, the speed of his swing, and the uncoiling of his hips are exceptional. He gets a better look and a better cut. Yeah, he could do it; he could hit .400." Ruth was merely shrewd on the mechanics; he wasn't privy yet, if he ever was, to Williams's elaborate theory of zoning the plate that made his selection of hittable pitches akin to Cartesian geometry.

One of the more fascinating and least known things about DiMaggio's streak was Williams's phenomenal performance during the early part of its run. For the first 23 games the two kept pace, each getting at least one hit daily. But Williams's .489 average for those games humbled DiMaggio's solid .374. Though Williams took the collar often enough during the remainder of DiMaggio's 56 games, he still edged DiMaggio .412 to .408 in overall average for the days included in the record streak. Williams recalls the wonder of DiMaggio's consistency; DiMaggio recalls the wonder of Williams's average.

Entries in the Streak Journal will plot out the details, but the performances by these marvelous ballplayers for a few weeks in May, June, and July weave only part of a tapestry that covers three brilliant years, including 1941, since Williams's arrival in the league as a rookie in 1939. No two players after them have ever courted parallel years like these, not even DiMaggio and Williams after the war. DiMaggio's cumulative batting average from 1939 to 1941 topped out at .363, Williams's at .359. Both hit the exact same number of home runs: 91. DiMaggio knocked in 384 runs for the 3 years, Williams 378. In slugging percentage Joe muscled ahead .647 to .646. Not since Ruth and Gehrig or Gehrig and Foxx of the 1920s and early 1930s had two players in the same league put numbers like these on the board during the same seasons. No other combo or any arrangement of players and seasons, selecting among Mantle, Mays, Snider, Banks, and Aaron, has approached the matchup of average and power achieved by the Yankee center fielder and the Boston left fielder during these years. DiMaggio's legendary streak and Williams's .406 average in 1941 crown mirror performances the likes of which may belong to an era whose glory resides not only in its achievements but in its very pastness.

III. Maydays

When the 1941 season began in earnest, several DiMaggios showed up handsomely in the initial weekly averages. Having hit in all 19 exhibition games following his contract dispute plus the first 8 of the regular season, Joe DiMaggio began the year with an unofficial 27-game hitting streak. He also opened on a first-week rampage, posting an average of .528, with four homers, four doubles, a triple, 13 runs, and 14 runs batted in. Dominic and Vince DiMaggio didn't get off to bad starts either; Dom was at .444 for the Red Sox, and Vince was hitting .400 for the Pirates. A few thousand miles away from most of the action, the *San Francisco Chronicle* ran a daily feature in its sports pages called the "DiMag-o-Log," which charted the day-by-day progress of the homegrown DiMaggio brothers in the big leagues. The log in early May was a bull market. Soon it would turn bear for Joe DiMaggio before it began in mid-May to mark the quickening pace of an incipient hitting streak.

As the Yankees opened a western tour early in May the euphoric days of their first homestand began to sour. They lost ball games in which they had built up big early leads, and the frustration came to a head in Detroit during one of those baseball moments which give the sport its folkloric timelessness. Yankee hitters complained unceasingly that the Detroit pitcher, Tommy Bridges, was throwing them nothing but spitters. In a second at bat after going down on three pitiful swings the first time, Joe Gordon cut at a tough Bridges pitch and missed by a foot. He groaned at umpire Bill McGowan, "The sonofabitch is loadin' it up." "Get in there and hit," said McGowan. Bridges then let one go that watered the grass on the way to the plate. Gordon rolled his eyes; McGowan took off his mask, ran halfway to the mound, and warned Bridges about a spitter so obvious that the weatherman could have called it. Bridges looked toward his manager, Del Baker, as if McGowan had accused him of molesting a child, and a huge brouhaha ensued. Baker: "What? Him?" Bridges: "Who? Me?" McGowan: "Yeah, you." Some things have changed in baseball; some have not.

If baseball is a game of concentration, diversion is one of its more persistent strategies. Players, managers, and coaches are always working not only to fool their opponents but to distract them. A story in the *Sporting News* in May revealed that wily third base coaches around the league had spotted a tip-off to Bobby Feller's fastball. When the fastball was coming, he wiggled his fingers after receiving the catcher's sign. The story was something of a setup, intended to get Feller thinking about what was second nature to him, his speed. When he heard it, he responded in kind: "Any hitter dumb enough to rely on a sign from the third base coach is going to end up picking red stitches out of his ear." Those for whom hitting against Feller was no picnic under ordinary conditions cried foul. It was criminal for a man with his fastball to talk about hitting anyone intentionally. "Who's talking intentionally?" Feller shot back.

In speaking with Feller about the 1941 season, I asked him if he remembered this incident, and indeed, he not only remembered it, he still fumed over it. "Sure, they were always picking up my pitches. That's why I won 25 games that year. The ball's coming over 90 miles an hour, and a hitter's going to take a sign from the coach telling him it's really a slow curve because my fingers weren't wiggling? Good luck! I never meant I'd start throwing at people—I just meant that anyone stupid enough to trust in someone else's guess might be stupid enough not to duck. It happened this way every year. Coaches are paid to say they can pick up pitches. But if I'm a hitter, I'm not buyin' it."

As the baseball season meandered through mid-May, the sweetening air of spring eased some of the year's early tensions. The dailies brimmed with warm weather ads, everything from Jantzen swimsuits to Spalding tennis rackets, from Realsilk "Tropics Nude" nylon stockings (three pairs for $5; imports from the Orient were at a premium) to Stetson Stratoliner hats at $6.50 up top. Kool cigarettes in the warming months of 1941 told their prospective smokers in full-page spreads to switch from "hots."

Along the coasts of California—Pacific Palisades or Santa Monica—the rotogravures advertised nine-room ranch-style homes for under $10,000, which seemed about right for the middle-class family as profiled in May by *Life* magazine. The average salary for a head of household ran around $2,500 a year, with normal family expenditures running $735 for food, $265 for clothing, $460 for rent, $135 for utilities, $97 for furniture, and $800 for miscellaneous flings. To gauge the range of things in the spring of 1941, a dozen eggs went for 47 cents, a quart of milk for 14 cents, a loaf of white bread for 9 cents, a gallon of gas for 20 cents, and a pack of cigarettes for 15 cents.

The neighborhood gallant in his springtime worsted at $17.50 could pick up a snazzy middle-of-the-line Packard for $1,345 or the De Soto of his dreams for $898. For $100 a month he could rent a six-room apartment on the Upper West Side of Manhattan near where Joe DiMaggio then lived with his wife, the actress Dorothy Arnold, in a ritzier and more expensive penthouse at 425 West End Avenue. For a nickel DiMaggio could have caught the subway to Yankee Stadium, trains that Mike Quill's Transit Union drivers ran for 99 cents an hour, his mechanics worked on for $1.01 an hour, and his change-makers changed for 65 cents an hour. But of course, DiMaggio never did take the subway; he took a cab at 35 cents for the first mile or Lefty Gomez drove down from his apartment at 800 West End Avenue and the teammates headed up Manhattan and across to the Bronx at the 155th Street Bridge.

A traveler in May 1941 could book a Pullman round trip to Miami from New York for $40; a more exotic itinerary encompassed a $395, 38-day sail to South America, including Rio and Buenos Aires. European vacations, of course, were beyond the pale. The *Philadelphia Enquirer* ran a man-on-the-street poll asking who would take a trip to England that May if offered $5,000 to do so. Only 1 in 10 found the notion or the nation attractive, and she had a sister in London. Nearer and safer, $30.95 purchased a 3-day cruise to Bermuda, $75 a 6-day trip to Cuba, $160 a 14-day tour of Trinidad and the Virgin Islands, and $241 two thrilling weeks in the national parks of the American west, the Black Hills, and the Dakota badlands, where Mount Rushmore sculptors were hurrying to put the finishing touches on presidential noses, ears, and eyelids so that this famous depression monument could open in the fall of 1941.

The restrictions of wartime might have kept Americans in their own hemisphere in 1941, but nothing kept them from getting to where they were going faster than ever before. America's new frontier in the '40s was up in the air. To understand this era is to imagine the airplane. An RKO-sponsored Gallup survey in May told moviemakers what they had already figured out: "The horse, symbol of adventure, is on the way out as a standby. His most likely successor: the airplane." Spring was both blessed and burdened with such films as *I Wanted Wings*, starring Ray Milland, William Holden, and that classic World War II pinup in her first role, Veronica Lake. However much the movie inspired those who wanted wings, there could be little doubt that it enraptured millions who wanted Veronica Lake.

The obsession with aerial adventure was as much visionary as actual in 1941. Air fares, by comparative standards, were expensive: $149.95, New York to Los Angeles; $71.75, New York to Miami; $44.95, New York to Chicago. Nonetheless, the major airlines (American heading the list with 81 planes) flew over 2.5 million passengers in 1940, an increase of nearly a million over 1939. Bookings for 1941 continued to increase despite a series of crashes such as the one in February, when Eastern's "Silver Sleeper" to Mexico smashed into the fog-shrouded hills north of Atlanta with the second most famous aviator in America, Eddie Rickenbacker, on board. A badly mauled Rickenbacker, president of the airline, acted with extreme courage in aiding passengers and crew even worse off than he.

Of course, the real aerial adventure in 1941 was not civilian flight but air power. The strategic implications of air defense and air attack permeated every stitch of the social fabric and dominated media time and space, especially the advertising columns, from Dallas urban development ads ("from Plains to Planes in 120 Days"), where the horse indeed meets the plane, to Parker pens: "Why is the Parker Vacumatic like a Flying Fortress?" "I have it, they're both super-charged."

If the American people aired it out like never before, the

American media responded in word and image. *The New York Times Rotogravure* ran a feature, "Air Minded America," whose title articulated what its pictures revealed. For those whose heads were in the clouds, a syndicated feature appeared in newspapers all over the country, "Know America's Planes," in which tabloid readers could experience on the installment plan the virtues of everything with wings on it, from the Curtiss "Helldiver" to the huge B-19, unveiled for the first time in all its massive glory during DiMaggio's streak. A springtime issue of the elegantly produced *Fortune* magazine featured a cover-to-cover review of air power in the warring world. The titles of the articles indicated the scope of the arena in which World War II was being waged and would continue to be so: "U.S. Air Power," "Air Power as World Power," "The New Battlefield," "A Portfolio of U.S. Military Airplanes" (the photographs in this feature are simply stunning). Most telling of all was the subtitle of the *Fortune* piece on U.S. air power—"If the future belongs to us"—which picked up a refrain—"Tomorrow belongs to us" (*Die Zukunft gehört uns*)— from a Nazi youth movement song of the earlier '30s, later sung with such frightful poignancy in the movie *Cabaret*.

The future, for obvious reasons, was on everyone's mind in May 1941, but no one spoke of it more often or more fearfully than the most renowned aviator in America and perhaps the most revered hero of the twentieth century, Charles A. Lindbergh. Lindy was a daunting and darkening presence in the days just before DiMaggio's streak, and this tortured American soul now seemed much more than 14 years removed from the magical moment of his solo Atlantic flight in 1927, when he landed to the nighttime cheers of so many delirious Parisians.

Late in May, Hollywood's Preston Sturges began filming one of his classic comedies with Joel McCrea, *Sullivan's Travels*. The story involved a famous movie director who finds himself, through a series of pathetic mishaps, condemned to a prison chain gang. When McCrea as Sullivan tells a wily trustee that he is actually a famous man and not a criminal, the trustee responds: "Sure—last year we had a fellow here said he was Lindbergh. Flew away every night. Flew back every morning." Sullivan insists he would be recognized if he could get his picture in the paper: "Who in these parts gets his picture in the paper?" The trustee stares balefully at him: "Baseball players."

The story of Lindbergh's meanderings back and forth across the country at the same time when at least one famous ballplayer got his picture in the paper almost every day provides a subtext or counterplot to DiMaggio's 56 games of glory. The ballplayer, in the midst of building a legend, crisscrossed in more ways than one with the aviator, who was already a legend, in the midst of compromising a reputation. No other individual during DiMaggio's streak days penetrated America's consciousness with such "surgical" (Lindbergh's word) precision, and no other individual predicted a worse fate for the patient.

For the 2 years since his return home after a hiatus in Europe, Lindbergh had grown feistier and more desperate in opposition to any American involvement in the European war. By May 1941 he had placed himself at seeming odds with much that he had inspired, America's confidence in air power. He had just joined Senator Burton Wheeler's isolationist crusade, America First. Wheeler wanted to keep America off European turf; Lindbergh wanted to keep America and all her planes out of European skies. In 1940 he had preached that England was finished, that Göring's Luftwaffe would annihilate what remained of the RAF. The great American aviator, the courageous Lone Eagle, the daring aerial pioneer, took his stand against the most heroic achievement of the war, England's struggle for aerial supremacy over her own skies in the Battle of Britain. England's victory in the summer of 1940 became the salient rallying point for the western democracies, the impetus for the American lend-lease program, and the inauguration of the greatest spurt of airplane production in the history of the world. And now, in the spring of 1941, Lindbergh was traversing the country saying that neither England nor America, if we were to ally ourselves with the English, would stand a chance against German aerial and ground forces more powerful and efficient than ever.

Lindbergh's detour from the remarkable flight of 1927 through the '30s and early '40s was a disheartening odyssey from euphoria to catastrophe. The brutal kidnapping and murder of his young son in 1932 changed the man and changed the times for the man.

His bitterness toward America made him a captive of his own agony. The Lindbergh family had moved after their horrible tragedy to an estate in Englewood, New Jersey, where hidden arms caches and camouflaged pillboxes dotted the grounds. This was no way to live. In 1933 the *San Francisco Chronicle* ran a huge spread in its Sunday magazine section on the Lindbergh estate, diagramming the fortifications and guessing at the distribution of ammo. The sports section of that day's paper bannered a different story: the extraordinary hitting streak of a young star playing for the 1933 San Francisco Seals by the name of Joe DiMaggio.

As the San Francisco headlines recorded the young Joe DiMaggio's assault on the Pacific Coast League streak record in 3-inch boldface, a new heroic aviator, Wiley Post, flew solo around the world. He made it just as DiMaggio set the record at 61 straight. It took Post 7 days and 18 hours, despite a journey that was almost halted twice, first in Russia when his monoplane went down in a storm and then in Alaska when he crashed it all by himself. Both times Post fixed his craft with a few tools from his cockpit kit, a hands-on approach that helped give early long-distance flying its panache. Post landed to the cheers of 55,000 screaming aficionados in Bennett Field, New York.

For a despondent Lindbergh the glory and raw excitement of such adventures were mere memories. It was time for him and his family to leave, and his absence from the country for several years during the '30s gave him an opportunity to reflect on what he considered the imperfect decorum and undisciplined moral hysteria of America, the voyeuristic obsession of its masses, the public necrophilia of its press, and, almost as an afterthought, the demagoguery of its President.

Lindbergh returned to America only when the European war broke out and when his ties to Germany—Field Marshal Göring had awarded him Germany's highest aviation medal—made him persona non grata in England. Back home he became a cause célèbre because of his opposition to lend-lease, his despairing assessments of England's chances against the Nazis, and his insistent notion that the German people had legitimate geopolitical rights in all of Europe. In a piece for *Reader's Digest,* "Aviation, Geography, and Race," Lindbergh wrote that "our civilization depends on a Western Wall of race and arms which can hold back either a Genghis Khan or the infiltration of inferior blood." Thus it was no coincidence that the Nazis translated the American flier's writings and speeches and distributed them to a German audience sympathetic to their content.

By May 1941 Roosevelt and Lindbergh were at each other's throats. A few weeks before the beginning of DiMaggio's streak, Roosevelt publicly called Lindbergh a "copperhead," a reference to those northerners during the Civil War who despaired of defeating the south. Lindbergh, in cold fury, quit his commission as a colonel in the Army, which caused Roosevelt's point man, Secretary of the Interior Harold Ickes, to refer to "Ex-Colonel" Lindbergh as the "Knight of the German Eagle," a barbed reference to Lindbergh's quitting his honorary commission in America while refusing to return the medal given to him by Göring and the Nazi government in 1938.

The President poured it on. He considered Lindbergh's radio speeches the most disturbing, shameless, and demoralizing apology for Nazism the war effort in this country had to face at a time when the land was trying to build the spirit necessary to oppose a German juggernaut that was overrunning the Greek peninsula, looking toward Crete and the Mediterranean, massing for an invasion of Russia, and readying itself to annihilate the populations of eastern Europe.

Given the predictable mixture of preparation and trepidation in Maytime America and in the world just before DiMaggio's streak, it is not surprising that two of the land's greatest, and perhaps two of its last, true heroes should capture, whether for good or ill, the national imagination. For several months, though for different reasons, the names and actions of DiMaggio and Lindbergh would dominate the news and stir much of the country. Joe DiMaggio would silently hit a baseball; Charles Lindbergh would loudly deride the weaknesses of the western democracies. DiMaggio would set a record; Lindbergh's embittered volubility against Roosevelt, Churchill, and certain unknown and unlocatable Jewish warmongers would besmirch an aviator's heroic countenance almost beyond the cleansing powers of memory and time.

Such were the days of May.

IV. Streak Week

A month into the 1941 baseball season, the Chicago White Sox arrived by train in New York City, registered as they always did at the New Yorker Hotel, and prepared to open a three-game set against the Yankees. DiMaggio was slumping badly this second week of May as the Yankees, in none too good shape themselves, had just gotten buried by Cleveland and were still muttering about Bobby Feller's pitching on May 13. DiMaggio took the collar that day, 0 for 4, and said of Feller: "He's the best pitcher living. I don't think anybody's ever going to throw a ball faster than he does. And his curve? It ain't human."

That week's *Life* magazine profiled Feller, who repeated the story of the test devised by Lew Fonseca to measure the speed of Feller's fastball by racing it against a cop on a motorcycle. A former big league utility player and a pioneer of sports filming, Fonseca explained to Feller what he expected him to do: "Just throw the ball at the exact moment the cop goes by." Sure thing! Feller still recalls the circumstances. "I started winding up in the middle of a road, and a motorcycle is revving over my right shoulder. You ever tried this? Jeez, the bike starts coming at me while I hurry to get my delivery in sync. The cop roars by before I even release the ball. But I let it go, and the ball catches up and beats the bike to the plate! Who knows how fast I threw it? Fonseca clocked the cop at 86.2 mph."

DiMaggio was happy enough to see Feller and the Indians depart on May 14, 1941. He hadn't done much better that day either, taking the collar again against a tough righty, Mel Harder. Then, if he listened to the radio at home, he had to deal with Feller yet again on Eddie Cantor's nationally broadcast nighttime show. Cantor had Feller read advertising copy for a sponsor so that he could technically qualify him as a member of the cast for an invented "on-the-air" game later in the season between the *Eddie Cantor Show* and the *Jack Benny Show*. Benny protested in his comically forlorn way, but it did him no good.

DiMaggio's troubles before the May 15 Thursday game with the White Sox had actually begun prior to the Indian series and Feller's high jinks on the field or off. Back on April 22 in Philadelphia at Shibe Park the Yanks blew a five-run lead and lost

6–5 to the A's Lester McCrabb. McCrabb was a journeyman junk ball artist, and though DiMaggio usually had little difficulty with him, he failed this day to drive the ball out of the infield. He recalled the game as the beginning of his skid. "I felt uncomfortable against McCrabb. You hit the ball on the handle a few times, you swing at a few bad pitches here and there, and then you start pressing."

Pressing indeed. For the next 20 games DiMaggio hit .194. It would have been worse except for a three-game sequence, dotted by rainouts, May 8, 11, 12, when he went 7 for 13. Without that spurt his average from April 22 to May 15 would have been .119. *Madonn'.* DiMaggio reacted to the slump with simple baseball wisdom: "There is always a remedy. Time and confidence." He put the pinstripes on, one leg at a time, and took the field with the Yanks for an afternoon game against the White Sox. That day at the Stadium would turn into a debacle, more of which later in the Streak Journal.

It might have been better to spend the afternoon in New York of May 15 at a matinee. Six bits purchased the best loge seat in the house for a string of first-run movies in the city: Disney's *Fantasia,* Gary Cooper in Frank Capra's *Meet John Doe,* Chaplin's *The Great Dictator,* Hope and Crosby in *The Road to Zanzibar,* Abbott and Costello in *Buck Privates,* Spencer Tracy in *The Men of Boys Town,* Joan Crawford in *A Woman's Face,* Henry Fonda and Barbara Stanwyck in Preston Sturges's *The Lady Eve,* and Marlene Dietrich in René Clair's *The Flame of New Orleans.*

Better yet, Orson Welles's *Citizen Kane* played at the RKO Palace, where it had premiered two weeks earlier on May 1. Welles and his producers had just triumphed in a struggle with Louis B. Mayer, then of Loews Theatres, who tried to purchase the film and scrap it after hearing rumors of its savage portrayal of his friend William Randolph Hearst. Having prevailed over Mayer, Welles preferred to tell a more humbling premiere story. He was mobbed by autograph seekers, including one young fellow who surged forward several times with pen and paper in hand. Each time Welles signed dutifully. Finally, the lad turned away and Welles heard him say to a pal, "Okay, here's my seven Welleses, give me your one Clark Gable."

If the rout of the Yankees that afternoon at the Stadium,

13–1, had been particularly trying, a relaxing springtime dinner and an evening at a Broadway play might provide recompense: a dollar for a seat in the balcony or $3.50 tops for the orchestra and a veritable history of the theater played out before one's eyes. The following were in extended runs on May 15: *The Man Who Came to Dinner, Life with Father, Arsenic and Old Lace, My Sister Eileen,* and *Tobacco Road.* Newly mounted that season were William Saroyan's *The Beautiful People,* Orson Welles's production of Richard Wright's powerful *Native Son,* Dorothy McGuire's nubile stage debut in *Claudia,* Raymond Massey and Katharine Cornell in Shaw's *The Doctor's Dilemma,* Ethel Merman in *Panama Hattie,* Gene Kelly in *Pal Joey,* Ethel Barrymore in *The Corn Is Green,* and Gertrude Lawrence in *Lady in the Dark,* where the young Danny Kaye originated his famous show-stopping mad Russian number by reeling off 57 Russian names in 39 seconds.

The Critics Circle Award–winning drama for 1941, Lillian Hellman's *Watch on the Rhine,* had opened in April, and Miss Hellman was still living in town this third week of May during the run of the play. In an interview she was less sensitive about the average American wage earner than she had been in her play about those serene older orders of Europe oppressed by a grotesque yet largely unperceived wave of the future. She told a theatrical beat reporter that it was absurd to rent an apartment in New York when you could live at the Plaza.

Perhaps a Yankee fan wished to do nothing on the afternoon of May 15 but tune in to the 3 P.M. start of the game on the radio. If so, the fan would continue doing nothing. There were no broadcasts during the season from Yankee Stadium in 1941 that day or any other. Only the Brooklyn Dodger games, with Red Barber at the microphone, were carried locally. Neither the Yankees nor the New York Giants were able to garner sponsors for the $75,000 they asked for the rights to air their games. Without full broadcasts, Yankee and Giant fans had to rely on brief radio re-creations from 7:15 to 7:30 each night on station WINS by a young announcer, Don Dunphy. Dunphy was soon to win national acclaim for his brilliant call of the Louis-Conn fight on June 18, but his baseball re-creations on radio were at best hit-or-miss affairs. For analysis and commentary, another radio name, Paul Douglas, who later gained prominence for his acting in Hollywood, broadcast *Paul Douglas's Sports Column* nationally from New York. Douglas that year won the *Sporting News* award as the best baseball commentator in the country.

The bulk of the radio day on May 15 filled the hours with soaps (*The Guiding Light*), news (H. V. Kaltenborn, Lowell Thomas), gossip (Walter Winchell), and chitchat and song (Kate Smith). Evening programs included Fred Waring's orchestra and the Fanny Brice, Bing Crosby, and Rudy Vallee shows on WEAF and *Amos 'n' Andy, Major Bowes' Amateur Hour,* and Glenn Miller's orchestra on WABC. Doing the news each weeknight on station WEAF in New York was a young man by the name of George Putnam, who later had a flashy career as a television commentator in Los Angeles but whose major contribution to American culture came when he served as the model for the profile-mongering, jaw-strutting, dim-witted anchor man Ted Baxter on the *Mary Tyler Moore Show* of the late 1960s and 1970s.

Passive and active listeners on May 15 heard on the radio or simply in the air the strains of *Billboard*'s best: Jimmy Dorsey's "Amapola" ("Amapola, my pretty little poppy..."), Bing Crosby's "Dolores," and the Andrews Sisters' "Apple Blossom Time." Jimmy Dorsey had two more songs in the top 10: "Maria Elena" and "Green Eyes." Brother Tommy chimed in that week with "Oh Look at Me Now" and "Let's Get Away from It All," and so did Guy Lombardo with "The Band Played On." A new song was in its way creeping up the charts, Xavier Cugat's "La Cucaracha." Soon Lawrence Welk's "Henny Penny" ("My black hen/She lays eggs for gentlemen") would take its rightful place among *Billboard*'s best, followed by the blockbuster of spring and summer, the "Hut Sut Song," whose lyrics sounded like the curses of a herniated Swedish cheerleader: "Hut sut rawlson on the rillerah and a brawla, brawla, soo-it."

For those who sought their pleasure from syllables that made sense, local bookstores on May 15 carried two current best-sellers slated to become American classics: Hemingway's *For Whom the Bell Tolls* and Bud Schulberg's *What Makes Sammy Run.* A fascinating new book had just appeared, *The Long Weekend: 1918–1939,* by Robert Graves and Alan Hodge, about the nature of British life between the wars. America's deep concern with English culture of this period, even elite English culture, had a distinctly elegiac ring to it, including two novels about England on the verge of attack at the very top of the best-seller lists: James Hilton's *Random Harvest* and Eric Knight's *This Above All.* On top of the nonfiction charts were two books about England beyond the verge of attack: Churchill's *Blood, Sweat, and Tears* and Edward R. Murrow's *This Is London,* soon to be joined by William Shirer's *Berlin Diaries.* The subject matter of these books touched the same raw nerves that had proved too much for one of the century's geniuses a few months before. Virginia Woolf drowned herself in March, leaving a note about the Nazi bombing raids over England: "I cannot go on any longer in these terrible times."

Too heavy? Then try the comic strips. The trials, traumas, and tribulations of besieged democracy could be gleaned from the week's fare. Daddy Warbucks, Orphan Annie's padrone, was at death's door after getting shoved by saboteurs and spies into the machine works of a factory manufacturing bomb sights. Superman confronted "the oncoming juggernaut" of a deadly armored car on the streets of Metropolis. Brenda Starr read the patriotic riot act to a young gentleman sleaze trying to use his influence in Washington, D.C., to gain an exemption from the military draft. Dick Tracy, who so often shot from the hip, had just been shot in the back. He lay in a coma in need of a massive blood transfusion, rather like America before the war. Joe Palooka was better off. As a draftee he had just participated in war games. A ranking general asked those in Palooka's company whether anyone thought it would really be like this in combat on the front lines. "General," answered Palooka. "You wouldn't be here if this was really the front lines."

As for the sporting life on May 15, some notables were active, some between engagements. Joe Louis was fine-tuning at Pompton Lakes for his upcoming fight with Buddy Baer, but the fight world also had its eye on a flashy speedster rising through the lightweight ranks who could move like a hummingbird and hit like a woodpecker, Ray Robinson. During a preliminary bout Robinson touched gloves with his opponent, Maxie Shapiro, at the beginning of the second round. "Hey, Ray," Maxie complained, "you're only supposed to touch gloves in the last round." "That's right," said Robinson.

In golf the major European tournaments were of course suspended, but Byron Nelson currently led the rankings in America, though challenged by Ben Hogan, who would surpass him, and by Craig Wood, winner that year of both the U.S. Open and the Masters. Sam Snead and Lloyd Mangrum were the best of the younger golfers in the land, and Gene Sarazen at 39 was still very much in the money. Bobby Riggs, Frank Parker, Ted Schroeder, Frankie Kovacs, and Jack Kramer led the ranks of amateur tennis in America (again, no European tournaments), though the most exciting new name among the top players belonged to a delightful little bow-legged Ecuadorian, 19-year-old Pancho Segura. Jimmy Evert, Chris Evert's father, reigned as the junior indoor champ in 1941. Don Budge, an aging Bill Tilden, and Alice Marble played the 1941 pro circuit.

During the opening week of DiMaggio's streak the whole world was deep in wonder at a story developing in and around Glasgow, Scotland. Headlines for the past two days had bannered the strange, war-related news of the inexplicable flight and descent into Scotland by parachute of the third-ranking official in all Nazi Germany, Deputy Reichsführer Rudolf Hess. What could this possibly mean? The sequence of events went back to the previous weekend, May 10 and 11. All seemed natural enough. The great colt Whirlaway, with Eddie Arcaro up, dashed to a five-length victory in the Preakness, the second leg of what would be the Triple Crown for the colt that year. That Saturday afternoon the new British ambassador to the United States, Lord Halifax, attended his first baseball game—a contest between the White Sox and the Tigers—though he understood precious little of it. The American League president, William Harridge, told umpire Bill Summers to keep the irascible Jimmy Dykes under control to avoid a spectacle in front of Lord Halifax. Summers said he would take care of it before the game by telling Dykes that the Lord himself was in the stands.

In Boston the same Saturday, the stripper Sally Rand was guest of honor in the evening at a Harvard freshman smoker. When in response to shouts of "Take it all off," she said, "I will if you will," 200 Harvard lads began to shed their shirts. The ensuing melee was calmed when a dour New York columnist in attendance, Ed Sullivan, who introduced Elvis Presley and the Beatles to television audiences, insisted on the restoration of clothes and sanity. Meanwhile, one lonely man, inspired as he later said by Charles Lindbergh's solo Atlantic flight of 1927, hunched in the cockpit of a specially souped up long-range Messerschmitt late Saturday and began to fly undetected from, of all places, Bavaria, the heartland of Nazi fanaticism, to, of all places, the estate of a British Air Force officer near the coast of Scotland.

While Hess was in the air, having told no one in the Nazi hierarchy about his plans, Göring and Hitler sent the German Luftwaffe on a bombing run over London, not an unusual occurrence, though on this sad occasion the targets were the great monuments of West End London: Westminster Abbey, the Houses of Parliament, and Big Ben. Pictures of these ruined structures covered the newspapers all week, and the images were heartbreaking for the western democracies. This much was in keeping with the Pulitzer Prize–winning political cartoon just announced; Jacob Burch of the *Chicago Times* had won for a wrenching sketch of a little girl kneeling in prayer next to her bed in her bombed and gutted London home. The caption read "If I should die before I wake."

Hess flew on through Sunday, despite the monumental London carnage. At eight o'clock Sunday night, with darkness approaching off the Scottish coast, he homed in on preset coordinates and prepared to ditch his plane. He pushed himself out of the cockpit and parachuted to the ground, landing a few miles from the rural seat of the Duke of Hamilton, an aviator in his own right, having in 1933 been the first to fly over Mount Everest.

Two days later, when this episode hit the newspapers with bold headlines half a page high, the world went crazy, with the *Times* of London calling the adventure "the most bizarre incident so far in the war." Correspondents marked the reaction worldwide as a global fit of "Hessteria." Bill Henry of the *Los Angeles Times* wrote that he would give his eyeteeth to know what went through Churchill's mind when his aides told him that Deputy Führer Hess had just dropped out of the sky into Scotland. Actually, Churchill was at a country house retreat watching a screening of the Marx Brothers' *Day at the Races:* "Hess or no Hess, we'll deal with the matter after the movie." Few, including

Churchill, had any real grasp of the details yet, though the prime minister sensed that "the maggot is in the apple." This strange adventure in the air was still momentous news when on May 15 Joe DiMaggio laced a single off Chicago lefty Edgar Smith in the first inning and launched a legend.

The rest is streak history.

STREAK JOURNAL

"In order to do the toughest thing there is to do in sport—hit a baseball properly—a man has got to devote every ounce of his concentration to it."

—*Ted Williams*

GAME 1: May 15

"Properly" is the rub. The baseball is a joy to hold and jiggle in the palm of one's hand but a terror to hit properly, to hit hard, and to hit consistently. There it sits according to 1941 specifications: a spheroid with a cork-centered pill (small percentage rubber) 3/16 of an inch in diameter; covered with four separate red and black rubber shells to a circumference of 4⅛ inches; wrapped in three layers of yarn, totaling 219 yards, and another layer of rubber-cement-soaked cotton, 150 yards, to a circumference of 8⅞ inches; covered again with two distended figure eight patches of taut horsehide 0.050 to 0.055 inch thick, nuzzled in the fetal position at cross-purposes; and sewn together with 108 raised cotton stitches.

If powerfully thrown, the baseball spins through the air at speeds ranging from 88 to 95 miles per hour, a blur with red highlights between 9 and 9¼ inches in circumference and between 5 and 5¼ ounces in weight. Hitters, who have subjected the baseball to the same scrutiny as physicists have the atom, differ as to exactly what it does under different conditions, though they have seen them all, even those never intended by Mother Nature. When a hitter is at a peak of concentration and in a comfortable groove, the baseball, according to Williams, seems to grow disproportionately as it approaches the plate: It looks bigger than it ought to. On the other hand, when a hitter is slumping, the ball looks like a cross between a white tablet and a firefly.

On Thursday, May 15, 1941, Joe DiMaggio was in the middle of a horrible slump. A slump is a streak in reverse. It is leveling in its agonies, equalizing the paying customer, who thinks he could do as well, and the player, who so desperately wants to do better. DiMaggio suffered from a doozy. In 3 weeks he had shorn more than 200 points off his average; he was hovering at .306 thanks only to a torrid opening week of the season but no thanks to his work for the past 20 games. Other astronomical early season averages in both leagues made it look as if the Yankee center fielder had fallen from grace. Roy Cullenbine of the Browns led the American League at .431, followed by the Senators' Cecil Travis at .394, and then a duo of Red Sox, Joe Cronin at .387 and Dominic DiMaggio at .368. Arky Vaughan of the Pirates led the National League at .395, followed by Enos Slaughter of the Cards at .388. DiMaggio's 1 for 4 on his first streak day dropped him another 2 points to .304.

The Yankees were a grim crew all around on May 15. Tommy Henrich was struggling so badly that McCarthy wouldn't play him against lefties; the rookies, Phil Rizzuto and Jerry Priddy, were tumbling toward the .200 barrier; and the largely rookie pitching staff was blowing early leads in the later innings game after game. Having just dropped two to Cleveland and, prior to that, two to Boston, the team had now lost four in a row and seven of the last nine. The Yanks were 5½ out of first and falling.

They were not the only ones. Three thousand miles west, about the same time as the ball game at the Stadium, an extraordinary aerial adventure took place over the skies of San Diego. It all began when Navy Lieutenant Walter S. Osipoff thought he was making a routine parachute jump from a Douglas transport. He leapt out the open door, but before he cleared the plane the shrouds of his chute caught on the wing supports. The jolt knocked him cold and left him dangling in midair. While base personnel stared up in horror, a marine pilot, Lieutenant W. W. Lowrey, and a machinist's mate, J. R. McCants, ran for an empty Navy biplane dive-bomber. They jumped in, hurriedly taxied along the runway, and took off. Moments later they sighted the

Douglas transport at an altitude of about 1,500 feet out over the ocean. Osipoff was still hanging unconscious as the transport banked and circled.

Then a miracle: Lowrey caught up to the transport and delicately edged his biplane toward the dangling chutist. While he steadied the plane underneath, McCants, a giant of a man, grabbed Osipoff and tugged as hard as he could against the pull of the air and the tangle of the chute. He finally managed to stuff the limp lieutenant headfirst into the open cockpit. But the shrouds of the parachute were still ensnared by the wing supports, so Lowrey maneuvered the biplane within inches of the larger transport and severed the tangled lines with his propeller, shearing off a few centimeters of metal in the process. He veered away and landed moments later with a battered and stunned extra passenger. Crowds on the ground cheered themselves hoarse. And Osipoff? He had a Hall of Fame headache and a cut on his arm that required 25 stitches.

The New York press reveled in this event on the first day of DiMaggio's streak, but the sportswriters had a different set of aerial motifs ready for the Yankees. "A non-stop flight toward the second division" was the lament of the *New York Herald Tribune*. The Yankees got pasted 13–1 by the White Sox, and the papers were merciless, muddling all distinctions between the linotype key and the panic button. The *Daily News* called the Yankees "ghastly" and their play a "shameless shambles." It reached the point where team president Ed Barrow had to plead for charity. "The vets can take it, but give the rookies, Rizzuto and Priddy, a break." Dan Daniel, writing for the *Sporting News* that week, finally concurred: "Rizzuto and Priddy had the hard luck to drop into a lineup that was not hitting. They could not carry everybody."

A cartoon on the sports pages of the *New York World-Telegram* depicted manager Joe McCarthy sitting in despair as his minions fell exhausted at his feet. If only the Yankees could switch places with their provincially named farm team in Atlanta, the Crackers, who had won 30 of 35 ball games so far. (The catcher and manager of the Crackers was a shrewd fellow named Paul Richards who would do a bit of managing in the majors before he was through.) Salvation, however, would have to come from elsewhere. Dan Daniel ventured a guess in his *World-Telegram* column for May 15: "Slumps are overcome suddenly, and once the bellwether shows the way, a whole club very often will follow him. It is possible that when Joe DiMaggio begins to hit again he will pull the other Yankees with him."

This was prescient, but Daniel was placing his money on a good bet. The revival of a blighted team by a kind of fisher king—an appropriate role for DiMaggio, the son of an immigrant fishing family—has its charm. On the more somber side, a few of the Yanks were still involved in genuine legal proceedings against a writer's tasteless charge that Lou Gehrig had blighted his buddies with a disease of mysterious etiology and debilitating symptoms. Rookie first baseman Johnny Sturm, about to be put into the lineup as a regular, remembers that the Gehrig situation was all the more unsettling because Lou was desperately ill then and getting worse fast. The times themselves were neither healthy nor happy for the Yanks. McCarthy, Sturm said, was unusually on edge. He was also about to lower the boom.

During the game Chicago jumped all over Ernie Bonham, Charley Stanceu, and Norman Branch for 14 hits and 13 runs. Bill Knickerbocker, a Yankee castoff, blasted four hits, including a home run. DiMaggio didn't do badly against Chicago lefty Edgar Smith on this otherwise woeful day. He hit the ball crisply and even drove in the only Yankee run. Things might have turned out better for DiMaggio if he had kept the ball away from his brother Vince's boyhood chum, Dario Lodigiani, now at third for the White Sox. Lodigiani snared one smash down the line on a bounce and deflected another to Luke Appling at short, who threw DiMaggio out. These drives were precursors for two later shots to third off another lefthander named Smith on a fateful July night in Cleveland. That time Ken Keltner would be at third.

DiMaggio's hit came early in the game. With two out in the bottom of the first and Phil Rizzuto, who had led off the inning with a double, on second, DiMaggio slammed a solid shot to center. Rizzuto scored, and the Yankees folded their tent for the rest of the day. They were already losing in the first because in the top of the inning DiMaggio had picked up Luke Appling's bouncing single to center and drew a bead on the runner, Knickerbocker, heading to third. The ball caromed off Knickerbocker's elbow into the box seats, allowing him to score. DiMaggio drew a rare error as Appling chugged all the way into third smiling.

Luke would end up returning the favor on a number of occasions during DiMaggio's streak; fate provided him more chances than any player to put the kibosh on the record early and late, but bad hops and hairbreadth plays deprived him of the honor. Appling was a great Hall of Fame shortstop whose brilliant career was capped, after a fashion, when in a 1982 nationally televised old-timers game in the nation's capital he stepped up to the plate against Warren Spahn, took a mighty ancestral swing, and launched one over the left field fence at the tender age of 75 years.

May 15, 1941, was roster cut-down date in the major leagues, and of much more importance on the first day of DiMaggio's streak than a game in which the Yanks seemed to be coming apart at the pinstripes was the fate of two of baseball's more incredible presences, White Sox player-manager Jimmy Dykes and the great right-hander Dizzy Dean, then barely hanging on with the Chicago Cubs. The fiery, loudmouthed, irrepressible Dykes was the umpires' scourge, and with his playing days by common consent near an end, he placed himself on the inactive list, though he continued to manage as actively as anyone in the majors. In pregame ceremonies, Dykes clutched at the bag near his customary position, third base, and wouldn't leave the field until a half dozen of his players dragged him back to the dugout.

As for Dean, he had never been the same since an injury to his toe in the 1937 all-star game threw his pitching delivery out of whack. The Cubs released him for good and made him a coach on the day DiMaggio's streak began. Dean would soon take a job broadcasting radio games for the St. Louis Browns, and his mangling of the English language would set the St. Louis Board of Education's teeth on edge: "He's standin' confidentially at the plate"; "The scar is nothin' to nothin' and nobody's winnin'"; "Don't fail to miss tomorrow's game."

Around the majors, Cleveland led in the American League over the Red Sox by 3½ games and added to that lead with a 6–4 win over Boston. Ted Williams, hitting .339, laced a single in the game, beginning a streak that would shadow DiMaggio's for 3 weeks. Bill Dietrich of the White Sox helped take Williams to the laundry the day before, starching him at 0 for 5. In the

National League, Brooklyn and St. Louis began the season by playing almost perfect ball for a month. Indeed, the Dodgers won 15 of their first 18 and still trailed the Cards, who had won 13 of 15, by 0.033 percentage point. By now both teams had cooled off just a bit and the Dodgers held a lead of a game and a half at the end of the day's action. All summer long it would be a see-saw race.

Meanwhile, the rest of the world was still abuzz over the Hess aerial misadventure, the deputy führer's solo mission, ditched plane, and parachute jump over the inland coast of Scotland. By Thursday afternoon Embassy Newsreels had hastily pieced together footage for a brief feature, *This Man Hess: Hitler's Right-Hand Man in Action,* and ran it at many neighborhood theaters. Fast work. The explanation for Hess's bizarre flight was still anybody's guess, and the *New York Daily News* reminded its readers of a 1940 novel by Peter Fleming (Ian's brother) called *The Flying Visit* in which none other than the führer himself fell out of a reconnaissance plane over England and parachuted to the ground. Locals picked him up, dusted him off, and entered him in a Hitler look-alike contest, which he won. In the London papers, the versifier A. P. Herbert caught the tone of the myriad rumors concerning Hess and the flight. The rumors would become odder still as the days rolled by.

> He is insane. He is the Dove of Peace.
> He is Messiah. He is Hitler's niece.
> He has a mission to preserve mankind.
> He's non-alcoholic. He was a "blind."
> He's fond of flying. He was racked with fear.
> He had an itch to meet a British peer.

More deliberate and less impish voices were no less absorbed by the Hess mission. President Roosevelt imagined the worst and feared Hess was in cahoots with German sympathizers in England who had connections to the noninterventionist movement in America, especially Lindbergh and the America First Committee. In Russia, the steel-willed Stalin suspected something that turned out to be closer to the truth, that Hess was in England to negotiate an alliance before the Germans engaged the Russians along an eastern front. For this, more than for his war crimes, the Russians refused to let Hess out of Spandau Castle in Berlin, where, according to the memoirs of Albert Speer, who was there with him, he walked the halls alone, a perfect martyr and a perfect loon. Hess killed himself at the age of 93 by wrapping an electrical cord around his neck and stepping off a chair in his cell at Spandau on August 17, 1987.

At home on May 15 Roosevelt continued a long series of provocations aimed at firming up a western alliance against the Axis powers. Next to the dangling Osipoff on the front pages of the papers were news photos of a great ship, the magnificent 85,000-ton Vichy French liner *Île de Normandie*. The President had just impounded it. For good measure he signed impounding orders for 11 other ships sailing under the flags of Axis-dominated nations. Ostensibly Roosevelt wished to protect these vessels from sabotage, but actually he was signaling that the Atlantic belonged to us and to the British. Noninterventionists and isolationists all over America saw in Roosevelt's actions the very incremental tactics that would edge us toward war, which is precisely what they were.

GAME 2: *May 16*

The Yankees ended the skid of a five-game losing streak on the second day of DiMaggio's embryonic streak with a clutch ninth inning rally to put the game away 6–5. Trailing the White Sox 5–4 entering their half of the last inning, the Yanks flexed a bit of muscle. DiMaggio tripled off the wall 415 feet away in left center for his second hit of the day. He barely had time to dust himself off after a headlong slide to the bag at third before Joe Gordon lined another triple to the exact same place in left. With the game now tied, Chicago manager Jimmy Dykes decided to have his pitcher, Thornton Lee, walk the bases loaded to set up a force at home. The Yankees then pinch-hit Red Ruffing, a frontline pitcher, for Johnny Sturm, inserted into the lineup this day to play first as veteran Joe Gordon moved back to his old position at second for Jerry Priddy and Frankie Crosetti took over at short for Phil Rizzuto. Ruffing, one of the best hitting pitchers in baseball history, promptly delivered a game-winning line smash over Appling's head at short to put Chicago and archstrategist Dykes out of their misery.

Ironically, a *Saturday Evening Post* profile on Rizzuto and Priddy, in preparation before their troubles, raved about the Yankee rookies, the "two kids who in four years have never hit under .300, played on any club but a pennant winner, or failed to be named on the All-Star team of whatever league they happened to be in. Paste that in your hat." McCarthy pasted it in, all right, and found a nice warm spot on the bench for his rookies to read their press clippings. Never one to mince words, McCarthy told the writers covering the game, "They could learn a lot looking on from the bench." Earlier in the day McCarthy had simply looked at Johnny Sturm and motioned him out to first. At the same time, Sturm recalls, McCarthy tossed a first baseman's glove at Tommy Henrich, a pantomime quiz to which Sturm guessed the right answer immediately: If I don't hit, I sit. Sturm's bat spoke eloquently for the next couple of weeks; his glove spoke eloquently all year. Unfortunately, an injury later during the war made 1941 not only his best year in the majors but his last.

The just demoted Yankee double play combination was not the *Saturday Evening Post*'s only interest. Extremely influential and previously isolationist, the magazine cartwheeled on May 16 and announced its support for Roosevelt's policies in regard to the war effort. This was a key move in the hastening march toward war of spring and summer. The *Post*'s editorial explained: "We are like a man who has jumped off a springboard and has not yet touched the water. He isn't wet, but he hasn't a chance of getting back on the board." Changing circumstances and new dramatic realities made the shift necessary for the magazine. The will of the western democracies to confront the Nazis was now in its words a "national crusade." The crusade at this point was more a supply line. In a recent poll, only one state in the union had favored open declaration of war against Germany in May 1941, Florida, a state stirred by the impassioned anti-Nazi tirades of its New Deal senator, Claude Pepper, whose golden vocal cords still ring in today's House of Representatives in support of the land's elderly and poor.

At the Stadium on May 16 the Yankees loosened a couple of buttons on their flannels in garnering their first win that week. In the opening inning Charlie Keller took one of Lee's pitches 440 feet to left center, and by the time anyone ran it down Keller was crawling up the back of Red Rolfe, who had just rounded third in front of him. Keller beat the throw for an inside-the-park homer. Stay tuned. This was neither the first nor the last of its kind, and Keller would in the next few weeks set some unusual standards in a category that if it had a name would be called power running.

When DiMaggio came up in the third inning, Thornton Lee didn't figure he could hit it any farther than Keller had in the first. But DiMaggio did. He launched a fastball beyond the bull pen in left and deep into the cheap bleacher seats. Only one other American Leaguer besides DiMaggio had ever hit one so far to eft at Yankee Stadium, Hank Greenberg of the Tigers. But Hank wasn't likely to get the chance to try it again this year, at least not from Camp Custer, where he was in his second week of basic training as an Army private. Detroit fans had organized letter-writing campaigns to members of Congress to get Greenberg back, even arguing that the size of his $50,000 a year salary, the highest in baseball, qualified him for exemption under essential employee status. No luck. Greenberg would serve until an Army doctor, possibly a Tiger fan, discharged him just before Pearl Harbor for bilateral pes planum, or flat feet. A week later Hank reenlisted.

Abroad on May 16, Hitler's propaganda ministry had gotten its hands on the Hess affair and began releasing stories that the deputy führer was entirely mad, was woefully under the influence of astrologers, and believed underwater streams were coursing in different directions under his bed. Göring was personally delegated to detain Willy Messerschmitt, the famous plane designer who reportedly had helped Hess fit out his escape plane. When the irate Göring asked Messerschmitt how he could assist such a lunatic, Messerschmitt reportedly replied, "How could such a lunatic be deputy führer of Germany?"

In regard to the Hess flight, the day's wire services out of Europe carried a story that in retrospect provided the clue to the entire affair. It was reported that the Gestapo had arrested a man by the name of Albrecht Haushofer in Germany for questioning. It turned out that 2 years before, in 1939, Hitler had indeed agreed to a Hess scheme to sound out England about an alliance through the offices of Haushofer, an Anglophile and a friend of the Duke of Hamilton. The duke and Haushofer were supposed to meet in Portugal. Nothing came of the plan, but Hess obviously brooded about it after falling out of favor with Hitler's new men, Goebbels, Göring, and Himmler.

It now seemed as if Hess had put the plan into action by eliminating Haushofer as middleman. Or had he? When Hess was arrested by the Scottish Home Guard, he carried fake identification as Luftwaffe Lieutenant Alfred Horn, and when he met the Duke of Hamilton, he gave him Albrecht Haushofer's greeting card. Even the fake name, Alfred Horn, bore Haushofer's initials. For different reasons, Hitler too put poor Haushofer, by then seemingly out of Hess's mad plan, back into it. Haushofer's father, by the way, was the founder of a branch of study called geopolitics that formed the basis of Charles Lindbergh's views on the rights of Germany in Europe. With all these tangential connections, including the one with the air pioneer Hamilton, it's understandable why Roosevelt was convinced, though incorrectly, that Lindbergh had something to do with the Hess affair.

In Vichy France on May 16, Marshall Pétain was beside himself over Roosevelt's impounding of the *Île de Normandie* (it later caught fire in the New Jersey docks in 1942 but was refitted as an American troopship). Pétain insisted that his nation's interest and now its honor dictated a firmer relationship with Nazi Germany, as if the choice were his. Pétain then threatened the United States and Britain regarding actions he deemed naval piracy, as if Vichy France were in a position to do much. The British responded to Pétain by sending bombers to blast Axis planes into oblivion near the Damascus airport in Vichy-mandated Syria. This was the second major humiliation of the week in a series of disasters for the Vichy regime through spring and summer. Free French General Charles de Gaulle was ecstatic, cabling Churchill on May 16: "We shall win the war."

Whatever Vichy France's national interest by this point in 1941, its national honor had much to answer for. A story on the back pages of *The New York Times* for this second day of Di-Maggio's streak noted that the Vichy government had just roused 5,000 Jews in the middle of the night for deportation to labor camps under something called the *Statut des Juifs*. This strange legislation authenticated Jewish inferiority under Vichy law, determining in precise degree what sort of grandparental bonds produce a predominance of Jewish blood. Oddly enough, the degree could rise or fall depending on whether one's grandparents attended synagogue.

GAME 3: May 17

In the Saturday afternoon rubber game of the series with the White Sox, the Yankees could only manage five hits while losing 3–2. The game was delayed by a passing rainstorm, and Mc-Carthy might have hoped for a lingering one. The Yankees got what hits they could muster off Chicago ace John Rigney, soon to have an intricate and complex set of troubles with the officials of the military draft, who wanted him much more that spring than he wanted to be wanted. DiMaggio managed a harmless second inning single, enough to chalk up the game for the streak but not enough to help his mates.

Saturday was the first week's anniversary of the Bavarian beginnings of the Rudolf Hess flight, with its vertical conclusion having taken place on the previous Sunday. Hess had been demanding all week long, with little luck, to speak to King George VI. Only the Duke of Hamilton so far had talked with him at length. With Hitler now deriding him, Churchill ignoring him, and British agents pumping him, Hess clammed up. For nearly a half a century he said little, right through the Nuremberg trials and his long imprisonment in Spandau. In fact, the real story of the Hess escapade was supposedly part of the new material in the Hitler diaries that were forged a few years back. But on this weekend of May 17, all Hess said was that his flight deserved to be written up in aeronautical journals the world over for its plan-ning and daring. He boasted to British intelligence on Saturday that the mission's conception and the precision of its execution were the equivalent of Lindbergh's transatlantic crossing in 1927.

Before the game at the Stadium that same Saturday, Mc-Carthy held a team meeting to explain to his men the shake-up of his infield. When he came out of the clubhouse, he told reporters: "Something had to be done, and relieving Rizzuto and Priddy of the strain was the obvious recipe. Maybe we expected too much of them." With Bill Dickey back at catcher after a couple of days' rest, McCarthy's infield had everyone in it from the late '30s but Lou Gehrig. It must have looked like old times to New York Mayor Fiorello La Guardia, who showed up at the Stadium for the game. La Guardia would soon get as caught up as any Yankee fan in his *compare* Giuseppe DiMaggio's streak, especially its key games near the Wee Willie Keeler record of 44. Giuseppe, by the way, is what Dan Daniel called DiMaggio in his 1941 *World-Telegram* columns. Around the league it was an oddly respectful "the Big Dago," which DiMaggio rather liked and sometimes used when referring to himself.

In the three outings with the Yankees this first series of DiMaggio's streak, Chicago White Sox pitchers tossed three complete games. Among managers, Jimmy Dykes was hardly a man of patience, yet the four men in his rotation—Smith, Lee, Rigney, and the veteran Ted Lyons—plus a few fill-ins tossed a remarkable 106 complete games in the 1941 season. No staff in the American League had proved that durable since the record set back in 1904 by the Boston Red Sox pitchers, led by Cy Young, of 148 complete games in a 154-game season.

About a hundred miles southwest of New York City—a $5.26 train ride in 1941—the Philadelphia Athletics on Saturday honored their 79-year-old owner-manager Connie Mack's fifty-fifth year in major league baseball. The A's Shibe Park became Connie Mack Stadium, that is, until Mr. Mack spotted the new sign and made his ground crew take it down immediately. Connie Mack had been with the Athletics since the origin of the American League in 1901, and he would stick with them until 1950, at which time the Connie Mack Stadium sign went up for good. Mr. Mack took a different attitude in 1941 toward the threat of the lottery draft than had Ed Barrow of the Yanks and Larry

MacPhail of the Dodgers. The old veteran, born during the Civil War and in his mid-30s by the time of the Spanish-American War, froze his austere face and said, "If they draft them, they draft them."

Elsewhere in the majors on May 17, Ted Williams heated up the action. He pummeled Bobby Feller for two doubles and a single during the Red Sox game against the Indians, though Feller weathered the storm 12–9. Williams had singled off the Indians' Jim Bagby the day before. His average was up to .353, and he was keeping what at so early a stage seemed an inconsequential pace with DiMaggio's streak. Cleveland was now 8½ games in front of the Yankees. In the National League, the Dodgers still played nip to the Cardinals' tuck.

Before the White Sox left town and the St. Louis Browns arrived, New Yorkers could catch three fine movies that had just opened. With production booming, 1941 was a banner year for Hollywood, and some of its best moments occurred during DiMaggio's streak. At week's end *The Devil and Miss Jones* premiered at Radio City Music Hall, a touchingly funny depression film about a tycoon (Charles Coburn) who takes a job in his own department store and finds himself befriended by union supporters Bob Cummings and Jean Arthur. The movie bears no resemblance to a much later film, somewhat different in intent, that borrowed most of its title. For the choral set, Paul Robeson's *Proud Valley,* about an unlikely collection of singing Welsh miners, opened on Thursday. Best of all, *Major Barbara,* adapted from George Bernard Shaw's witty play about salvation, greed, and love, opened at the Astor. Filmed during the previous year's aerial blitz of London, *Major Barbara* starred British actors Rex Harrison, Robert Morley, and Wendy Hiller, and its ad campaign featured cartoons of Shaw himself carrying a placard: "YOU SENT US 50 DESTROYERS...I SEND YOU MAJOR BARBARA." This referred to the obvious end run around the Neutrality Act earlier in the year whereby the United States simply decommissioned 50 destroyers and sent them to England in return for access to British naval bases. It was hard for Shaw or anyone else to imagine conditions under which the English would *not* provide us access at this time in the war.

W. Somerset Maugham arrived in New York on the weekend

from his home in France. He planned to remain for the duration of the war. At the inaugural dinner of European PEN, an organization for exiled writers, Maugham delivered the keynote address. After dinner he told friends about a conversation in Paris several years before the war with the composer Maurice Ravel, of *Bolero* fame. Ravel wanted to set to music Lincoln's Gettysburg Address because he thought it was the best speech he had ever heard. "But I have forgotten it completely," he said to Maugham. "Perhaps you could recite it for me."

GAME 4: May 18

Sunday, May 18, 1941, was "I Am an American Day" all over the country. While 30,109 headed to the ball park for the Yankees' game against the St. Louis Browns, over 700,000 gathered in New York City's Central Park for a rally presided over by Mayor Fiorello La Guardia, Eddie Cantor, and the immensely popular black entertainer Bill Robinson, who personally guaranteed the crowd that he would stop Hitler at Yankee Stadium if the crazed führer ever marched on Harlem. La Guardia cast his nets wider and informed "Adolf, Benito, and Joe" that "we are not afraid to defend our democratic institutions." "Joe" was Stalin, who took it on the chin this day not only from La Guardia but from Arthur Koestler's just published novel, *Darkness at Noon,* a brilliant account of the Soviet purge trials of the 1930s.

Under less dire circumstances at the Stadium, Lefty Gomez, DiMaggio's road roommate, pitched the Yankees to a 12–2 romp over the American League's patsies. Every American in the lineup hit well for the Yankees on "I Am an American Day," including Gomez, who was notoriously poor at the plate. Gomez was married to June O'Dea, of the musical comedy stage and a good friend of DiMaggio's actress wife, Dorothy Arnold. It was not unusual for the two ballplayers and two wives to step out for a full evening on the town in New York, except on nights preceding games in which Gomez pitched. Johnny Sturm remembers the solicitous Gomez, whose concern for DiMaggio's energy level bore a direct relation to the pitching rotation: "Lefty took DiMaggio under his wing the nights before he pitched. And Joe was rested and ready—he hit pretty good when Lefty was on the mound. You have to remember, Lefty was getting towards the end of his career and DiMaggio put out a little extra for him. We had a lot of rookies on our staff waiting to take over." DiMaggio confirmed as much in an interview a few years after: "When El Goofy pitched, I usually came through." Of course, Sturm also remembers other times when DiMaggio would wander into the clubhouse, perhaps on days when the rookies were pitching, muttering about the previous night's action and the range of his wife's interests. "I don't suppose it would do any harm to mention it now," said Sturm, with an early '40s sense of what constitutes harm, "but Joe used to complain sometimes that he had to change clothes three different times in a night for three different parties." Harm or no, DiMaggio had the wardrobe to do it.

In the middle of the Yankee rout of the Browns, DiMaggio recorded a perfect 3 for 3 day, though the perfection had a more elegant cut to it in the box score than it did on the field. The *New York Herald Tribune* quibbled that "DiMaggio was credited with three hits on drives manhandled by fielders. Twice he handcuffed the third baseman and the other time Laabs [the Browns' right fielder] must have been worrying about backing into the railing when he let the ball jump out of his glove." Matters were even more complicated than the *Tribune* reported. In the fourth, DiMaggio popped to Clift at third for an apparent easy out. But on his swing the bat nicked Grube's glove for a catcher's interference call and, according to the vagaries of the rule book, an automatic single. DiMaggio trotted to first.

There was only one other game during the streak in which DiMaggio had a perfect day at the plate, a 3 for 3 game against the White Sox on June 19, and in that game he hit the ball with considerably more authority than he did in this one. Everything seemed slightly jaundiced. His grounder to third in the first just squirted off Harland Clift's glove. Dan Daniel, the official scorer, claimed quite rightly that Clift would have had no throw on DiMaggio even if he had fielded the ball cleanly: hence, a hit. The next time up, in the second, DiMaggio sliced a high, drifting fly down the right field line. Chet Laabs, playing over toward center, got on what served for his horse and headed straight for the angle of the short foul pole and the low right field railing. He ran a long way, coasted underneath the fly, speared it on the way down, and, having so far done everything right, did one last thing wrong: He dropped the ball. Dan Daniel rewarded Laabs for his long run by not penalizing him with an error for the muffed fly. DiMaggio coasted into second with a cheap double.

Joe DiMaggio's charmed hits for the day brought his streak average to an even .500 (7 for 14), edging him ahead of Williams, who had matched the fledgling four-game streak so far at .375 (6 for 16). The hottest Yankee at the moment was a rejuvenated Bill Dickey, at .375 for the season and moving in on Cronin and Travis for tops in the league. Dickey had also hit in 19 straight of the games in which he had an at bat (there were a few in which he played but didn't get up). Arky Vaughan of the Pirates still led in the National League at .384, followed by Enos "Country" Slaughter of the Cardinals at .365.

Among those on the St. Louis Browns squad agape at the day's festive events but probably none too happy with the day's score was their starting shortstop, who was nursing a leg injury, a slick fielder by the name of John Berardino. With the second of two r's taken out of his name, he now appears on television five days a week as Dr. Steve Hardy on the immensely popular soap opera *General Hospital.* In another fitting "I Am an American Day" show business note, a young Hollywood couple appeared in the Sunday *Chicago Tribune* magazine supplement feature on movieland marriages. The two looked confident and coy, in masculine-feminine order, climbing out of their movieland pool: a lovely Jane Wyman and an ex-lifeguard, ex-radio announcer, Ronald "Dutch" Reagan. The stars, parents of a brand-new baby daughter, Maureen, had just been voted Hollywood's happiest in a Los Angeles poll.

GAME 5: *May 19*

New York citizens and fans were exhausted after Sunday's all-day extravaganza, and only 5,388 showed up at Yankee Stadium on Monday afternoon to watch the lowly Browns rear up and beat the Yankees 5–1. While the nation celebrated everything American at the expense of everything Axis on Sunday, on Monday news reached the land of a disaster at sea perpetrated by the very Nazis who had been vilified so roundly the day before. An Egyptian steamer, the *Zamzam*, with 138 Americans on board (including 35 children), had been out of contact for about a month somewhere between Brazil and Africa. The State Department in Washington and the Foreign Office in London had feared the worst for some time, but the worst became clear only on this day. The Berlin command boasted that a Nazi surface raider had shelled the ship and blown it to pieces because it was carrying a small American ambulance corps headed circuitously for east Africa, where, ironically, its services would no longer be needed. This day the aristocratic, humane, and terribly sensible duke of Aosta, commander of Italian forces for the east African Ethiopia campaign, surrendered Mussolini's Africa corps of 38,000 men to the British. Mussolini's troops found the British tank forces more formidable than they had Haile Selassie's spearmen.

In boasting of their action against the *Zamzam*, the Germans declared that transporting an ambulance corps was a violation of the U.S. wartime Neutrality Act. Roosevelt was furious; he felt we ought to be the ones to determine when the Neutrality Act was violated. Although "Remember the *Zamzam*" was never to have the resonance in American history of "Remember the Alamo" or "Remember the *Lusitania*," the fate of this sorry steamer remained on Roosevelt's mind for his famous "unlimited emergency" speech in a few days, one of the most galvanizing of his entire presidency and a watershed in readying America for war. DiMaggio and the Yankees would be playing in Washington, D.C., at the time of the speech, where the streak's progress would first be picked up by the media right after Roosevelt's stirring words about efforts and increments. In one way or another, everyone in 1941 was either tracking or counting or doing both.

At the Stadium on Monday, May 19, St. Louis pitcher Dennis Galehouse, who in his previous outing against the Washington Senators had pitched a one-hitter, stifled the Yankees on four hits. One of them was Joe DiMaggio's two-out double to left in the seventh inning. DiMaggio mustered just enough energy to extend the streak on his last time at bat, but the Yankees could not muster enough to pick him up from second, where he remained at the inning's end. On his other trips against Galehouse, DiMaggio flied out twice and walked.

Marius Russo, the quick Yankee left-hander, pitched well against the Browns, but his teammates made life difficult behind him. The new double play combination of veterans Crosetti and Gordon started doing what the old double play combination of rookies Rizzuto and Priddy had been doing before McCarthy benched them: dropping balls. Gordon fumbled a double play ball in the first, and Crosetti did the same in the fourth. On each occasion the Browns scored clumps of runs on doubles by Heffner and Cullenbine, respectively. Bill Dickey was the only Yankee who made an afternoon of it. He homered in the fifth inning for the one Yank run and extended his substantial hitting streak to 20 straight. By losing this day, the Yanks followed a pattern they had sustained for over 2 weeks. They had not won two ball games in a row since beating Cleveland twice earlier in the season.

There is no charity in the hearts of rival borough fans. Only on one occasion this day did the Yankee crowd roar its approval—when the scoreboard operator posted nine runs for the Chicago Cubs in the second inning of a game against the Dodgers. The Cubs went on to win 14–1, knocking the Dodgers out of first place half a game behind the Cardinals. But the Dodgers weren't ready to take the loss or a 7–6 loss the day before lying down. An ever-vigilant Larry MacPhail protested that the Cubs had exceeded their roster limit of 25 because an extra outfielder was in the hospital when he should have been optioned to Montreal. Here's the way MacPhail finagled. Three days earlier he had traded minor leaguer Charlie Gilbert to the Cubs in exchange for second baseman Billy Herman. But Gilbert had a bum leg, and the Cubs had him checked out at a hospital before sending him on his way to Montreal. MacPhail and the Dodgers protested that picking up Gilbert's hospital tab was tantamount to exceeding their roster limit. He demanded that Chicago's last two wins over the Dodgers be forfeited. The National League president, Ford Frick, listened to MacPhail with even less charity in his heart for the Dodger cause than the Yankee fans displayed when Chicago posted all those runs: "Baloney, the violation is merely technical." He fined the Cubs $500. "Well," said MacPhail, "it was worth a try."

GAME 6: May 20

Several hours before the Yankees and Browns slugged it out in a donnybrook at the Stadium on Tuesday, news poured over the wire services about the launching of one of the most daring and, it turned out, excruciating campaigns of the war. At 8 A.M. on the morning of May 20, an aerial shock force of German paratroopers 10,000 strong, *Fallschirmjäger*, or "hunters from the sky," appeared in transports and glider planes over the northwest horizon of Crete. Coincidentally, an article in the Sunday magazine section of *The New York Times*, "Invasion from the Sky," had the week before reviewed the tactics and risks of just such an aerial invasion, claiming that the Germans planned to send paratroopers onto the island of Great Britain.

On Crete, following incessant and violent Stuka dive-bombing attacks at daylight, German paratroopers, mostly former Hitler Youth, descended in wave after wave of multicolored parachutes from hundreds of silent gliders. British defenders on Crete watched in awe as an armed invasionary force dotted the skies over the island, the ancient home of the Minoans and the exilic place of the fabulous artificer Daedalus, the inventor of manned flight. The official British history of the campaign recalled the almost deadly elegance of the battle's opening moments as the paratroopers descended: "Each man dangling carried a death; his own, if not another's." British forces commenced firing as soon as they had taken in the haunting spectacle, and hundreds of German chutists died literally before setting foot on Crete.

Project Mercury, as the Germans dubbed the battle, naming it after the messenger of winged flight, was not a foregone conclusion. The British had a sound chance of winning with a 3 to 1 advantage in troop strength, with control of key landing strips and tactical positions, and with excellent intelligence information on the German invasion plan from deciphered codes. If the Germans failed to capture the landing strip for reinforcements, their first wave of paratroopers would be slaughtered on the ground. As it was, their first wave casualty rate was an extraordinary 40 percent; the Germans had experienced nothing like this kind of resistance in any other ground campaign so far in the war.

The sheer intensity and high drama of the Cretan invasion all but obscured another bit of Nazi action this day that would generate the monstrous shape of things to come in the war. The General Office of Emigration in Berlin sent a circular letter to key Nazi officials banning emigration of Jews from all German-occupied territories because of what Göring referred to as the "doubtless imminent final solution" (*Endlösung*). This was the first time Göring had employed such phrasing for what the Germans had in mind, though he was so vague about what the solution entailed that even those victimized failed to recognize the horrific scope of the Nazi project for the Jews of Europe.

On this historic day for World War II in the Mediterranean and in the consular offices of German-held territory, the Yankees and Browns slapped each other around at the Stadium with little mercy. When the dust settled, the Yankees came out on top 10–9. Despite the buzz of activity around him, DiMaggio went hitless until the eighth inning, when with none out he singled sharply to center off submariner Eldon Auker. Later, in game 38 of the streak, Auker would figure again in another eighth inning at bat, one of the most desperate moments of the record for DiMaggio. But now there was no streak pressure to speak of, just game opportunity. Earlier in the fifth inning DiMaggio had ripped one down the line toward Harland Clift, only to have the Brown third baseman make a spinning, backhanded stab and a fine throw to force Henrich at second. If DiMaggio was robbed early, he was mortified later. An odd baseball occurrence in the ninth inning involved a would-be DiMaggio hit that became a freak DiMaggio out. Fortunately, the streak was already locked in—it would have been a heartless way to lose it. With Rolfe on second and Henrich on first, DiMaggio looped one behind second. But Lucadello and Heffner were moving a little in on the dirt for a double play, and neither made much of a gesture toward the short fly, assuming Walt Judnich could come in to field it. Wrong. Judnich came in, all right, but the ball dropped untouched at his feet. Where was Rolfe? Not on third, where he might have wished. Instead, he lingered at second because he was sure Judnich was going to get the short fly. Judnich picked up DiMaggio's would-be single, fired a strike to third, and hung Rolfe out to dry. No hit for DiMaggio—just a complicated force-out.

The lead changed hands all day as the Yankees held out against the only team in the American League playing worse than they were at this time in the year. The Browns committed six errors. It was a mad day, including a bizarre play, also in the ninth inning, in which Tommy Henrich scored from second base on a ground ball back to pitcher George Caster. Henrich just kept motoring around third and so stunned Browns' first baseman George McQuinn, who had grabbed the throw from Caster, that McQuinn took a header in the dirt before throwing home. His sorry humpbacked toss arrived too late to get the speeding Henrich. Bill Dickey's three hits on the day put his average at .391 and his streak at 21. Roy Cullenbine of the Browns still led the league at .414. Ted Williams matched DiMaggio's streak at 6 straight with a single off Hal Newhouser in Boston's 4–2 win over the Tigers. His streak average was .348 to DiMaggio's .409, but Williams was gearing up for a 3-week tear that in his view would make his season, and what a season it was.

GAME 7: May 21

The Detroit Tigers, American League pennant winners in 1940, came to town on Wednesday. They played a marvelous ball game against the Yankees, with New York winning it in the tenth inning 5–4 after scoring two to tie in a dramatic ninth inning rally. DiMaggio extended the young streak easily with a run-scoring single in the first off Schoolboy Rowe; he added another clutch base hit off reliever Al Benton to drive in a run during the rally in the ninth. The great Tiger left fielder, Hank Greenberg, also played a game this day, but not for Detroit. Warming up for a stint with his division's hardball team, Greenberg starred in a recreational softball game with the antitank company sluggers. He was called out on strikes his first time at bat on a ball that was 6 feet over his head: "That's no worse than some umps in the American League," he grumbled.

May 21 was one of those spring days when events all around the world crescendoed. Normal interludes at the ball park, even brilliant games like this afternoon's, paled in the greater historical light. Hitler, prodded by his downtrodden Vichy allies and aware that Roosevelt intended reprisals for the sinking of the *Zamzam,* decided that the time was ripe to expel all American consular diplomats from declared war areas, including 2,000 officials in Paris. Roosevelt had been regularly deporting German aliens living in America all through the winter and spring of 1941. Before DiMaggio's streak was over both the Axis powers and the western democracies would clear all diplomatic decks, so to speak, by expelling and counterexpelling every portfolio-carrying official of the wrong stripe in their rival spheres of influence.

On Crete, May 21 was do or die day for the British. Because of strategic bungling, they died when they might have done. During the wee hours of the morning a few hundred German paratroopers moved into position around Hill 107 at the Maleme heights while the British, saving virtually all their troops for daylight, left positions around the airstrip vacant. When the German field commander probed the hill, he couldn't believe it was unoccupied. In the dark the German paratroopers secured the hill, and by daylight they were dug in to cover the Maleme airstrip. The Germans could now gain reinforcements by flying in troop transports. Wave after wave of troops began landing on May 21, including the former heavyweight champion of the world, paratrooper Max Schmeling. His story would capture attention in the next several days.

In a theater of action far from the Mediterranean, another climactic wartime adventure began this day. Through their Enigma decoder, stolen from the Germans without the Germans' knowledge, the British had information that two large battleships were under way in the Kattegat Channel between Denmark and Sweden. One of these was the brand-new *Bismarck,* the newest, fastest, and most deadly ship in the German fleet, fresh from its shakedown cruise in the Baltic. With British naval superiority over the Germans at a 7 to 1 ratio, Hitler had put enormous energies and resources into a massive ship-building program. The *Bismarck* was the pride of that effort and the apple of his naval eye. The British Admiralty wanted to track it down and blow it out of the water before the Germans moved it into the open Atlantic, either to harass the convoy lines or to serve as support for an aerial invasion of the Hebrides akin to the attack on Crete.

On the afternoon of May 21, a British Spitfire reconnaissance plane sent out to scout for German ships spotted the *Bismarck* and the *Prinz Eugen* in the Grimstad Fjord south of Bergen. The British home admiral, Sir John Tovey, initiated the most sustained and exhaustive sea and air hunt in the history of naval warfare. He dispatched his battle cruiser *Hood* and his battleship the *Prince of Wales,* but miserable weather made it impossible to sight the German ships. Instead, the British Admiralty played its latest ace. One of its sleek cruisers, the *Suffolk,* was equipped with a sophisticated new radar system, as yet untested against such prize targets. In the next days the cruiser *Suffolk* would have more to tell Admiral Tovey about the movements of the *Bismarck* and the *Prinz Eugen* than the Germans thought was technically possible in 1941.

With all the action around the world on May 21, the ball game at the Stadium struggled to meet the competition. The Tigers almost iced this wonderful game in the eighth inning after Pat Mullin's home run, but Rudy York ran them out of a big inning by getting hung up between first and second when Red Rolfe cut off a relay throw. After a rally, led by DiMaggio, to tie in the ninth, the Yankees pulled it out in the tenth when Red Rolfe, who had four hits on the day, contributed the gamer, a triple to drive in Johnny Sturm. Sturm had smashed six hits in the last two games, raised his average over 100 points, and worked his hitting streak up to 5 games. Every paper in New York City commented on Sturm's performance since his insertion in the lineup, cynically wondering when the rookie would begin to fade.

The best play of the game occurred in right when Tommy Henrich reached into the stands over the fence and pulled a Charlie Gehringer drive out of the collective clutches of several 2d Signal Corps trainees visiting the ball park from Fort Monmouth, New Jersey. All the trainees in the right field seats, a contingent of 200, were delighted with the play, and Henrich became an adopted member of the corps for the rest of the ball game. Though the Yankees were able to put together a winning streak of two games in a row for the first time since May 8, Bill Dickey's

21-game hitting streak ended this day. In Boston, Ted Williams was luckier. The Browns had come to town, and Williams had a chance to feed on St. Louis pitching. With four hits on May 21, the Red Sox star eased among the league's leading hitters for the first time that year at .367. So far he had matched DiMaggio's hitting streak at 7, shooting up to a .429 (12 for 28) average during the run, compared with DiMaggio's .407 (11 for 27).

In America on May 21, prominent isolationists across the land celebrated the fourteenth anniversary of Charles A. Lindbergh's heroic and pioneering 1927 solo flight across the Atlantic, but the Philadelphia Municipal Transportation System picked the Lindbergh anniversary to announce its refusal to carry advertisements for the aviator's upcoming appearance on behalf of the America First Committee in the City of Brotherly Love. Furthermore, John Fredrick Lewis, president of the Philadelphia Academy of Music, refused to allow the scheduling of Lindbergh's appearance at the academy's auditorium. Lewis said he intended no direct insult to Lindbergh, but he could not bear the thought of the fascist goons who so often attended these meetings showing up at his beloved hall. *The New York Times* took its almost daily shot at Lindbergh by printing text of a congratulatory telegram sent to the aviator on his flight's anniversary by a shadowy group of South American Nazis, Afirmación Argentina.

More than ever on this anniversary, false rumors circulated that Lindbergh and Rudolf Hess were collaborating to set up an Anglo-American-German alliance against Russia. Even the British papers were linking the two aviators, both of them former, if not present, Anglophiliacs: "Hess was—as good old Lindbergh was— a friend." Lindbergh, of course, met Hess while being shepherded around Berlin by Hermann Göring in 1938, and the two had spoken about long-distance flying. With Lindbergh on his mind, Hess imagined a world capable of being moved and influenced by a single, precise heroic act. Indeed, the paranoid Hess shared with the gloomy Lindbergh the fear that world events were escaping the control of the truly gifted and the heroically blessed. Oblivious to the scorn of others, Hess took the burden of the historical moment upon himself when the historical moment had already passed him by. The parallel with Lindbergh in America was not exact, but that did not prevent Lindbergh's enemies, especially in the Roosevelt administration, from making it. The famous aviator's saga, at once glorious and immensely sad, fascinated everyone during the days of DiMaggio's streak, and there were more twists before Lindbergh's final turn prior to Pearl Harbor in 1941.

GAME 8: May 22

The Yankees closed out their two-game series with the Tigers at the Stadium on May 22 by holding on to win a squeaker 6–5. DiMaggio got but one hit in the soggy, rain-interrupted game, a clean single off lefty Archie McKain in the seventh. He tried to stretch it into a double, saw that he was about to get thrown out by 20 feet, and reversed course back to first. There Rudy York waited for him with ball in hand, but DiMaggio slickered the less than acrobatic York and slid around him to the bag. Rookie Steve Peek got the win for the Yankees, the third rookie in a row to do so—Norman Branch and Charlie Stanceu had won the previous two. It was Peek's first major league win. Bobo Newsom took the loss for Detroit.

On Crete, the day's action got more desperate for the British defenders. The Germans began moving in enough troops to even out the odds, though they held but one airstrip while the British, mostly troops from New Zealand and Australia, still held much better tactical positions on the rest of the island. Churchill desperately wanted Crete kept in British hands for strategic access to North Africa and for home front morale. A year before he had ordered Crete heavily fortified, but the man Churchill called his "muddle east" commander, General Archibald Wavell, had virtually ignored the prime minister. Instead, Wavell concentrated on defeating the duke of Aosta's Italian forces in east Africa. With the commanding officer on Crete begging for military supplies 5 days before the Germans attacked, Wavell sent an emergency shipment of tablecloths and veterinary kits for sick mules.

May 22, 1941, in America turned out to be a black day for

another fervent isolationist, a staunch supporter of Lindbergh's efforts and one of the few who would employ the aviator after war broke out, the elder Henry Ford. Workers at the Ford Motor Company voted for the first time ever to allow union representation, selecting Walter Reuther's recently formed UAW affiliate of the CIO. Henry Ford tried to stave off the union vote by beating Reuther's mid-May GM settlement with a 15-cents-per-hour across-the-board raise for his workers, but the tactic failed. Ford called the union vote a miserable mistake for his company and for the American automobile business.

Reuther's contract with General Motors called for the lowest paid worker in the plant, a janitor, to receive 86 cents an hour and the highest paid, a master welder, $1.60. The president of General Motors, Charles E. Wislon, did a bit better at $278,324 a year, but not as well as Louis B. Mayer of Loews Corporation, the highest paid executive of the year at $697,048. Bob Hope and Gary Cooper that year pulled in about $600,000 and $500,000, respectively. By these comparative standards, as astronomical as Joe DiMaggio's $37,500 salary for 1941 looked to some, it looked modest to others. Moreover, when DiMaggio tried to negotiate a few thousand more during spring training he was under the eagle eye of the commissioner's office because the year before Judge Kenesaw Mountain Landis had had his suspicions that several unsavory types hanging around Toots Shor's on Broadway were acting as DiMaggio's agents. The notion of a ballplayer in 1941 negotiating through and cutting in an agent was anathema to both leagues. One gambler friend of DiMaggio's in particular, Joe Gould, was on the commissioner's hit list, and Landis threatened to stomp all over Gould's zoot suit if he ever tried to influence DiMaggio's salary dealings with the Yankees. In a private chat with DiMaggio, Landis advised the Yankee center fielder to lose some of his flashier New York friends.

With the first week of DiMaggio's streak rounding out, two mildly memorable films opened in New York City: *Penny Serenade,* with Cary Grant and Irene Dunne; and *Blood and Sand,* a Technicolor remake of an old Valentino bullfight extravaganza with Tyrone Power, the rising starlet Rita Hayworth, and the lovely Linda Darnell. But a more notable piece of coming attractions news slipped into the entertainment section of the *New York*

Herald Tribune. John Huston, a young screenwriter, reportedly began work this week on his first project as a director, something called *The Knights of Malta.* The information proved to be slightly distorted; the correct title had a little more mystery to it, and the actual movie had Humphrey Bogart in it: *The Maltese Falcon.*

GAME 9: *May 23*

The orchestrated sea hunt for the *Bismarck* was still top secret when the Boston Red Sox came to New York on Friday for an afternoon game at the Stadium. Though the German battleship was locked in on the radar systems of the cruiser *Suffolk,* the British Admiralty was frightened of losing it in fog-shrouded northern waters. The Yankees and Red Sox were also stymied this day by a kind of invisibility. They stayed until dark and pounded each other into moot submission 9–9 before the umpires called it a day because there was no light left to call it anything else. DiMaggio garnered a simple single off Dick Newsome in the eighth inning of a slugfest in which a total of 47 men on both teams reached base. The game would not count in the standings, but the statistics from it remained on the books. DiMaggio's streak single therefore stood, as did a two-run single by Ted Williams that kept him even with DiMaggio through the first 9 games of the streak. This debacle would be replayed as the second game of a doubleheader on the day DiMaggio chased Wee Willie Keeler's all-time hitting streak record of 44. DiMaggio would get a chance to make the same game count twice in his streak, though the hits registered in them counted only once each.

The Red Sox used virtually their entire roster in the 3-hour game, which was plagued by ineptitude and miserable weather throughout. At least one team scored in every inning as nine weary pitchers misapplied their skills. The Red Sox player-manager, Joe Cronin, drawing upon the dregs, had to resort to a pitcher to pinch-hit in the seventh inning. Lefty Tom Judd stroked a single through the box and drove in two runs to tie the game at 9–9. King Kong Charlie Keller did most of the damage for the Yankees with a triple and two doubles. In 1939, when Keller had first come to the

Yanks, Lefty Gomez took one look at his mug and said, "That's the first ballplayer Frank Buck ever brought back alive." But a simple piece of advice in regard to Keller floated from clubhouse to press room for the benefit of everyone's general good health in the late '30s and early '40s: "Don't call him King Kong to his face."

On this Friday night a much greater sports spectacle than the sorry affair at Yankee Stadium took place under the brand-new lights at Griffith Stadium in the nation's capital: Joe Louis defended his title against Buddy Baer. When the two men stepped into the ring, Baer looked like an affable square-shouldered cardboard cutout next to the supple Louis. The champ was an odds-on favorite to retain his title in his seventeenth defense, and the odds seemed perfectly reasonable. But in round 1 Baer caught Louis with a stunning left hook and knocked him through the ropes onto the ring's apron. Long before the count approached 10, Louis stepped back into the ring, and Baer's best moment of the night was history.

For the rest of the evening the big, cumbersome Baer took a savage beating round after round. At one point near the end of the sixth, Louis hit him so hard that Baer slowly corkscrewed to a sitting position in the center of the ring. When he got to his feet, Louis stalked him and put him down again, this time leaving Baer lying supine in the corner. He haltingly raised his tottering body, winchlike, before Louis came on at the referee's signal and drove him to the canvas for a third time with a smashing right. The blow came after the bell ending the round, which no one could hear in the din and which Baer might not have been able to distinguish from the hundreds of others ringing in his head.

Two of Baer's corner men jumped into the ring to drag their unconscious hulk back to his seat; another Baer attendee, all done up in a white suit and Panama hat, headed for the champion's corner and began berating Louis for hitting after the bell. Meanwhile, Baer's manager, Ancil Hoffman, took off after the referee, Art Donovan, and refused to leave the ring at the start of the seventh round. Donovan had no choice but to forfeit the bout against Hoffman's fighter. Baer all the while sat slumped in a state of semiconsciousness on his stool; he couldn't have risen for a replay of the national anthem. Next on Louis's agenda: Billy Conn. This heavyweight title defense during DiMaggio's streak would turn out to be one of the greatest fights of the century.

On the same night as the Louis-Baer fight, but back in New York City, 20,000 people showed up inside Madison Square Garden and another 14,000 listened to loudspeakers outside as Charles A. Lindbergh and Senator Burton K. Wheeler led an America First Committee rally, one of several during the days of the hitting streak. Tonight's was crucial because it marked the beginning of a schism within the isolationist movement. John T. Flynn, liberal politician, author, and leader of the New York chapter of America First, was appalled at the profascist and anti-Semitic support that America First was receiving nationwide, though he thought his organization was being set up by warmongers. The problem was one that haunts many large organizations: the strange bedfellow syndrome. In this instance, a hooligan, one Joe McWilliams, showed up at Madison Square Garden with his racist and pro-Nazi thugs.

At the Garden rally Flynn publicly fumed at McWilliams and his assortment of yahoos: "Just because some misguided fool in Manhattan who happens to be a Nazi gets a few tickets to this rally, this meeting of American citizens is called a Nazi meeting. And right here, not many places from me, is sitting a man named McWilliams. What he is doing here, whose stooge he is, I do not know, but I know the photographers of these war-mongering newspapers can always find him when they want him." *Life* magazine was more balanced on the issue in a profile of Burton Wheeler and America First: "To suppose that all isolationists are pro-Nazi or pro-Communist is as naive as to suppose that none of them are."

Lindbergh said in his diary on this occasion that he wished Flynn had acted with dignity in these matters, but he kept his own counsel on the likes of McWilliams. In his speech, the aviator argued that Roosevelt would have to become a dictator to confront one. "If we go to war to preserve democracy abroad, we are likely to end by losing it at home." Noninterventionists at this time were apprehensive about new moves planned by Roosevelt for his upcoming "unlimited emergency" broadcast. Presidential aide Stephen T. Early had just provided a blunt forecast of the speech whose prospect made Lindbergh so nervous: "The foes of democracy abroad or at home are not going to like it."

Roosevelt had been so irritated by the Germans' sinking of the *Zamzam* with hundreds of Americans on board that the isolationists feared he was ready to use the incident as a pretext for convoys or, worse, open naval hostilities. One isolationist who lately had been keeping a low profile, the former United States ambassador to the Court of St. James's in England, Joseph Kennedy, Sr., resurfaced to volunteer advice to the President. Kennedy did not want Roosevelt to talk the nation into war over the *Zamzam* incident or any other. He dreaded the thought of a European engagement and did not wish to contribute any of his sons to an Axis bloodbath. On May 24 he spoke out in a way that friends like Burton Wheeler wished he would have done more often. Kennedy warned that we "cannot divert the tides of the mighty revolution now sweeping Asia and Europe." Any attempt to do so "would end in failure and disgrace abroad, in disillusionment and bankruptcy at home."

These remarks were a much less subtle version of a brilliant little tract, *Why England Slept,* written in 1940 by Kennedy's then 23-year-old son, Jack. Jack Kennedy argued in 1940 that democracies could not hope to confront fascist states with tactics reserved for and in fact fashioned for democracies. But by May 1941 Jack and his older brother, Joe, Jr., had second and different thoughts. Both volunteered for active military duty, though Jack's bad back would delay his actual service until late summer. The Kennedy sons tried to mollify their father's antagonism to Roosevelt or, at the very least, to have the elder Kennedy keep his distance from Burton Wheeler and America First.

Wheeler, the model for Jimmy Stewart's character in the 1939 Frank Capra movie *Mr. Smith Goes to Washington,* had directed his ample energies against Roosevelt in the early months of 1941 just as he had against the Harding administration and its kingmaker attorney general, Harry M. Daugherty, in the 1920s. He was under something of a national cloud at present for incurring Roosevelt's wrath by describing lend-lease as the "New Deal's Triple-A foreign policy to plow under every fourth American boy." Roosevelt said of the senator's remark that "it was the rottenest thing said in public life in my generation." This is the man from whom the Kennedy sons wanted their father to cut bait. In a notorious incident, Wheeler came to visit Joe Kennedy and almost sensed his presence in the vestibule as the maid insisted that the elder Mr. Kennedy was not at home. Kennedy later chortled to friends how he had stood out of sight and watched Wheeler come to a slow boil before stalking out.

GAME 10: *May 24*

The Yankees came from behind with four in the seventh to beat Boston 7–6 in Saturday's game at the Stadium. They had now won four in a row—discounting the previous day's tie—to match their longest winning streak of the young season. DiMaggio's single off Boston lefty Earl Johnson, a line drive to left with two out in the seventh, drove in the last two Yankee runs. In the sixth inning Dominic DiMaggio had all sorts of trouble with a long fly Joe hit to center, perhaps sensing with brotherly intuition the birth of a streak no one else had yet noticed. But the official scorer, Dan Daniel, shook his head and signaled a big three-base error as DiMaggio's fly ball dribbled out of his brother's glove.

This play would muddle Joe DiMaggio's later recollection of a long fly in the direction of right center on the day he tried to break Wee Willie Keeler's record of 44 straight. Stan Spence got that one after momentarily misjudging it, but Joe DiMaggio later supplemented Spence's catch with the invention of another made by his brother that robbed him of a hit in a tense moment. More than likely he superimposed the earlier image of a dropped ball—what he wanted—over a snagged one—what he dreaded—and credited Dominic with both.

Johnny Sturm, who had singled in the first two runs of the Yankee seventh, had now hit in 8 straight games since taking the collar the first day Joe McCarthy played him at first. Local reporters continued tracking Sturm's streak but said nothing of DiMaggio's or Williams's longer ones. Williams singled twice in three trips this afternoon and remained even with DiMaggio at 10 straight, outhitting the Yankee center fielder for the course of the streak so far .447 to .350. Ted was now firecracker hot.

He was in the middle of a run of games that would extend over 2 weeks in which he would hit only a few decimal points below .600. Without this spurt, Williams recalls, he could have kissed his .406 season good-bye.

On May 24 the British retreated eastward and southward in Crete as their positions deteriorated in the western sector of the island. Staff officers on the scene wanted to mount a counterattack against the Germans at Maleme but later reported that their commanders "were utterly without any offensive spirit." Churchill cabled his command: "The whole world watches your splendid battle on which great things turn." This cheery note came just as the only "turns" were by British regimental leaders—in the wrong direction. Infantry units began to trek over the central mountain range to Crete's hazardous southern coast for naval evacuation. The king of Greece and his government in exile, harbored on Crete by the British, had already hiked over primitive mountain trails to a disembarkation point for Egypt.

As things grew worse for the British in Crete, they grew better in the north Atlantic pursuit of the battleship *Bismarck*. On May 24 the British announced publicly that the chase was on. The news thrilled the western democracies and electrified those who hoped for a naval victory this year as devastating to the Germans as the victory in the air at the Battle of Britain had been in 1940. Two British capital ships, the newly commissioned *Prince of Wales* and the much older *Hood*, finally caught up with the *Bismarck* and the *Prinz Eugen* in waters well off the coast of Greenland. Unfortunately for the *Hood*, the largest battle cruiser afloat at 42,000 tons, both German ships trained their guns on her. When the *Bismarck* finally put a shell directly into the *Hood*'s ammunition magazine, the huge British ship, whose hull was too lightly armored, went under in minutes, losing the entire crew of over 1,400 men. Only three survivors remained afloat in the cold northern seas. The *Prince of Wales*, virtually unfired upon, managed to score a glancing hit on the *Bismarck*. But with the *Hood* sinking and the odds temporarily changed, the new British battleship scurried from the scene under a smoke screen. It signaled to Admiral Tovey the chilling news: "*Hood* has blown up." The mission now took on new urgency: not merely to bag the

Bismarck as the prize of the German navy but to avenge its first capital victim, the *Hood*.

Admiral Tovey called in his aircraft carrier, *Victorious*, and sent a squadron of Swordfish bombers up in the midnight sun on May 24 for a scouting mission. When the bombers sighted the *Bismarck*, they also sighted, to their amazement, an American Coast Guard cutter, the *Modoc*, steaming near the huge German ship but apparently unaware of any of the circumstances of the last few days, indeed, of the present moment. The bombers regrouped, primarily because of the confusion the *Modoc* posed, and under a tremendous barrage of antiaircraft fire from the *Bismarck* one of the Swordfish pilots snuck in a torpedo bomb. The torpedo dealt a glancing blow to the German battleship and caused a nasty, debilitating oil leak. Scores of British ships were now on their way from the Mediterranean to converge on the *Bismarck*, a wounded but still dangerous naval behemoth.

GAME 11: May 25

The Boston Red Sox won easily against the Yankees 10–3 at the Stadium to conclude their series before a large New York Sunday crowd of 36,461. Given the lopsided score, a contingent of sailors was able to leave the park with no regrets in the eighth inning when the PA announcer called for "all personnel of the *USS George E. Badger* to report back to ship immediately." The announcement was related to a general alert of U.S. naval forces in light of the ongoing *Bismarck* adventure. By the early morning of May 25, British intelligence had picked up coded German messages that the *Bismarck* had been hit and that destroyers and U-boats were to cover her as she turned south and made a run for the French coast in the wake of the *Prinz Eugen*. At the same time, feeling a bit heady about the sinking of the *Hood*, Grand Admiral Erich Raeder of the German Navy, later imprisoned with Rudolf Hess at Spandau, warned that if the President of the United States intended in his publicized upcoming speech to order armed convoys for British merchant ships across the Atlantic, this would be tantamount to a declaration of war on the German Reich.

Roosevelt did not yet intend to order armed convoys, but he must have been sorely tempted. Moreover, Admiral Raeder would have been surprised to learn exactly what the President had on his mind this morning. According to his speech writer, the dramatist Robert Sherwood, Roosevelt began speculating on what might happen if the *Bismarck* escaped the British dragnet and approached American waters in the Atlantic: "Suppose the *Bismarck* showed up in the Caribbean. We have some submarines down there. Suppose we order them to attack her and attempt to sink her? Do you think the people would demand to have me impeached?" The noninterventionists' fear that Roosevelt was staying awake nights trying to figure a way to get us into the war was not far from the mark in this instance.

Before the *USS Badger* crew left Yankee Stadium late in the game on May 25 as part of a preparatory scenario in which Roosevelt's *Bismarck* pipe dream might be parlayed into reality, a future navy cadet and fighter pilot, Ted Williams, led Boston's onslaught against the Yankees with four hits: three singles and a double. DiMaggio countered with a single to center on his first at bat against 41-year-old Lefty Grove to keep the streak intact at 11. By giving up a hit to DiMaggio, Grove participated unwillingly in two of baseball's most famous hitting records; he had also given up a home run to Babe Ruth on September 27, 1927, during Ruth's 60-home-run season. One other veteran pitcher later in the streak earned the same dubious distinction of gophering Ruth in '27 and sustaining DiMaggio in '41. His name will turn up on July 13.

Ted Williams wrote of this day's game at some length in his autobiography. Most teams in the American League adjusted their infields clockwise—though not yet to the extent of the 1946 Lou Boudreau shift—when Williams came to the plate, since he was a dead pull hitter. But Yankee manager Joe McCarthy did not like to wrench his players too far out of the normal alignment. Needless to say, Williams put all four of his hits between Sturm at first and Gordon at second. His double not only found that slot but continued in the outfield past a startled Henrich, who ought to have been positioned to play it on a hop. Sturm remembers the double in particular because he claims that neither he nor Gordon picked it up off the bat from the white-shirted background of the box seats. When he got back to the dugout, McCarthy was all over his infielders: "Christ, you could at least wave at it." Years later Williams remained puzzled by Yankee defensive strategy, wondering "why they didn't pull the shift on me that day." His wonderment is slightly anachronistic, yet his four-hit binge brought him to a league-leading .404; his game-for-game matchup during the streak now had him at .488 (21 for 43) and DiMaggio at .341 (15 for 44).

New York's baseball writers continued tracking Johnny Sturm's streak at 9 without noting that DiMaggio's was at 11. They were, however, on top of another set of numbers. This day's win put Lefty Grove on flight approach toward his goal of 300 major league victories: 296 down and 4 to go. As the weather heated up and his old dehydrated bones took the brunt of it—the man still threw hard and needed reserves of energy—wins were few and far between. But Grove wouldn't call it a career until he hit his milestone. He began as a rookie with the Philadelphia A's in 1925 and came to Boston in 1934. From 1927 to 1933 he won at least 20 games a year, including a remarkable 31–4 in 1931. During one 4-year stretch beginning in 1928, Grove had a winning percentage of .817 (103 and 23).

Another great Red Sox veteran whose career after 1941 had only a couple of sputtering years left, Jimmie Foxx, found the game this day a more troubling effort than had Lefty Grove. Foxx was playing third for the injured Jim Tabor, and during the Yankee fourth he fumbled a DiMaggio grounder for one error and then dropped a Charlie Keller pop fly in foul territory for another. With two men on and Keller given another life, "Don't Call Me Kong" stroked one into the nether regions of Yankee Stadium 457 feet away in left center for an inside-the-park home run. This was the second inside-the-parker for Keller in the last 10 games. Wearying of this unusual sort of home run, he would begin hitting grand slams in a few days. When I recently asked Keller how fast he was in comparison to the Yankee rookie Rizzuto and the Yankee Clipper, DiMaggio, Keller said, "I could beat both of 'em."

Keller generated a special kind of awe among many baseball writers of 1941, the kind associated with Williams, DiMaggio, and nonentity. None of the rare social encounters with the opposite sex that are recorded in his diary even merit the description of 'flirtation'. There is considerable evidence that Heinrich Himmler did not have his first sexual experience until he was twenty-eight – after getting married to his wife Marga. 'And about time too', commented a Nazi official, Otto Strasser, at the time.

To judge from Himmler's reading list and his own writings, he found an escape from the failures of his daily life by increasingly taking refuge in the strange, make-believe world of his books. In ancient Hindu epics he discovered a troop of fearless warlords, who impressed him greatly. They were the Kshatriya caste, the landowning aristocracy of ancient Indian society. 'That is what we must be. That is our salvation', he claimed in 1925. Elsewhere we find admiring comments about the Japanese samurai or Rome's Praetorian Guard. To belong to an elite like that would be the solution to all his problems – Heinrich Himmler, a member, or better still, the leader of a caste of carefully selected and totally dedicated warrior heroes. His dreams turned into an obsession, a self-administered cure for his painful inferiority complex. The naïve aspirations of a young man who had problems with entering adulthood became the blueprint for the SS.

He found kindred spirits in the 'Artamanen League', one the many conspiratorial societies in the *völkisch* milieu. 'Artamanen' was a name concocted from Middle High German: 'art' meaning 'farming', and 'manen' meaning 'men'. They saw themselves as a chivalric order, whose aim was the German colonisation of eastern Europe. At their evening meetings these would-be settlers argued over the introduction of labour service for young people or a programme to stem the flight from the land. From the very beginning, conquest by force, dispossession and enslavement of the Slav population were key elements in the plans of the Artamanen, though they numbered scarcely 2,000. In his diary Himmler described how the settlements of the 'Germanic paradise' should look. Between the fortified villages of the people of 'Nordic blood' there would be camps 'of labour-slaves who would be forced, with no regard to their welfare, to build our towns, villages and farms'. Among the Artamanen the obsessive notion of the master-race was growing with a vengeance. It was

Gomez and Charlie Keller skipped the game and headed straight for the capital, but DiMaggio played in the exhibition, making two fine running catches in center, walking, and scoring a run before popping out twice, to third and short center. He left the game in the seventh as Tommy Henrich moved over to center field to replace him. A purist's question: What southpaw pitcher held DiMaggio hitless for the whole game in the middle of his record 56 straight in 1941? Answer: Jimmy Halperin of the Norfolk Tars.

The Yankees broke open a 2–2 tie against their farm team by batting around in the seventh inning and scoring four runs. Phil Rizzuto, very popular in Norfolk from his stint there as a minor leaguer, did most of the damage with a two-run double as New York ended up winning 7–4. Rizzuto was the toast of the town, along with local revel master Genial Gus ("Hotfoot") Meloni, who escorted the Yankee shortstop right up to the dock where the team boarded a steamer for a leisurely voyage up Chesapeake Bay to Washington, D.C.

While the Yankees were on exhibition in Norfolk, up the eastern seaboard in New Jersey another kind of exercise was the order of the day or, better, of the early morning. At 12:15 A.M., Newark city officials, in cooperation with National Defense Forces, attempted a total blackout as a trial run for similar procedures in case of air attack. This had little significance in itself except in juxtaposition with another event that provides insight into the tone and temper of America in spring 1941. A man named John Cudahy, a friend of Charles Lindbergh and a former ambassador to Belgium, had recently gotten a solemn promise from Hitler that he wouldn't bomb American territory. Cudahy wired *Time* magazine this reassuring news from Europe after a personal interview with the führer at his Bavarian Berghof. Hitler wanted to inform the American people that he had nothing but the best intentions toward them and would never even think of an aerial assault in this hemisphere. Cudahy longed to get his interview, prepared for a larger feature in *Life* magazine, printed quickly to counter Roosevelt's major foreign policy address scheduled for this day, but *Time* refused. The editors stalled him partly because they did not want to serve as an uncritical conduit for Hitler's messages to the American people, especially messages delivered through the obliging mediation of a staunch isolationist. Cudahy was furious; he joined many of his compatriots in blaming the media, with some reason, for stifling their views.

When the Yankee ship steamed up the Chesapeake into Washington, the capital was abuzz with rumors about the President's talk that night. Something big was about to break. But first DiMaggio broke loose in grand fashion himself at Griffith Stadium in the afternoon game. He had four hits—three singles and a three-run homer smashed 425 feet to left—in the Yankees' 10–8 win over the Senators. Sturm, Crosetti, and Joe Gordon chipped in with three hits each in the New York rampage. Sturm had now hit in 10 straight, Crosetti in 9. DiMaggio's streak, almost 2 weeks old, continued to go unnoticed, though Dan Daniel in the *New York World-Telegram* first marked Crosetti's in addition to Sturm's, which he had posted almost daily. The Yankees had a 9–1 lead until a Washington uprising in the sixth, when the Senators sent 10 men to the plate, most of them against Yank ace Red Ruffing, narrowing the gap to 9–6. But Washington couldn't quite catch up. The report of the game in *The New York Times* boasted that "Joe DiMaggio's bat spoke with unmistakable authority today at Griffith Stadium." When DiMaggio later tried to reconstruct his sense of the progress of the streak around the time of his assault on George Sisler's modern-day record of 41 straight, he remembered this game but got it confused with another nearer the beginning of the season against the Senators in which he also had gotten four hits. The day-by-day pressure of the streak was not yet significant enough for DiMaggio to recall which of his early games fell inside its perimeters and which outside.

Shortly after the day's game ended, Franklin Roosevelt spoke to the entire world. Estimates of between 50 million and 85 million people listened to Roosevelt's address that evening on radio, including the New York Giants and the Boston Braves in the middle of the first night game of the year at the Polo Grounds in Manhattan. The game was halted for 45 minutes as Roosevelt's speech was relayed over the loudspeakers. Translated into 15 languages, the President's speech rallied the western hemisphere to its core. Addressing his words to "steelworker or stevedore, barber or banker," Roosevelt mustered all the moral conviction and sentiment he had stored in him for England's cause and for its plight. The bravery of that lonely nation characterized the passion of the address as Roosevelt hammered at the economic and political realities of the war. We required open sea-lanes and a free Europe for our nation to prosper, and we had no way of competing with a major industrial German nation if the Nazis enslaved the populations of Europe, controlled the Atlantic, and threatened England with annihilation.

For the President, there was no negotiating out of this war. Roosevelt ridiculed those seeking such a course, thinking, without saying so, of Hess and Lindbergh. And he openly challenged the Germans in the sea-lanes of the western world by playing on a historic tactic in American policy: He extended his notion of the boundaries of America to an almost complete Atlantic sphere of influence from Greenland to the Cape Verde Islands. We would defend the seas as we defended our borders: "When your enemy comes at you in a tank or a bombing plane, if you hold your fire until you see the whites of his eyes, you will never know what hit you. Our Bunker Hill of tomorrow may be several thousand miles from Boston." In what came to be known as his "unlimited emergency" speech, Roosevelt echoed the energy of his attack a decade before on the great depression: "We must not be defeated by the fear of the very danger which we are preparing to resist." If this phrase sounded familiar, Roosevelt made the connection implicit by rounding out his speech with his famous depression rallying cry, "The only thing we have to fear is fear itself."

Roosevelt's broadcast could not have come at a better time for the British. His Majesty's Royal Navy on May 27 had put the pride of the German fleet, the *Bismarck,* to the bottom of the sea. After a week of tracking and a relentless pursuit across 3,000 miles of open ocean, a combined British naval force of six battleships, two aircraft carriers, four 8-inch-gun cruisers, seven other cruisers, and 21 destroyers converged on the lone and limping *Bismarck.* The German ship was hundreds of miles out in the Atlantic south of Ireland and far east of her destination, the port of Brest in Vichy France.

The day before, May 26, an American-built Consolidator Aircraft scout plane with an American copilot had sighted the *Bismarck* in the morning, and the British launched an aerial torpedo attack from the newly arrived carrier *Ark Royal.* By nightfall at least one torpedo had scored a direct hit, damaging the giant ship's steering device. When the British first saw the *Bismarck* turn north, they assumed it was making a run back to the Baltic, but in reality the ship was fated to sail in maddening, unalterable circles. British intelligence decoded a signal from the *Bismarck* during the night from its commander, Captain Lütjens: "Urgent. Ship unmaneuverable. We shall fight to the last shell. Long live the führer."

British destroyers moved in during the night, and the *Bismarck*, in another wartime first, began firing radar-controlled torpedoes. But by morning, the big British ships, the *Rodney* and the *King George V*, had arrived, joined by dozens of others in a massive flotilla. The British ships fired at a range of 7,000 yards, and then the *Rodney* moved in to fire at point-blank range of 3,000 yards. The *Bismarck* was helpless, its guns silenced and fires raging on all its decks. A smaller ship, the *Dorsetshire*, sank the German battleship at 10:40 A.M. on the morning of May 27. Lloyds of London rang its historic bell on this day upon news of the *Bismarck*'s fate. In the eighteenth and nineteenth centuries the company rang the bell only when ships insured by Lloyds were lost at sea. How fitting that they chose to ring it on May 27 in jubilation at the sinking of a ship decidedly without a Lloyds of London policy.

In a final American footnote to the *Bismarck* sinking, an 86-year-old retired rear admiral, Bradley A. Fiske of the U.S. Navy, claimed credit for the weapon that had led to the German battleship's demise. Back in 1912 Fiske had taken out a patent on a torpedo device launched from an airplane and offered it to the Navy. They had shown no interest, claiming the torpedo would be wildly inaccurate if dropped from a plane. The British Navy listened more favorably to Fiske, and nearly three decades later an advanced version of his patented product did a nifty piece of work against the deadliest ship in the German fleet.

The celebration in London over the sinking of the *Bismarck* was unrestrained; symbolically the naval victory meant dominance in the Atlantic. There was nothing left to celebrate for the British on Crete, however. On the afternoon of May 27, the commander of the middle east for the British, General Wavell, issued orders to abandon the island after receiving a telegram from its commanding officer, Brigadier General Freyburg: "Crete no longer tenable." The weary commander called it the worst day of the war. A frustrated Hitler couldn't understand why it had taken so long. He cabled his own commanding general, Kurt Student: "France fell in eight days. Why is Crete still resisting?" Meanwhile Churchill was still writing his regimental commanders on Crete to reinforce and hold. Such a thorough misapprehension on Churchill's part could only mean that he had been lied to egregiously for months about the degree of preparation for the island's defense. As the battle for Crete entered its mop-up phase, the British managed to get about 11,000 men off the island by ship, the Italians landed on eastern Crete to secure positions the Germans had taken days before, and the Australian forces, which had fought best, hardest, and most successfully against the initial shock of the invasion, were captured almost to a man by the advancing Germans.

GAME 13: May 28

The Yankees and Senators played the first night baseball game in the history of Griffith Stadium on May 28, but another first made the game historic. For the first time a sportswriter noticed DiMaggio's daily performance as contributing to a sustained hitting streak. Dan Daniel was out of town traveling with the Yankees, and he was making something of a feature out of Johnny Sturm's daily hits in his columns. When on the road, Daniel would submit game accounts back to his home paper, the *New York World-Telegram*, under the anonymous tag "special to." With Daniel's daily column appearing side by side with the day's report on the ball game, the paper obviously did not wish its readers to think that Daniel wore every hat in the shop. But the "special to" correspondent and Daniel were one and the same: "Last night's battle saw all three hitting streaks on the Yankees continued.

DiMaggio hit in his thirteenth consecutive contest. Sturm in his eleventh and Crosetti in his tenth." It may have sounded as if Daniel had been tracking all three for days. He hadn't. In fact, he even stopped noting the streak games for a couple of days after Sturm's parallel effort collapsed; Daniel's real interest was in the rookie. He would pick up DiMaggio's sequence again in Cleveland.

Before the beginning of the night's game, former Washington great Walter Johnson threw the ceremonial first pitch past an electric beam at home plate, tripping the switch that flooded the park with lights. It took "Big Train" three tosses to trip the switch. His first two hard ones were wild—perhaps he was simply setting the beam up for the strike that eventually did the trick. The Griffiths paid $120,000 to install the lights, and their park now took its stand along with others equipped for night ball: Crosley Field (1935), Ebbets Field (1938), Shibe Park (1939), and the Polo Grounds, Comiskey Park, Municipal Stadium, and Sportsman's Park (1940). The Senators drew 25,000 fans, 10 times the attendance of the previous day's game. Counting the usual take on peanuts and Cracker Jacks, libations, and all other baseball paraphernalia, the Senators on May 28 probably made back half what the lights had cost before the evening was out. But the specialness of night baseball in 1941 was still such that Washington officials had to request permission to raise the flag after sundown in order to play the national anthem.

The game to inaugurate Clark Griffith's new attraction was a good one. Washington took a 3–1 lead into the eighth inning but not out of it, as the Yankees erupted for five runs, having little difficulty in that one inning, at least, seeing the nighttime ball. Joe DiMaggio got his first and only hit of the day to knock the Senator starter, Sid Hudson, out of the game with one gone in the eighth. He tripled off the right field fence. An error by Cecil Travis at short and two walks loaded the bases and allowed DiMaggio to score. Then George Selkirk, pinch-hitting for Crosetti, blasted one far into the night air for a grand slam home run. The Senators scratched for a couple of runs in the last two innings but came up shy, 6–5.

Around Washington, D.C., and throughout the rest of the

country on May 28, Roosevelt's speech of the previous evening evoked a tremendous reaction. The pace of things all across the land appeared heated and accelerated. At a press conference, the President explained that the new powers he sought in his speech would give him the right to commandeer industrial plants and transportation systems, take over communication resources, requisition vessels for sea duty, and monitor all the workings of the financial sector, industry, and labor. He reserved the right to initiate armed convoys whenever he deemed it appropriate, without notifying the Nazis.

Noninterventionists throughout the land fumed. Lindbergh literally wished to make a federal case of the President's speech. An entry in his journal for the date reads, "I must find out exactly what is involved in this proclamation—and that requires specialized legal advice." The rabidly isolationist *Chicago Tribune* printed an editorial accusing Roosevelt of conspiracy and "secret actions" to alter our naval policy—our "Jap policy" as the *Tribune*'s lead so eloquently put it—and move our entire Pacific fleet to the Atlantic. Had the President done so, the Japanese might have found fewer targets at Pearl Harbor later in the year.

A curious announcement came from the British regarding Crete on May 28, as the evacuation of thousands of exhausted troops proceeded over 30 miles of treacherous terrain on the Askifou plain. The Foreign Office was sorry to report that the former heavyweight champion of the world, Max Schmeling, the only man to defeat Joe Louis in his prime, had been killed in action on Crete while trying to flee from captors on the second day of the invasion. No one took the time to check these facts, and obituaries for Schmeling appeared throughout the west. Buddy Baer, recently battered into a state of semiconsciousness by Joe Louis, said he hated war and was certain that Schmeling felt the same way. Jack Dempsey claimed that Hitler had forced Schmeling into the Cretan fracas as a Nazi publicity stunt. The very next day, the British somewhat abashedly retracted their previous bulletin on Schmeling's death. He was indeed a casualty on Crete, but far from dead. The nature of his condition, for which he was now in an Athenian hospital, turned out to be a severe "tropical" infection rather than a fatal British bullet.

GAME 14: May 29

Attendance slipped to a paltry 1,500 on May 29 in almost un-bearably humid 97-degree heat as the Yanks and Senators played to a 2–2 tie. This inconspicuous and dreary game was one of the closest calls for DiMaggio during the course of the streak, though no one remembers its details with the exception of Johnny Sturm, who had good reason. With the skies threatening thunderstorms from the opening inning, the game was an uncomfortable or-deal for everyone. Tommy Henrich's home run in the top of the fifth put the Yankees ahead 2–1, but Senator first baseman George Archie singled home the tying run in Washington's half of that inning. In the top of the sixth, with the heavens about to burst, the Yankees scored five times, though they would dearly have liked to cut their rally short and give the Senators time to bat, therefore getting the win on the record as official.

Try as they might, the Yankees couldn't kill themselves off in the top of the sixth. Johnny Sturm slashed a clean single to ex-tend his hitting streak to 12, or so he hoped. He even tried to steal on a halfhearted hit and run play, recalling, "I wasn't ex-actly running at top speed." He was out by so ludicrous a dis-tance that the Washington manager, Bucky Harris, protested to the umps on the field that the Yanks were intentionally giving themselves up in order to get to the bottom of the inning before the rains came. As Harris ranted, the downpour began. The umps, players, and fans left the field so fast that only the echo of Harris's lament sounded round the ball park. Mother Nature made the day's final call.

Johnny Sturm lost his streak. The inning reverted to the fifth, the Yankee runs ebbed down the drain, and Sturm's single was declared unfit for the record books. But Joe DiMaggio, who also lost a solid single to the rains in the canceled sixth, had sin-gled earlier off righty Steve Sundra in the fourth inning to con-tinue the streak. Sturm paid attention to this play because he wondered at the time how long the ball game would go and what would happen to his own streak, to Crosetti's, and to DiMaggio's. Fortune smiled on the veterans in the fourth. Sturm remembers: "DiMaggio hit it down on the plate. It bounced straight up, and the fellow at third—Archie, or maybe he was at first—had to wait until it came down. Joe just beat the throw to first." DiMaggio scored that same inning on Crosetti's base hit. Both Italian streaks were sitting pretty.

With Dan Daniel keyed to Sturm and not to DiMaggio, mention was made about the loss of one streak but not about the continuation of two others. Instead, Jack Smith of the *New York Daily News* became the second baseball writer to pick up DiMaggio's trail, still 4 days before traditional lore has it that the streak was noticed by anyone. Smith reported that "Crosetti was up to eleven straight and Joe DiMaggio to fourteen." Along with his lucky streak hit, DiMaggio did something else this day he had done only twice before so far in the season—he struck out. *The New York Times* saw fit to report this rare event, as yet unaware of the streak: "It was the third time this year that Joe went down on strikes. He fanned twice on April 25. In the interim he went to bat 113 times." DiMaggio would whiff an unusual four times in the next week and then, in an astounding statistic for a power hitter, would not strike out again until July 26. Making perpetual contact had one drawback. Sometimes DiMaggio hit a pitch poorly for an out that mere mortals would have missed entirely. But for a hitter like DiMaggio, keeping the ball in constant play during the streak proved crucial to its longevity. In a phone conversation, DiMaggio agreed emphatically, "That's the one thing I always tried to do, and early in the count: hit the ball hard somewhere." One of the reasons the 56-game record is so tough to approach has to do with the subtle relation of bat contact and defensive positioning. A streaking slap hitter can be defensed by ignoring the power alleys. Not so for a streaking power hitter who hits the ball consistently and with authority.

Around the league on May 29, Bobby Feller won his tenth game of the young season, shutting out the Detroit Tigers 9–0. The Cleveland Indians had been struggling a bit of late, losing even to the lowly St. Louis Browns, but Feller remained on top of his game; the day's shutout gave him a string of 29 scoreless innings. Ted Williams, still on fire, collected six hits in nine at bats against the Philadelphia A's. He now led the league with a .421 average. His own hitting streak moved one ahead of DiMaggio's 14 straight (the Red Sox played a doubleheader on May 27), and Williams's average since May 15 stood at .500 (29 for

58) to DiMaggio's .375 (21 for 56). A *Sporting News* story at the end of this week had the real scoop on hitting during these wartime days: "The war in Europe has nothing on the bombardments being staged almost nightly in the Cotton State League. Two official scorers resigned in succession as the Hot Springs Bathers lost a series to Texarkana. There were 94 hits in three games, 44 in the third alone as 112 batters came to the plate in Texarkana's 25–12 win."

As the Yankees left Washington by train on the evening of May 29 and sped past Philadelphia on their way to play a Memorial Day doubleheader in Boston, they crisscrossed with Charles Lindbergh, who got his first chance to react publicly to Roosevelt's "unlimited emergency" speech. Lindbergh spoke at an America First rally distinguished by Philadelphia's reluctance to hold it. The aviator seethed at the President's actions. By calling the war in Europe or on the high seas "our" emergency Roosevelt had out-Hitlered Hitler: "Roosevelt, not Hitler, seeks world domination by one power." The very idea of rearranging our border to suit the defenses of Europe exasperated Lindbergh: "If we say our frontier lies on the Rhine, they can say theirs lies on the Mississippi." Lindbergh alluded to what he knew of the interview conducted by his friend John Cudahy with Hitler at his Berghof: One of Hitler's attempts at wit in the interview disclaimed Germany's interest in western borders marked by the Mississippi River. Despite Lindbergh's and Cudahy's efforts, the noninterventionists were losing ground fast. The majority still opposed, as did Roosevelt, an open declaration of war, but a Gallup Poll recorded that 85 percent of the American public expected war by year's end and that nearly 80 percent agreed with Roosevelt's current policies in staking out the terms under which we would fight it.

As postlude to Roosevelt's toughening policy, the State Department ordered a German official, Dr. Kurt Heinrich Rieth, whom they called the number one Nazi in America, out of the country. Rieth claimed he was here on business, but immigration officials, distrustful of both his claim and his business, whisked him to Ellis Island and took the liberty of packing his bags for him. Meanwhile, in an action unrelated to war, another set of federal officials on May 29 nabbed the famous Hollywood and

Las Vegas gangster Bugsy Siegel and escorted him to Brooklyn to face a federal indictment for conspiring to harbor Louis "Lepke" Buchalter, the notorious industrial racketeer. The end of the second week of DiMaggio's hitting streak was not a good time for undesirables of international or domestic coloring.

GAMES 15 and 16: May 30

The Yankees traveled to Boston for a Memorial Day doubleheader on May 30, and the Red Sox management had to turn away 25,000 fans at the gate. Fenway was already bulging with a capacity crowd of 34,500. Tens of thousands also showed up for Memorial Day in Indianapolis and the 1941 version of the 500. Driver Mauri Rose, a toolmaker in a defense factory, won an unusual Indy in a car different from the one in which he had started. Rose got 177 miles into the race before he retired the sleek pole position Maserati he was driving because of what the newspapers charmingly described as "carburetor catarrh." Since Rose had made no other plans for the afternoon, he took over driving duties from Floyd Davis, by then hopelessly off the pace in the same car Rose had driven to a third-place finish the year before. Rose drove like a souped-up demon until he caught the man who had won the last two Indy 500s, Wilbur Shaw.

About 150 miles from the finish, Shaw's car threw a tire, skidded toward the wall, and smashed, although Shaw managed to escape with minor injuries. Meanwhile, Mauri Rose ended up in first place with Davis's car. His average of 115 miles per hour clocked in at 2 below the Indy record of 117 set by Floyd Robert. A Hollywood stunt driver, Cliff Bergere, drove to a fifth-place finish, but did so in a fashion that had been accomplished only once before in the history of the race: he completed the 500 without making a single pit stop. The last racer who had managed this drove a diesel and finished far out of the money.

The holiday ball games at Boston were the first of six doubleheaders for the Yankees during DiMaggio's streak, and New York would sweep all of them but this one. In a tense first game, Boston lefthander Earl Johnson took a 3–1 lead into the last inning, a lead Joe DiMaggio helped build when he dropped a fly in center, allowing a Boston run to score. But trouble arrived in the ninth for the Red Sox. Red Ruffing began the inning for the Yanks pinch-hitting for Tommy Henrich. He slammed a long single off the green monster in left field. DiMaggio followed Ruffing to the plate; so far he had no hits, two walks, and only one official at bat. Johnson took a look at Frenchy Bordagaray at first, running for Ruffing; then he let go with a fat pitch that DiMaggio drilled to right field for a clean single. The streak was alive at 15 and breathing again. An out and an error later, Charlie Keller walked with the bases full to force in the first Yankee run of the inning. Crosetti then lined a single to drive in two more and extend his own hitting streak to 12 straight. The Yankees held in the bottom of the ninth to win this tight game 4–3.

The second game turned into an absolute nightmare for the Yankees and their star center fielder. DiMaggio almost scratched himself from the lineup, suffering the pain of a miserable stiff neck and sore shoulder, but finally kept mum because manager Joe McCarthy already had his own list of woes. The day before Bill Dickey had hurt his knee on a foul tip—his shin guards were too small—and he sat out the Boston games awaiting special delivery of a new pair. DiMaggio steered clear of sick bay and an anxious McCarthy. Instead, he warned the Yankee infielders about coming out to help him with the cutoff throws. Johnny Sturm remembers DiMaggio telling him before the games that his neck and shoulder were so sore that he wouldn't even risk warming up. He hoped he could get by in the games without throwing. No such luck.

DiMaggio's horror show included a muffed ground ball single through the middle by Ted Williams, then two balls heaved against the box seat railings. All in all Joe chalked up four errors for the doubleheader—the worst fielding day of his career. The large Boston crowd experienced a rare kind of delirium. Chants of "Meatball" greeted the Yankee center fielder in his later at bats, which, during an epoch freer with ethnic epithets, seemed appropriate for Italian errors. A Gene Mack cartoon in the next day's *Boston Globe* offered up a little drawing of a forlorn DiMaggio and a balloon caption: "Seldom on any field has anyone equalled his wild throwing."

If DiMaggio's sore-necked fielding was atrocious, his hitting fared better only through the good graces of the elements. In the fifth inning, batting against Mickey Harris, he poked a wind-blown high fly into right that looked like a duck soup out. But right is a particularly brutal sun field in Boston later in the afternoon, as many can still attest from the famous 1978 playoff game between the Yankees and Boston when Lou Piniella almost lost a line drive in the sun. On DiMaggio's fly, Pete Fox circled around helplessly but couldn't accommodate sun and wind at the same time. The ball fell near him, untouched. A newly installed HIT sign on the scoreboard at Fenway flashed HIT, and the crowd groaned. Only a few parks around the league relayed such information; usually it was between the official scorer and a select few who could see him in the press box. The same Gene Mack cartoon that had DiMaggio throwing the ball all over Boston also depicted Pete Fox running himself dizzy under DiMaggio's fly, with the caption "Not since Snodgrass in 1912 has a muff at Fenway caused such a furor as Fox's of Joe DiMag's." Mack's reference was to the famous incident in the 1912 World Series when Fred Snodgrass dropped a pop fly and lost the series for Christy Mathewson and the Giants. In any event, DiMaggio stood at second, rubbed his neck, and savored his streak hit for a fortunate sixteenth straight.

The New York Times commented on the 13–0 humiliation of the Yankees in game 2: "To say that their first shut-out of the year was the worst beating of the campaign for the Yanks doesn't begin to tell how bad they looked." With the Red Sox ahead 10–0 in the fourth, both managers began replacing their regulars. In this comedy of Yankee errors, the Red Sox pulled a startling triple steal in the sixth, with Skeeter Newsome dashing for the plate as his teammates headed for third and second, respectively. Newsome had already stolen second that inning. Reserve Yankee catcher Buddy Rosar must have thought he was at a penny arcade.

DiMaggio's windblown, sun-drenched double was the only Yankee hit of the second game until rookie Jerry Priddy got another late in what by then was a fruitless cause. Jim Tabor, Boston third baseman, led the Red Sox 16-hit attack with two doubles and a home run. Ted Williams got two hits in the nightcap to extend his streak to 17 (one ahead of DiMaggio), but Frankie Crossetti lost his 12-game hitting streak by taking an "ofer" in the Yankee defeat. With his 3 for 5 on the day, Williams stayed ahead of DiMaggio for the streak games .510 to .377. Overall at this point in the season, Williams was hitting .429 to DiMaggio's .331.

In addition to the indignity of the doubleheader's nightcap this Memorial Day, the Yankees had to share a train out of town with the Red Sox, at least as far as Buffalo. The teams thankfully rode in different cars which would then make different hookups. From Buffalo, the Yanks headed to Cleveland, the Red Sox to Detroit. In New York on Memorial Day the Dodgers and Giants played two at the Polo Grounds in front of a packed house of 59,487 fans. Brooklyn took both games to gain ground on the surging St. Louis Cardinals, who had won 11 straight in the National League before losing this day to Cincinnati.

In New York City, Memorial Day brought out the veterans of all stripes from most wars, including a dozen old gentlemen, 2 down from last year's 14, willing and able to parade in their original Civil War uniforms. Amid the patriotic fervor of the day and continuing what amounted to a minipurge after the anti-Nazi sentiment in America fired by Roosevelt's "unlimited emergency" speech, federal officials gave the go-ahead to local law enforcement agencies in New Jersey to bust up a German Bund rally in Andover and confiscate photos of Hitler plus an assortment of pamphlets, emblems, and maps. The government feared sabotage emanating from the Bund groups within the country and began beefing up the forces guarding defense plants, now contracted for $10 billion worth of war matériel.

Japan picked this Memorial Day to reaffirm its bonds to the Axis alliance and to announce that it might find it necessary to end its peaceful policy in the Pacific. Japan's peaceful policy in the spring of 1941 was something like Vichy France's national honor. One would have had to look far and wide to find any traces of it. But eyes in the United States were for the most part turned away from the rattling sabers of Japan at this time in the year and in the war.

The festive American mood of the day and season in New York took on more cheerful proportions when the owner of the

Copacabana leased Madison Square Garden on May 30 for a hundred days at $1,000 a night for an enormous palm-grove-style nightclub. Benny Goodman, Larry Clinton, and Charlie Barnet opened. It cost 66 cents to get in on weeknights and 88 cents on weekends. Armed forces personnel could bring dates for free. One advantage of the arrangement for those who supported the President's position on the war rather than Lindbergh's: with the dance bands in the Garden, the America First Committee would be out of it.

On Broadway this Memorial Day weekend, the longest-running play on the boards, *Tobacco Road,* closed after 3,180 performances. A tremendous, though steamy, popular success, the play earned its New York investors close to $2 million for its run in the city and nearly $2.5 million on the road. Out in Hollywood on May 30, Warner Brothers Studio found itself in a pitched battle with one of its stars, John Garfield. Garfield was placed on Warner's idle list when he refused to take the lead in a movie called *Nine Lives Are Not Enough.* The studio threatened to give the lead to Ronald Reagan, as if that were supposed to intimidate Garfield. It didn't, and Reagan ended up starring in this 1941 movie, whose title reflects something of the nature of his future political career.

GAMES 17 and 18: June 1

Saturday's game in Cleveland was rained out, but with a day's rest the Yankees beat the Indians in a doubleheader on June 1 and knocked them out of first place. The Chicago White Sox took over the league lead as the Yankees found themselves in third just 1½ games back. DiMaggio extended his streak with a two-out single to left field in the third inning of the first game off Al Milnar and an eighth inning single off Mel Harder in the nightcap that nicked Keltner's glove and shot by him down the third base line.

An odd story is attached to this play. DiMaggio came to the plate hitless for the game in what was to be his last at bat of the long day. Harder was tough for DiMaggio and tough against the

Yankees. He had collared DiMaggio back on May 14, the day before the streak began. DiMaggio settled in and drove a hard bouncer down the third base line. The ball kicked off the tip of Keltner's extended glove hand; he chased it down in short left but had no throw. At the inning's end DiMaggio passed Keltner as the teams exchanged positions on the field. Keltner heard DiMaggio say something, but the noise of the big crowd made it difficult for him to discern what. Perhaps DiMaggio mentioned his good fortune in sustaining the streak on a close play. This was the day the streak went public, as it were, and he would have been less than human if he hadn't been gratified to have squeaked one past the league's premier fielding third baseman. Keltner recalled the muffled hum of a comment he never quite picked up and later said the vague memory encouraged him to play DiMaggio deeper and closer to the line the next Yankee series in Cleveland. One of the games in that series was on the fabled night of July 17.

Municipal Stadium in Cleveland packed in 52,081 fans on June 1, the largest baseball crowd of the year so far, to witness DiMaggio extend his streak and see the Yankees defeat the Indians for the fourth straight time this year in their home park. Only Bobby Feller had been able to hold things together for Cleveland in the last few days, and fortunately for the Yankees, Feller wasn't out there this day—he would be on the morrow. Red Ruffing shut out the Indians 2–0 in the first game, with the Yankees scoring single runs in the second and third innings, enough to win. The 5–3 win in the nightcap proved tougher. Indian third baseman Ken Keltner put Cleveland ahead with a home run off Lefty Gomez in the first. The Yanks tied the game in the fifth, and it remained that way into the eighth, at which time Johnny Sturm hit his first major league home run with Crosetti on base. George Selkirk added another with Rolfe on base. The Indians rallied for two in the ninth but fell short against Marvin Breuer in relief of Ruffing.

The two Yankee home runs in the second game of the day's doubleheader began another sequence running parallel to DiMaggio's hitting streak in which the Yankees would challenge a major league record. The challenge at issue was for at least one member of the team to hit a home run in the day's ball game.

The record was 17 straight games by the 1940 Detroit Tigers, the previous year's pennant winners. As this sequence mounted, the possibility of a new Yankee home run record provided both a distraction from and a supplement to DiMaggio's hitting streak. In a way, the entire team could take some of the strain upon its shoulders that otherwise DiMaggio would have taken alone. There were occasions, however, when it remained for DiMaggio to oblige himself with a hit and his team with a home run to keep both streaks alive.

After DiMaggio's two hits this day in the doubleheader, the *New York Herald Tribune* and *The New York Times* caught on to the hitting streak at the 18-game mark, as did the *Cleveland Plain Dealer.* These papers joined the *New York World-Telegram* and the *New York Daily News,* whose correspondents were a little quicker and a little more savvy. Now that a number of papers had the streak in their sights, no one ever lost it again. Ted Williams, playing with the Red Sox in a doubleheader against the Tigers, continued his brilliant hitting with four on the day to raise his league-leading average to a whopping .430. Williams kept one up on DiMaggio by now hitting in 19 straight, sustaining a .500 average (36 for 72) since the inception of both streaks. DiMaggio's streak average was at .362 (25 for 69). Trailing Williams in hitting in the American League were Bill Dickey at .376, Joe Cronin at .375, and Roy Cullenbine at .363.

In the National League, New York Giant Mel Ott reached a personal milestone this day by hitting the 400th home run of his career. Rookie Pete Reiser led the league in batting at .369, followed by Enos Slaughter of the Cards at .359 and Stan Hack of the Cubs at .357. Behind the pitching of Kirby Higbe, the Brooklyn Dodgers beat the Cardinals 3–2. The two teams were in a dead heat, tied for the lead. Brooklyn had now won 9 straight, allowing them to creep up on the Cardinals, who had wilted a bit after their own recent surge of 11 straight. The National League pennant race couldn't get any closer, nor were the two teams fated to get much farther apart.

Babe Ruth was in Cleveland while the Yankees were in town, and the *Plain Dealer* gave him space for a visitor's column. He told "long ball" stories, longer even than the longest he remembers hitting himself, a 550-foot blast in Tampa, Florida, during spring training a few years back. "As a big leaguer," Ruth began with only slightly veiled modesty, "I hit quite a few home runs," but nothing close to the one he saw while on a barnstorming tour with Bob Meusel "about 15 years ago." Ruth hunkered down for the yarn.

The two Yankees were up in Sleepy Eye, Minnesota, for a pickup game with a local team in the chill of late October. It was pouring rain, but the promoter had filled his little park and wasn't about to call it a day. Ruth played in the game, managed his team, and announced. Meusel complained so bitterly about the rain and the chill that Ruth told him to go back to his room—he would find a pinch hitter. A big husky fellow came out of the stands at Ruth's request and let Babe know he was willing enough to hit. "So I put him in," writes Ruth, "and he hits one to left into the teeth of the wind and driving rain that disappears into a cloud bank." There were no fences in the ball park, just empty grass-land. Ruth remembers hollering at the big fellow to start running. "Nope," says the local, "when I hit 'em that far I don't run." With that the man walked over and handed the promoter a dollar bill for the baseball. "Here, buy another. That one's lost." Ruth obviously relished this story.

The fervor in America stirred by Roosevelt's great "unlimited emergency" speech played itself out in a flurry of activity on the floor of Congress before the Memorial Day weekend. A new bill was hastily rammed through authorizing the President to seize whatever foreign ships he wanted and forgo the usual ruse of protecting Axis-registered vessels from sabotage. This upped the ante in what might be called the undeclared war of the Atlantic sea-lanes. Sabotage, however, may well have been more than a ruse on May 31 in Jersey City. From across the Hudson in Manhattan, it seemed as if the entire horizon were aflame. Over $25 million worth of matériel intended for shipment to war-ravaged England burned in an inferno along the New Jersey docks, and hundreds of cattle were incinerated in the adjacent stockyards. Local and federal officials spent most of June 1 trying to deny, with little effect, that sabotage was involved.

Two other stories that began during the largely unnoticed phase of DiMaggio's streak came to conclusions of a sort on Saturday. News reached the United States that most of the Americans aboard the ill-fated freighter *Zamzam*, sunk by a Nazi gunship, had crossed safely into neutral Portugal after their release by the Germans. The Nazis were still detaining the American ambulance corps members taken off the freighter. Also, the final numbing casualty figures arrived from Crete. In just over a week of brutal and intense fighting, the British had suffered 1,742 dead, 1,737 wounded, and 5,000 taken prisoner. At sea, the British Navy had lost 1,828 men and dozens of ships during the evacuation. The Germans had suffered over 4,000 dead and 2,000 wounded, the first infantry battle in the war in which they purchased victory at so dear a price. With Cretan resistance never entirely abating, the Germans held on to the island until after VE Day and gave it up only on May 15, 1945, the fourth anniversary of the beginning of DiMaggio's streak.

GAME 19: June 2

The game in Cleveland on June 2, played before a meager crowd of 6,000, seemed an afterthought to the celebratory weekend in which the visiting Yankees had attracted over 85,000 fans and had another 25,000 turned away. Surely the holiday mood evaporated entirely when after the game the Yankees arrived in Detroit by train from Cleveland. They were told by club officials the devastating news that Lou Gehrig had died early on the evening of June 2. He was almost 38 years old. Despite his severe amyotrophic lateral sclerosis, Gehrig had been serving faithfully on the New York City Parole Commission and continued to do so until 2 weeks before his death. That evening the Yankees were a shaken ball club.

Before the bad news and still in Cleveland, Bobby Feller went against the Yankees that afternoon. He was the only pitcher to have won for the Indians in their last 10 games, and he won this day 7–5 to help his club move back into first place past the White Sox. Feller pitched sloppily against the Yankees, but until New York scored in the second inning, he had pitched 30 scoreless innings in a row. He already had 11 wins in the young season. DiMaggio singled and doubled against Feller to continue the streak, and for the first time a staff writer on the *San Francisco Chronicle*, DiMaggio's hometown newspaper, took a look at the "DiMag-o-Log," a *Chronicle* feature that charted the day-by-day doings of the DiMaggio brothers, and noticed that the log had recorded a hit for 19 straight games. DiMaggio's single in the second began a Yankee rally that resulted in two runs, but Feller ran into most of his trouble against Tommy Henrich, who crashed a home run off him in the fourth and another in the eighth to drive in DiMaggio, who was on second after doubling 415 feet away off the left field bleacher wall. The Indians moved out in front to stay in the fifth when Marius Russo walked both Feller and Lou Boudreau with the bases loaded. In the sixth, Cleveland right fielder Jeff Heath hit his tenth home run of the year with Ken Keltner on third.

Now that the White Sox were contesting Cleveland for the American League lead, it came as bitter news to manager Jimmy Dykes that his ace pitcher, John Rigney, faced induction into the armed services on June 20. The draft lottery had been kind to the major leagues so far in 1941, but what the call-up lacked in numbers it made up for in quality. The players the Army selected were top of the heap. Unlike the Tigers' Hank Greenberg, however, Johnny Rigney tried everything in his power to finagle his way out of the service while the season was still in session. His saga for the next few weeks proved at once intense and comic. Bobby Feller had also recently received notice that his draft number indicated a possible late-August call-up, but Feller, pennant race or not, intended to honor it.

The international news was hot on the wire services this June 2. A good deal happened, not all of it clear at the time. Another piece of the Hess puzzle fell into place when a news bulletin was picked up from Berlin: The Gestapo had arrested Professor Karl Haushofer, father of Hess's friend Albrecht, for questioning in the deputy führer's escapade. Why the Germans should suspect this revered old man, a Hitler "brain truster" and originator of the *Lebensraum* policy so crucial to the Nazis, seemed odd. The Hess mission in effect had been an attempt to put Haushofer's theories of a natural Anglo-German alliance into practice. Hitler had figured out the theory—one to which he had once adhered and to which others, like Lindbergh in America, probably still did—and now he wanted if possible to round up its practitioners. Meanwhile, Hess still brooded as a prisoner at Mytchett Palace, where the British had bugged the walls in case he talked in his sleep.

Hitler had other fish to fry this day, June 2, 1941. Germany's führer and Italy's duce met in the Alps at the Brenner Pass, a fitting summit for a summit. Hitler and Mussolini conferred for 5 hours, and Hitler raised every issue but the one of most interest to Mussolini, the possible expansion of the war eastward into Russia. Instead, Hitler fulminated about Hess, boasted about Crete, dismissed the sinking of the *Bismarck,* and belittled Roosevelt's "unlimited emergency" speech. Mussolini's foreign minister, Galeazzo Ciano, tried to pry the Russian invasion plans out of the usually loose lipped Nazi minister, von Ribbentrop, but to no avail. Mussolini reportedly said to Ciano after the meeting, somewhat miffed at Hitler's withholding of information, "I wouldn't be at all sorry if Germany in her war with Russia got her feathers plucked." The secret invasion plan was not all that secret among the Axis allies. Nor was it to the British, who already knew the plan's intricate details from their Enigma decoding operation.

On June 2 the British, having just put down a nagging rebellion in their mandate of Iraq, began to mass troops around Vichy-mandated Syria. Vichy's territorial holdings were clearly the Achilles heel of the Axis-influenced operation throughout the world in 1941, and now that Crete and Iraq were settled for worse or better, crack British divisions in the middle east got ready to humiliate the troops of Vichy France. Since the British intelligence operations at Bletchley Park knew of Hitler's invasion plan for Russia, they knew as well that the Vichy regime could count on no help from the Germans. Meanwhile, in London, Parliament derided Churchill about the Cretan fiasco. Fighting wars in a democracy posed accountability problems for a nation's leaders then as now. Where were the island's fortifications? Where was the vaunted British Air Force? Why weren't the airstrips destroyed since the British seemed to be flying no planes of their own? Churchill remained mum but now realized that his command in the area, headed by General Archibald Wavell, had sandbagged him. The prime minister had plans for Wavell.

The big news in America on June 2 was the announced retirement of the Chief Justice of the United States, Charles Evans Hughes, the last "bewhiskered" judge, as a *New York Herald Tribune* article so thoughtfully pointed out. Another retirement of sorts took place on June 2 at the Bronx Zoo when the veteran favorite, Alice the elephant, fell to her knees and required a derrick, block, and tackle to lift her to her feet. Alice was now 44 years old. Over 30 years before, in 1909, she had entertained the folks by answering an old-fashioned crank telephone with her trunk, trumpeting her greetings into the receiver. Officials at the Bronx Zoo decided to test the fabled memory of elephants and set up the same stunt in Alice's pen before the old girl rang off for good. But Alice just looked at the phone and lazily lifted a floppy ear. While Alice was on her last legs, so to speak, the Bronx Zoo turned toward youth by opening for the first time in its history a children's zoo. Attendance was so great that the zoo had to bar adults from some of the special contraptions in the children's section.

In news from the entertainment world on June 2, the lovely Hollywood starlet with one of the sexiest overbites in the world, Gene Tierney, eloped with Italian aristocrat and bon vivant, Oleg Cassini. Gene's father, an insurance broker in New York, was furious. Family squabbles of this sort had a way in the '30s and early '40s of titillating depression-era readers of the local society pages, a facet of American cultural life capitalized on in movies like *It Happened One Night* and *The Philadelphia Story*. In this instance Gene's dad neither liked nor trusted Cassini, but there wasn't much he could do about it except vent his spleen to the newspapers. After the war, the lovely Gene, adrift from Oleg, met a young Boston politician by the name of Jack Kennedy and the two had a brief though flaming liaison that was to launch the dashing member of Congress on what would be a lifelong attraction to the community of starlets.

GAME 20: *June 3*

Stunned by news of Lou Gehrig's death when they arrived in Detroit, several Yankee players remember lingering in the lobby of their hotel to make the decision about who would return to New York for the funeral. Marius Russo still recalls the concern of those who had known Gehrig well—Bill Dickey, Lefty Gomez, Red Rolfe, and DiMaggio—for the immediate well-being of Eleanor Gehrig. It was troubling for these friends and former teammates to be out of town at this time.

The weather was damp and dreary on June 3, and few of the Yankees had their hearts in the day's work at Briggs Stadium. At the beginning of the game the teams lined the front of the dugouts for a silent tribute to Gehrig. DiMaggio stood alone, facing the flag with his head bowed. It was in the same ball park 2 years before, on May 2, 1939, that Gehrig had told manager Joe McCarthy that he wanted to be taken out of the lineup after playing in 2,130 consecutive games, a record spanning 14 years from June 1, 1925. The record was so much beyond anything like it that Gehrig surpassed Everett Scott's previous iron man sequence of 1,308 games almost 6 years before he ended the new one. At the time Gehrig passed Scott, August 17, 1933, a young Joe DiMaggio had just completed his 61-game Pacific Coast League hitting streak for the San Francisco Seals. When Gehrig's iron man record came to an end in 1939, DiMaggio was in his fourth year in the big leagues.

Gehrig played through almost anything during his record sequence, including the worst day of all, in 1934, when he woke up one morning with excruciating lower back pain. He got to Yankee Stadium with great difficulty and required the assistance of the Yankee trainer, Dr. Painter, to dress for the game. Joe McCarthy put Gehrig in the leadoff spot to get him in the game and out of it with dispatch. In the bottom of the first, Gehrig took a cut at the first pitch and singled; he had to inch his aching body to first before the throw beat him to the base from right field. He just made it, and McCarthy took him out immediately for a pinch runner. Gehrig's best day had coincidentally occurred on this date 9 years earlier, June 3, 1932, against Connie Mack's

Philadelphia A's. He had already hit four home runs in the game when he came to bat in the ninth and blasted one on a line toward the right field fence. Al Simmons just managed to reach up and grab it with his back against the wall. Gehrig had come within inches of hitting five home runs in a single ball game.

McCarthy now had a difficult time controlling his emotions as he spoke to reporters in the same visiting clubhouse where Gehrig had spoken to him when he asked to be taken out of the game 2 years before: "He was the greatest player of all time, the grandest man." The Yankee president, Ed Barrow, was the last representative of the club to see Gehrig alive, having visited him on Memorial Day. As he left the room, Gehrig told him, "I'm going to beat this thing." Late in the afternoon of June 3, McCarthy and Bill Dickey, Gehrig's former roommate, boarded the night plane for New York to attend the funeral in upper Manhattan. Tributes to Gehrig arrived from across the nation. NBC radio provided a hookup to various cities in America. Lefty Gomez, Bill Dickey, and Joe DiMaggio spoke for the Yankees in addition to Babe Ruth, then in New York and joined there by Carl Hubbell and Mel Ott of the Giants. Umpire Bill Klem also spoke from New York. Jimmy Foxx spoke from Boston, and Bobby Feller from Cleveland.

Babe Ruth's remarks struck an unusual, though moving, chord, as if the things he remembered about Gehrig were things he missed in himself: "I never knew a fellow who lived a cleaner life. He was a clean-living boy, a good baseball player, a great hustler. I think the boy hustled too much for his own good. He just wanted to win all the time." Ruth called this great man a boy almost as if he had forgotten the intervening years and chose to recall what Gehrig must have been like in Ruth's eyes early in the '20s, when the "boy" had just broken in with the magnificent Yankees of that era.

The day's game, once it started, took but 1 hour and 39 minutes to play. Yankee rookie Steve Peek had his troubles early, with the Tigers jumping all over him for four runs in the first on doubles by Pinkie Higgins and Birdie Tebbetts. The Yankees got one run back in the fourth on a DiMaggio leadoff home run off Dizzy Trout, who went the distance for the Tigers, and another back in the seventh, but that was it: 4–2. DiMaggio's blast to left field continued his own hitting streak at 20 and the team's brief streak of consecutive-game home runs at 3. Earlier in the spring Lou Gehrig had spoken with reporters about DiMaggio. He thought DiMaggio the finest ballplayer in the major leagues, not merely because of his superb hitting but because of his outstanding skills as a fielder: "Joe DiMaggio is the greatest defensive outfielder in the game. Scarcely has to be told to move. And when told, he knows how." For Gehrig, it was not only a matter of whether a ballplayer could catch a ball and throw it when the opportunity presented itself but what a player did before the opportunity presented itself. There are small moves and adjustments in the field, some of them imperceptible and some of them intuitive, that make baseball as much a game of anticipation as one of execution.

In America on June 3, the new war powers frenzy had gotten out of hand. Roosevelt found himself in a more ticklish position than he had bargained for when Congress rushed through a bill that would give him emergency powers to seize any real or personal property in the nation in the name of national defense. Astute politician that he was, Roosevelt saw this legislation as too sweeping for the present and as providing too ready confirmation of the noninterventionist charges that he sought dictatorial powers. He hinted that the bill ought to lie fallow in Congress for the time being until war was imminent. He did, however, take heart from a new national opinion poll revealing that a majority of Americans favored our convoying war matériel to England. Since the United States was now spending $27 million a day on defense and lend-lease, five times the level of the previous June, most people wanted to ensure that what was sent to England arrived there. In secret, Roosevelt and Churchill had already begun to formulate a de facto convoy policy, the nature of which would soon become clear.

GAME 21: June 5

The ball game in Detroit on June 4 was rained out, with McCarthy and Dickey in New York for Gehrig's funeral. A different epoch ended this day with the death of another figure whose life reflected a bygone part of the century. Kaiser Wilhelm of Germany died at Doorn in the Netherlands on June 4 at the age of 82. The kaiser symbolized the old Germany, from the blood and iron policies predating World War I to the broken dignity of the German nation after the Versailles humiliation in 1919. He had been living in exile since the end of World War I. The führer sent his obligatory condolences to the family of the man whose very presence in Germany was anathema to the Nazis.

In Detroit, when the skies cleared on June 5, the Yankees lost their third in a row, this one in extra innings, 5–4. DiMaggio lined a shot to left off Hal Newhouser that rattled around in the corner near the foul line for a triple. The big hit extended his streak to 21 games, but it took Tommy Henrich's clutch home run in the ninth to extend the Yankee consecutive-game home run streak to 4. New York moved ahead in the game by two runs after their DiMaggio-aided rally in the sixth inning, but in the bottom of the sixth Yankee right-hander Atley Donald wild-pitched in two runs and allowed another to score when he dropped catcher Buddy Rosar's throw to the plate. Henrich's home run tied it in the ninth, but Detroit got the run it needed to win in the tenth when, with the bases loaded, Red Rolfe at third waited for Bruce Campbell's high chopper to come down and watched helplessly as the winning run scampered unmolested across the plate.

Joe Gordon, Yankee second baseman, got the longest single of his life in the sixth when he belted one about as far as possible to left center in Briggs Stadium. Buddy Rosar, thinking the drive would be caught, held his base, stalling traffic and forcing Gordon to stop at first in disgust. The Yankee loss dropped them back into fourth place, 3½ games out. With the Red Sox playing Cleveland, Ted Williams had another great day at the plate, garnering three hits in four at bats and raising his league-leading average to a blistering .434. He had hit in 22 straight since May 15, one more than DiMaggio, and remained at .500 (40 for 80) during that run. DiMaggio's season average was at .326, and his streak average was .354 (29 for 82).

The current issue of the *Sporting News* picked up one of those wonderful items which are bound to occur if enough players play for enough teams. One Joseph Morjoseph, playing for St. Joseph, Michigan, in the Michigan State League, was traded up to St.

Joseph, Missouri, of the Western Association. Unless an imp in the front office had made up this item, Joseph Morjoseph, formerly of St. Joseph and now of St. Joseph, reserved his playing time for teams that clearly appreciated his nominal talents. Another back page note in the *Sporting News* about the league from which Morjoseph had come mentioned that a fledgling 18-year-old ballplayer led the Michigan State League in hitting in the first week of June at .431, almost matching Ted Williams in the American League. His name: Gene Woodling.

While the Yankees were waiting out their rain delay on June 4, a sorry event took place in the halls of the House of Representatives in Washington that touched upon one of the undercurrents in America, indeed in the world at large, during the days of DiMaggio's streak. John E. Rankin, a Democrat from Mississippi, rose to speak about a rally for the free world that had just been held in New York City. He ridiculed the rally as "inspired by Wall Street and a little group of our Jewish brethren." The condescension and prejudice were appalling to Michael Edelstein, a member of Congress from Brooklyn. Edelstein took the platform and spoke passionately about the values of the United States and the plight of the dislocated populations in Europe. He was so upset by Rankin's words and tone and by the blindness to the situation in Europe that he worked himself into a near frenzy: "Hitler started out by speaking about 'Jewish Brethren.' I deplore the fact that anytime anything happens in America, whether it be for a war policy or against a war policy, men in this House and outside this House attempt to use the Jews as their scapegoat."

Edelstein then left the floor, and moments later in the Speaker's Lobby, he collapsed dead from a heart attack. The next day, June 5, the day after Gehrig's funeral in New York City, 15,000 mobbed the streets for the representative's funeral. Edelstein was eulogized as a "martyr to democracy." Though most in the crowd had little idea of the enormity of the Jewish policy just beginning to take final shape in Nazi Germany, the sense of victimization was getting clearer and nearer day by day.

The notion of the complicitous figure of the warmongering Jew in a world whose Jewish populations were increasingly outlawed and finally annihilated struck a disturbing chord in 1941.

Committees in Congress such as the Nye-led Senate Committee investigating possible Jewish influence in antiwar films, and, of course, figures in America such as Charles Lindbergh and Henry Ford ended up following similar low roads against Jews whom they improbably dubbed as unscrupulous policy-fabricating manipulators of the western democracies. In fact, Lindbergh's downfall as an effective voice for the noninterventionist cause came later in the summer, when during his infamous Des Moines speech he went too far and blamed the Jews for Hitler's hatred of them. Behind the rather primitive and primitively confused fear of the "international Jew" lay the deeply anti-Semitic notion that the periodic purging of Jewish influence from the affairs of Europe was not only inevitable but desirable.

With the overseas war news at something of a lull on June 5, an interesting item came off the wire from Japan. Admiral Nomura proclaimed his confidence that the United States and his country could end the strain in their relations amicably. What Nomura did not say was that the Japanese Admiralty had just finished drawing up and refining plans for a surprise attack from aircraft carriers on the American naval installation at Pearl Harbor. The only question was when, and the answer awaited a favorable shift in the Japanese cabinet. As conciliatory as Nomura seemed toward the United States, he took mock umbrage at the boasting of the Luftwaffe commander, Hermann Göring, that the Germans had proven by the performance of their air and ground forces on Crete that they could take any island in the world. Göring meant England, but Nomura reminded the Nazi field marshal that Japan was also an island.

Back in America, the movie *Billy the Kid*, starring Robert Taylor, opened all over the country this week. Though the film could in no way rank with the better ones enjoying premiere engagements during DiMaggio's streak—*Citizen Kane, The Lady Eve, Major Barbara, Man Hunt, Sergeant York*—it had a curious secondary claim to fame. Its release delayed that of the Howard Hughes movie, *The Outlaw*, all set to screen in 1941 with a steamy new starlet outfitted in such a way that during the war she would wreak havoc with the hormonal flow of U.S. fighting forces. Hughes held back the film for this season because *Billy the Kid* was too close in subject matter to his own movie. He wanted the decks cleared, as it were, to introduce his discovery: Jane Russell. Hughes canceled the premiere, but *The Outlaw* was a scandal around the country because publicity stills of the lovely Miss Russell managed to burst out all over even before June did so. The Hays film censorship office was bug-eyed and up in arms, targeting the movie industry for displaying its starlets in revealing sweaters and skimpy blouses, and Jane Russell was exhibit A. Eventually, the still of Jane that caused all the furor ended up much more famous than *The Outlaw*. Her inviting torso rivaled Veronica Lake's golden hair, Rita Hayworth's sultry and silk décolletage, and Betty Grable's tush and gorgeous legs as classic military pinups of World War II.

GAME 22: June 7

The Yankees arrived in St. Louis after a travel day to play the Browns on June 7. Three games before, St. Louis had changed managers: Fred Haney departed, and Luke Sewell replaced him. The Browns had won every game for their new manager until they ran into the Yankees. Sewell watched in disbelief as the Yanks scored five times in the last inning to blow his sad team off their home field 11–7 before 2,394 loyalists. Joe DiMaggio contributed three singles to the Yankee effort, and his streak was never in jeopardy. His ailing neck and shoulder, bothering him less and less since his error-laden debacle in Boston, began to feel much better.

After only a brief lull, the overseas war heated up again on the Yankee off day, June 6. The British Air Force launched an extensive and devastating bombing raid on Vichy France–mandated Syria, if for no other reason than to stem the tide of criticism that raged in London about the fiasco on Crete. RAF bombers annihilated what little there was of the Vichy Air Force on the ground at the Aleppo and Tadmur airfields. British ground forces the next day, June 7, spearheaded across the Iraqi border. The French were helpless without Axis support, and support was not forthcoming from Hitler. Vichy forces tried frantically to fit out the inadequate defenses in their Syrian mandate. Meanwhile, Pétain appealed to the world for sympathy, claiming Vichy's neutrality. Hitler, in what the Vichy regime must have thought an instance of backhanded graciousness, announced that France had every right to defend Syria, implying that it had every right to do so on its own, since Hitler had no intention of committing forces to the middle east just before his invasion of Russia. Free French General Charles de Gaulle, headquartered in England, saw the move on Syria as the beginning of France's liberation from the Nazis.

On the train into St. Louis, any Yankee inclined to do so could have picked up the current issue of *Life* magazine, which finally ran the interview that Lindbergh's friend, the former United States ambassador to Belgium, John Cudahy, had conducted with Hitler, which he had been trying for 2 weeks to get into print. The lyrical awe and sycophantic whine of Cudahy's interview were appalling, and it was now obvious why *Time* magazine didn't want to run any of it, though their kissing cousin, *Life,* which had commissioned it, went ahead on June 6: "Through the largest bay window I have ever seen, the snow-sheeted Alps seemed startingly close and white as antimony in the spring sunshine. Far down, the green valley was polka-dotted with spring flowers. The distant silhouette of Salzburg looked vague and fluttering against a cumulus cloud embankment, like a phantom city." Cudahy was as interested in the decor of Hitler's Bavarian Berghof—"The whole color scheme has a garnet tint"—as he was in the brutality of the führer's policies. *Life* felt compelled to run a rider before the piece: "*Life* is well aware of its grave responsibility in printing this article at such a critical time. It does so because it is confident its readers can intelligently recognize this interview for what it really is—an essential part of Hitler's political strategy of 'softening up' the U.S. with large denials of aggressive intentions."

Cudahy's lips moved as Hitler spoke: "Convoys mean war." We hear the strains of an aggrieved Hitler: "He said that he never heard anybody in Germany say that the Mississippi River was a German frontier," which had been the very observation of an outraged Lindbergh just after Roosevelt's "unlimited emergency" speech. Cudahy ended the first installment of his interview with these palliative words of the führer: "He said that time after time he had tried to emphasize that the position of Germany and his plans were not inimical to the U.S. but that his efforts had always proved futile." *Life* then found it appropriate, in a gesture that must have infuriated their correspondent, to reprint part of Roosevelt's May 27 "unlimited emergency" speech and at the same time run a picture review of the fate of nations whose positions were supposedly not inimical to Germany's: Poland, Czechoslovakia, France, Denmark, Romania, Yugoslavia, Greece.

In the ball game on June 7, Lefty Gomez had some difficulty adjusting to the western time zone in St. Louis and walked four men in the first inning to force in a Brown run. But by the top of the third the Yankees had forged way ahead on the strength of Charlie Keller's bases-loaded home run, his first grand slam of the season, a nifty variation to go along with the inside-the-parkers he had recently been hitting. St. Louis kept pecking away at Gomez and finally snuck ahead in a wild eighth inning featuring a Walter Judnich home run, a run scored on a sacrifice bunt that went unplayed, and a DiMaggio peg to third that nabbed George McQuinn trying to sneak a base on a run-producing sacrifice fly to center. In the top half of the ninth the Yankees scored five times and sent nine men to the plate. Walks, errors, and hits filled the bases for matching two-run singles by Johnny Sturm and Bill Dickey.

Around the American League, Bobby Feller won his seventh straight game on June 6, shutting out the Philadelphia A's while striking out 11 of them. And around the track on Saturday, June 7, another young sportsfigure, the great colt Whirlaway, won the third and final leg of the Triple Crown for 1941, taking the Belmont Stakes to add to his Kentucky Derby and Preakness titles. Whirlaway left the average bettor at Belmont with but scant change in his pocket, approaching the gate a 1 to 4 favorite and crossing the line a 3½-length victor.

A dramatic story was breaking even farther west than St. Louis on June 7. At North American Aviation in Los Angeles a wildcat strike crippled a plant essential for wartime defense production. This was the first confrontation between labor and Roosevelt's new priorities for national defense, and the President immediately flexed his muscles. He was not about to put himself in the position of making an impassioned speech on emergency conditions before the entire world and then having workers at a crucial aviation plant take a hike on him. If the strike was not settled by Monday, June 9, the first workday of the new week, the workers of the local CIO union would find themselves looking down the barrel of a presidential gun. There had been nasty strikes earlier in the year at International Harvester and Bethlehem Steel, and Roosevelt knew from a recent Gallup Poll that the majority of Americans opposed strikes in any defense-related industry. Fully 85 percent wanted a federal labor board to settle disputes in such instances.

June 7 was one of those days stocked with back-page newspaper items of interest and curiosity. The brand-new superdreadnought, the *South Dakota,* costing over $70 million to build, first slipped into the Atlantic on this day; it would later take a considerable beating at the pivotal battle for control of the Pacific near Guadalcanal in 1942. Another item off the wire services relayed the story of a 98-year-old Civil War veteran, David Sisk, who had just gained a divorce decree by claiming that his 55-year-old wife, Margaret Livingston (he presumed), had not told him she was on parole from the Davenport Institution for the Mentally Insane when she had married him in October 1940. One wonders if he told her he was a Civil War veteran.

From Hollywood on June 7 came the story of Clark Gable returning from a fishing trip during which he had put on 15 extra pounds. A friend of his on a specially concocted and foolproof diet convinced the actor to give his regimen a try. It worked so well that Gable called up this June day to offer thanks. He was told to try the hospital—his friend was in serious condition, suffering from malnutrition and severe anemia. "Good God," said Gable, hurrying off to Perino's for dinner. In another medical story, *The New York Times* reported that the world-famous violinist Fritz Kreisler did something on June 7 he had first done as a child and had not done since April 26, 1941: he took a step. Back in April he had made the mistake of trying to cross Madison Avenue with a violin case as his only protection and was hit by a truck. He lay unconscious for days, near death with a fractured skull, and when he finally came to, his first words were about the safety of his violin, as if it were a near relation. The violin was well; Kreisler was getting better.

Two new movies opened in New York City by the week's end: *Love Crazy,* with William Powell and Myrna Loy battling over divorce procedures; and *Million Dollar Baby,* starring Ronald Reagan and Priscilla Lane. Reagan in this depression hangover comedy played a "stumble bum composer in a swing band" who teaches the baffled Priscilla Lane that a million dollar inheritance can't buy happiness. We have all heard that before. In a feature also screening in New York and everywhere else in the country at the time, Reagan played the good guy to Wallace Berry's eponymous *Bad Man.* Such early training has stood him in good political stead.

GAMES 23 and 24: June 8

The largest crowd of the year so far for St. Louis, 10,546—monumental for the Browns—witnessed the home team lose twice to the Yankees this Sunday, 9–3 and 8–3. DiMaggio thrived on St. Louis pitching with a marvelous display of power: two home runs in the first game and a home run and a double in the second, driving in a total of seven runs for the heady afternoon, the best power day of the entire streak, though some others came close. Meanwhile, Ted Williams took the collar in both ends of a Red Sox doubleheader against Chicago. He had kept pace with DiMaggio for the first 22 games of the legendary streak and, given a schedule difference, had actually hit in 23 straight since May 15, averaging .487 (43 for 88) to DiMaggio's .368 (32 for 87). Williams still insists that the numbers he put on the board during his early matchup with DiMaggio's great hitting streak made the difference in his finishing over .400, and the numbers do not lie.

When I recently asked him how aware he had been of matching DiMaggio early in the streak, Williams answered in no uncertain terms. "I certainly was conscious of my streak, and DiMaggio's was just starting to get in the papers then. I went to Chicago with twenty-three games, and I did a big and glorious zero for eight [he went none for five, walking four times] in Comiskey Park against Ted Lyons and Thornton Lee, and Joe carried on. Don't think for a moment that because a hitter hits .400, every pitch looks like a balloon. Some days getting a hit is the hardest thing to do in the world. Plenty of pitchers that I knew would be extremely difficult on any given day, either because of their stuff or a ball park's background."

At the time in 1941, Dan Daniel made a point of talking to Williams about his torrid weeks in May and early June for one of his *New York World-Telegram* columns. Williams reminded Daniel that he had just taken the collar in two games on Sunday: "I know how tricky percentages can be." But what Williams really wanted to do was wax lyrical on another subject, the cagey pitching of two seasoned vets: "Say, you should have seen Grove and Lyons fight it out for ten innings on Sunday. It was the greatest exhibition of pitching I ever hope to see. Certainly Feller is tops. But you should have watched those two old-timers maneuvering, outwitting hitters, making their heads do for them what their arms used to do. It was beautiful. I became so engrossed watching them, I guess I just forgot to hit."

The Yankees surely didn't forget in St. Louis. Their power proved devastating to the Browns' pitching on Sunday. Red Ruffing coasted to a win in the first game as four Yankee home runs sailed out of Sportsman's Park. In addition to DiMaggio's two, Henrich unloaded one in the eighth and Rolfe hit one in the ninth. But the most interesting Yankee play of the game occurred in the second inning. Bill Dickey caught Bob Swift's foul along the first base line and looked up to see Johnny Berardino motoring into second base without having tagged up. Berardino for some reason thought the foul would bounce fair. Dickey just kept legging it to first with the ball in his catcher's glove and stepped on the bag for an unassisted double play, home to first in one easy motion. Rare indeed.

Marius Russo pitched the distance in game 2, aided by Charlie Keller's three-run home run in the first inning followed almost immediately by Joe Gordon's two-run blast to knock Browns' starter Bob Harris out of the box early. After St. Louis scored two in their half of the inning, DiMaggio doubled to right in the Yankee top of the second, driving in two more. In the sixth DiMaggio iced the game by putting one of Bob Muncrief's deliveries over the right field roof. The shell-shocked Brown pitching staff offered little resistance this Sunday as the Yankees extended their consecutive-game home run streak to 7. This was a rough day all over the country for St. Louis. Between them the Browns and the Cardinals lost four games before sundown, with the lowly Giants taking two from the Cards in New York. Brooklyn lost as well, so the Cardinals fell only a half game behind the Dodgers. Brooklyn center fielder Pete Reiser pumped his league-leading average up to .373 on June 8. Williams, of course, at .416, still led the American League.

The strike situation at North American Aviation in Los Angeles had by now captured the attention of the nation, especially that of the parent CIO union to which the wildcatting strikers belonged. As the renegade strikers tested not only Roosevelt's new determination in the face of world war but labor's relation to a revivifying U.S. economy, the national CIO office turned against its local in cold fury. *The New York Times* flung its usual antiunion mud as well, noting that the Los Angeles local's leader, Elmer Freitag, had admitted to Congressman Martin Dies' Special Committee to investigate un-American Activities that he had registered as a Communist in a Los Angeles election in 1938. Roosevelt didn't really need this sort of help from the *Times,* but they were ready enough to provide it.

In contrast to the happenings at North American Aviation, with the National Guard alert and ready to move in to ensure the continued manufacture of vital aircraft, a woman from Virginia, Mrs. Kelly Evans, dug into her own pocket and purchased a complete Spitfire fighter, fully equipped with eight guns, for England's war effort. It cost Mrs. Evans $32,000 for the honor, and she forwarded the cash to the Wings for Britain Fund in Montreal, Canada. For months the British had come up with whatever ideas they could to enlist support in America for their solo enterprise against Hitler. Dressmakers in England had even forgone the usual floral print on items intended for export and substituted war-scene designs to help their nation's cause. One dress depicted a Home Guard trooper, bayonet in hand, facing down a Nazi fighter-bomber. Another simply recalled Churchill's words to the Royal Air Force after the Battle of Britain: "Never was so much owed by so many to so few."

At the same time that such pathos-ridden pleas for aid to England were heard and seen in America, a fascinating and complex international story about inadvertent aid for Nazi Germany began to break through leaks in the Justice Department. On June 8 bits and pieces of a government investigation came to light concerning a series of insidious, entangled, and far-reaching multinational negotiations involving oil, synthetic fuel, and rubber patents. The revelations this day focused on special deals and financial links between John D. Rockefeller's Standard Oil and the Nazi Germany conglomerate I.G. Farben.

In effect, two major conglomerates in nations whose interests were growing violently apart had made contractual arrangements that yoked them firmly together. Furthermore, the area of their shared interests was essential to the war-making capacities of the Allied and Axis powers. In 1926 I.G. Farben began to build a huge synthetic fuel plant to produce oil from black coal. Carl Bosch, a name still famous in German industry for spark plugs, directed the project and opened the plant in 1928. I.G. Farben, with cash-flow problems at the time, arranged to sell Standard Oil the rights to market the process in America and outside Germany. Standard did not want the synthetic fuel so much as the right to keep other nations from getting it.

For its part, I. G. Farben was given ownership of 20 percent of Standard Oil of New Jersey and shared an affiliate company, Jasco, set up for any new patents and processes. Hitler knew about the Standard deal in the late 1930s and instructed I.G. Farben to get whatever patents they could from Standard Oil without providing any themselves. Standard Oil did not bother to review the arrangement and kept sending Farben the results of work at Jasco. But by late 1939 some Standard executives got nervous. They asked our ambassador to England at the time, Joseph Kennedy, to set up a secret meeting between Standard and I.G. Farben officials at The Hague. All Europe was a cinder box, and as one Standard executive remembers it, "We did our best to work out complete plans for a modus vivendi which would operate through the term of the war whether or not the U.S. came in."

What turns out to be especially significant about the state of these affairs on June 8, 1941, is that not only the Justice Department but the United States Senate had the matter under investigation. A midwestern politician from Missouri headed the effort which would boost his reputation throughout the country and put him in line to run for Vice President in 1944: Senator Harry S. Truman. By the time Truman was done with the Standard Oil–I.G. Farben scandal, his committee had raked John D. Rockefeller's company over a public bed of hot coals, fined Standard Oil for what amounted to their foreign policy, and forced John D. himself to purge the company of executives with ties to Nazi Germany.

Lindbergh was again in the news on June 8. He simply couldn't keep himself out of it during DiMaggio's streak, and he became a national obsession matched by his own obsession with Roosevelt's war policies. For several days Japan had been dropping thousands of leaflets over Chungking that contained translations of Lindbergh's May 29 speech in Philadelphia attacking Roosevelt for his "unlimited emergency" speech. The Japanese, playing on the famous Lindbergh name, wanted the Chinese, whom they were currently butchering, to think that America was in turmoil about its commitments abroad. Lindbergh now had the dubious honor of having his speeches translated and distributed by Nazi Germany and imperial Japan, two nations with which we would be at war by the end of the year. If this were not enough, the famous Mexican artist Diego Rivera launched a public tirade against Lindbergh and America First. He claimed that Lindbergh had no right to speak for all the Americas; indeed, his hemispheric bullying had made him "just as dangerous as the head of the Gestapo." Though one of the least subtle of the attacks on Lindbergh during the spring and summer, it echoed the same general theme: Lindbergh's previous activities, and presumably his current ones, had the mark of the Third Reich upon them.

Before this spring weekend in June came to a close, the actress Madeleine Carroll, voted by her fans the most desirable of movie stars with whom to be marooned on a desert island, was marooned on a desert island. Madeleine and actor Sterling Hayden, aboard a small yacht near the Bahamas, were forced by a squall into a small island cove for protection. There they spent the night out of contact with those who expected them to return late Sunday. Fortunately or, as the case might be, unfortunately, the yacht had a crew and the actress and actor had company.

GAME 25: June 10

June 9 was a travel day, and the next day, before a small crowd of 2,832 in Chicago's Comiskey Park, Yankee rookie Steve Peek went the distance for the first time in his career and notched the win. Peek had difficulty sweeping up in the ninth; he took a shut-out into the inning but allowed the Sox five hits and three runs to whittle the final Yankee margin to 8–3. DiMaggio was fortunate this afternoon. His hard bouncer to third in the seventh handcuffed the slick-fielding Dario Lodigiani, the same San Francisco family friend who had made two great defensive plays that held DiMaggio to one hit on the day the streak began. The official scorer ruled the grounder too tough to handle, and the streak continued intact at 25.

Having won four in a row, the Yankees edged ahead of the White Sox into second place, still 4½ games behind the Indians, who beat the Senators behind Feller's thirteenth win. White Sox ace John Rigney, perhaps with his June 20 Army call-up date in mind, just didn't have it against the Yankees on June 10. He left the game in the sixth when New York batted around, with Frankie Crosetti's grand slam home run capping the outburst. In commenting on Crosetti's blast, the *New York Herald Tribune* picked up the Yankee consecutive-game home run streak and began its count at 8. Rigney's induction day count was at zero minus 10, though he was able to bear the day's loss more easily when he learned after the game that his induction appeal had gained him an additional 60-day delay under a complicated hardship regulation. Soon the hardship appeal became more trying for him than the draft notice in a nation whose consciousness of its role in the war was increasing day by day.

Jack Smith's column in the *New York Daily News* for June 10 focused on a story that would later play a significant role in DiMaggio's streak, though Smith had no idea at the time and neither did anyone else. Tommy Henrich had come alive with the bat recently for the Yankees, and Smith explained that Henrich had been slumping badly prior to DiMaggio's streak, not even playing against left-handed pitchers because his frustration was so great and his performance so slipshod. In a game with Detroit on May 21, Henrich had borrowed one of Joe DiMaggio's bats, heavier than the model he usually swung, and got three hits, all to left or left center. Several Yankees, ribbing Henrich about his day at the plate, claimed that the bat swung him instead of he it. But Henrich told Smith he felt comfortable with the DiMaggio model no matter how amusing his mates found his swing. He borrowed a few more from DiMaggio's available stock and started honing and boning them. Soon he got his swing down pat, and since muscling up with the heavier bats he had hit seven home runs in 18 games. Smith's column on Henrich swinging DiMaggio's lumber would add color to the lore of the great streak 16 games from this one when a fan stole DiMaggio's bat on the day he was after George Sisler's modern-day record of 41 straight. One can guess what happened, but the details would fall into place on June 29.

The weekend did not defuse the tense situation in Los Angeles at the striking North American Aviation plant. On Monday, June 9, Roosevelt lowered the boom. True to his word, he sent in the troops, 2,500 strong, to force open the plant for business and production. With its bluff called, the renegade local capitulated and voted to return to work immediately, leaving all wage demands in limbo. Meanwhile another locally sanctioned CIO union walked off the job in a Cleveland Alcoa Aluminum plant for one day but quickly announced its intention to return when Roosevelt threatened to bring in the Army reserves for another "consultation." The President meant business in more ways than one. Labor had twice tested the President's new unlimited emergency powers and twice had buckled. In many ways and in many sectors, Roosevelt's moves were less ideological than historical. Preparedness took precedence over negotiation in these critical months. The national leadership of the CIO shared most of Roosevelt's sentiments. They began this very day to purge the feistier left wing of their organization.

On June 10, 1941, a story broke that, like so many during DiMaggio's streak, was brief in duration but intense in terms of wartime outrage. In this instance a Brazilian merchant vessel came upon a forlorn lifeboat in the middle of the Atlantic Ocean. Those in it had been drifting aimlessly with the currents for 18 days. The rescued castaways, mostly American, revealed that their ship, the *Robin Moor*, on its way to South Africa with a crew of

28 plus seven passengers, had been torpedoed and sunk by a German U-boat a thousand miles off the coast of Brazil. The U-boat surfaced, and its captain gave the threatened freighter a half hour to lower crew and passengers into lifeboats. Thirty minutes later the U-boat fired a torpedo into the ship at point-blank range and then sailed away, leaving four lifeboats adrift. Those picked up on June 10 were unsure of the whereabouts of the other three boats—they had separated some 2 weeks before in the dark of night. Among the missing were three women and a toddler.

According to the survivors, the Germans knew that the freighter sailed the seas under an American flag but blew it up anyway. The *Robin Moor* thus became the first American ship to fall victim to German submarines, and many in the United States, including some of Roosevelt's closest advisers, urged armed retaliation. The President thought about it but was then in the middle of drawing up more controversial and comprehensive plans for the strategic protection of the Atlantic shipping lanes. Meanwhile, the question still remained: Where were the other lifeboats of the *Robin Moor?*

A superb and haunting war-espionage film opened in New York City on June 10, Fritz Lang's *Man Hunt* with Walter Pidgeon, George Sanders, and Joan Bennett. It was adapted from Geoffrey Household's novel *Rogue Male,* about an English big-game hunter who stalks Hitler at Berchtesgaden. The bizarre plot of this extraordinary film charted the regression from hunter to hunted, from sportsman to victim, in a thinly disguised fable about the effect of Nazi pressure on the British psyche. George Sanders headed a menagerie of Nazi agents sinister enough to strike fear into a stone wall. Joan Bennett, having pleaded to get the role, brilliantly played a down-class seamstress. In the novel on which the film was based her character walked the streets, but in deference to the Hays office she was censored into merely sewing where once she had reaped.

Later in the summer *Man Hunt* came before the Nye investigating committee in the Senate as one of the year's films supposedly packaged by warmongers to whip the American population into a frenzy of unreasoned Nazi hating. If so, Lang's *Man*

Hunt did its job with exceptional skill. When the Nye committee launched its summer attack, *Man Hunt* was in good and bad company. *I Wanted Wings, I Married a Nazi, Escape, Convoy,* Chaplin's *The Great Dictator, Sergeant York,* and Churchill's favorite movie, *That Hamilton Woman,* were all branded by the committee as insidious interventionist ploys. Senator Nye charged among other things that the movie industry was run by Jewish financiers intent on provoking a war with Hitler. Former presidential candidate Wendell Willkie, the primary lawyer for the film industry before the committee, would deliver such a blistering attack on Nye and his staff that the Senate voted to cut off funds for the committee's work until it resumed doing what it was meant to do, whatever that was.

Overseas on June 10, the British invasionary force in the middle east knifed into Syria and Lebanon, approaching Damascus on one assault line and occupying Tyre on another. Though headlines bannered the attack, another front-page story anticipated something far more ominous for June. A dramatic rift began to appear in Nazi-Soviet relations, a rift that in a matter of days would widen beyond anything previously known to modern war. The British had already decoded Hitler's invasion directive for Russia, Operation Barbarosa. When they attempted to tell Stalin, he refused even to see the British ambassador. Either Stalin wouldn't believe what he was about to hear or he believed it all too well and didn't require that the British tell him. For months Stalin had been making substantial preparations for war by training troops and readying arms in the hinterlands of his vast country. No one imagined the extent of these preparations, including an American, Charles Lindbergh, who in 2 weeks would begin mocking Russia's chances against Hitler just as he had mocked England's in the Battle of Britain. On a trip to Russia in the late 1930s Lindbergh had been shown a few flivvers and some bailing wire and told that he had seen the bulk of the Russian Air Force. He, like Napoleon and Hitler, underestimated the reserves of Russia and its people when faced with an invading army.

GAME 26: *June 12*

The Yankees were rained out June 11 on a day when headlines around the country reported the most recent tally of American lend-lease funds since March: over $4.5 billion for the production of wartime matériel slated for overseas delivery. On June 12 New York and Chicago played under the lights at Comiskey Park before 37,102 fans, a crowd 16 times larger than that which had attended the afternoon game 2 days before. The night game at Chicago was of the sort that Roosevelt wanted to see more of so that defense workers could spend all their afternoons producing and not skip out to the ball park. DiMaggio opened the Yankee fourth inning with a sharp single to center off Chicago's Thornton Lee to extend the streak to 26. But his big hit of the day sent the local multitude home unhappy: he homered with two out in the top of the tenth off Lee to break a tie and give the Yankees and their pitcher, Spurgeon Chandler, a 3–2 win over the White Sox.

Joe Gordon's home run for the Yankees in the sixth extended the team's consecutive streak to 9 games and drew them to within a run of Chicago, who had scored single runs in the second and the fifth. Gordon started things again in the ninth inning with a single. He scored when the amazing Yankee pinch-hitting pitcher, Red Ruffing, entered the game and jolted one off the left field wall for a double. The White Sox manager, Jimmie Dykes, came roaring off the bench protesting to the umpires that a fan had touched Ruffing's shot and that Gordon should be held at third. The umpires disagreed, and Dykes went into typical hysterics before the large crowd. It did him no good.

White Sox pitcher John Rigney, who just won a 60-day extension of his June 20 induction date, changed his mind under the pressure of publicity surrounding his appeal as a family hardship case. The only hardship that many saw in his case was the threat to Chicago's pennant chances. Actually, Rigney filed the extension form when he thought all ballplayers had the right to do so while the season was in progress. The hardship clause seemed to him a mere technicality. Dan Daniel, the patriotic and interventionist sportswriter for the *New York World-Telegram,* tried

A pensive Joe DiMaggio
contemplating the 1941
season. (*The Sporting News*)

(*Left*) Rookie New York shortstop Phil Rizzuto, during spring training 1941. (*National Baseball Hall of Fame Library, Cooperstown, New York*)

(*Below*) Bill Dickey, Hall of Fame catcher for the Yankees. (*National Baseball Hall of Fame Library, Cooperstown, New York*)

(*Right*) Johnny Sturm of the '41 Yankees. (*National Baseball Hall of Fame Library, Cooperstown, New York*)

(*Above*) Joe D's classic batting
stance as demonstrated
during game 43 of the streak.
(*National Baseball Hall of Fame
Library, Cooperstown, New York*)

(*Right*) Joe DiMaggio relaxing
after equaling the major
league record by hitting in
44 consecutive games.
(*The Sporting News*)

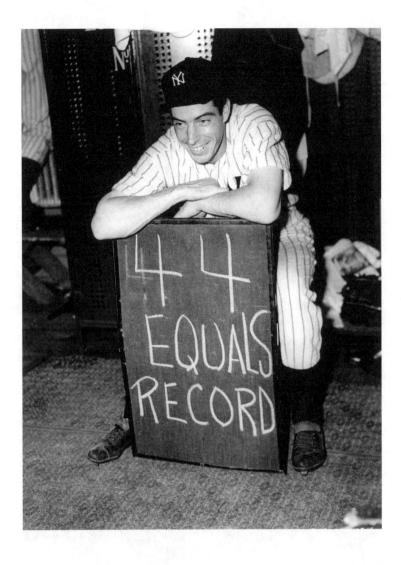

(*Above*) A rare newsphoto records the last swing of DiMaggio's streak, during the eighth inning of the July 17th night game at Cleveland's Municipal Stadium. DiMaggio has just bounced a hard shot to Lou Boudreau, which the Cleveland shortstop will turn into a double play. (*Cleveland Plain Dealer*)

The World Champion 1941 New York Yankees. (*National Baseball Hall of Fame Library, Cooperstown, New York*)

to stand back a bit and take a kinder look at Rigney. In so doing he marked the fervent if conflicted mood of the time: "Life seems to be rather jumbled these days, ideas and ideals are confused, and a lot of people who all insist they are right are tugging in different directions. One cannot be too tough on the ball players for being a bit muddled with so many others." In any event, Rigney now proclaimed himself ready to serve and hoped the fans would appreciate his gesture. One consolation for Rigney was that as of June 12, 1941, all servicemen were admitted to major league ball games for free. But his story had one more wrinkle in it: Rigney versus the army doctors.

The Cleveland Indians, trying to win their games and fend off the Yankees, who were pacing them for a move on the league lead, had other problems this day. Their starting center fielder, Roy Weatherly, was in the hospital after a severe beaning the day before in a game in which they had almost lost Ken Keltner as well in a runaway headhunter exchange. Therefore, the Indians took up the offer made during spring training by Larry MacPhail of the Dodgers to supply any major league team that wanted them with his recently patented protective helmet liners. It was about time for Cleveland to give the liners a try.

MacPhail got himself into the national news for a different reason on June 12. He was charged with being rude and insulting over the phone to one William T. Leonard, head of the Brooklyn chapter of the America First Committee, who was trying to rent Ebbets Field for an isolationist rally. Leonard probably didn't know he was talking to a man who had tried to kidnap the German kaiser before the peace talks ending World War I.

In any event, MacPhail let Leonard have it full broadside. Leonard was mortified and complained to the press that the Dodger executive had "applied unseemly terms to such outstanding Americans as Colonel Lindbergh, Senator Wheeler, Senator Nye, and to the entire membership of the America First Committee." In response to Leonard's demand that he apologize, MacPhail might have pointed out that Lindbergh was no longer a colonel, but instead he pretended to be contrite to a fault, agreeing to apologize at a future date: "Yes, indeed. Right on the steps of Borough Hall in the year 1999, if the America First Committee is still in the National League."

GAME 27: June 14

June 13 was Baseball Hall of Fame Day. The Yankees had the unlucky Friday off, which was just as well for DiMaggio. On the other hand, the gravel-voiced but always sultry Tallulah Bankhead considered it her lucky day: she showed up in Reno on June 13 to get a divorce from her husband of 4 years, John Emery. Tallulah, the daughter of the former speaker of the House of Representatives, William B. Bankhead, appeared for the proceedings leading a leashed pet lion cub which she had named Winston Churchill. Though mental cruelty served as the grounds for divorce, Tallulah told reporters that her husband, John, was a darling man: "Why just the other day he wrote me a beautiful letter."

Back in New York on June 14, the Yankees readied themselves to face the Cleveland Indians, and DiMaggio prepared in this home series to pursue the first of many records that would tumble during the hitting streak: the Yankee individual mark of 29 straight held by Earle Combs and Roger Peckinpaugh. Now managing the Indians, Peckinpaugh was on hand to watch the Yankee center fielder fly past him. A crowd of 44,161 turned up at the Stadium for the showdown series and for the two Yankee streaks, DiMaggio's and the team's consecutive-game home run string. The hottest pitcher in baseball, Bobby Feller, was on the mound trying to grind everything to a halt. He had not lost a game since May 9, winning 8 in a row for a season's record of 13–3. The Indians, with and without Feller, had won their last six; the Yankees, in second place four back, had won their last five. As for DiMaggio, the last time he had faced Feller in New York he had been completely frustrated and handcuffed.

On this occasion the Yankees broke Feller's spell early, touching him for four runs by the fifth inning. Tommy Henrich, who usually hit Feller well under any circumstances, began the Yankee scoring in the first with a solo home run. In the third, DiMaggio sliced a double to right, extending the streak to 27 and driving in a run. The count on DiMaggio at the time was three balls and no strikes, but Joe McCarthy gave DiMaggio the hit sign. Batters take whatever edge is given them, and the hit sign is a baseball inspiration; it means "swing" but conveys the confidence with which it is flashed: "Hit." With Feller grooving the cripple, Di-

Maggio sliced one into the right field alley that rolled to the fence over 415 feet away. This was the only DiMaggio at bat off him during the streak that Feller still remembers: "Yeah, he hit a cripple once. I put it over the plate to get a strike on the 3–0 count. If it's not 3–0, he gets nothing fast from me over the outside part of the plate. That's murder. I tried to get him out tight at the waist—I didn't want to get it up any higher."

Babe Ruth showed up at Yankee Stadium for the game and saw the powerful Yankees extend their consecutive-game home run streak to 10, amassing 24 homers in their last 15 games. The New York fans were so delighted to see Ruth at the game that a special stadium cop had to keep autograph seekers at bay. The mood was getting festive as the Yankees made a run at the American League lead. In the National League, the pennant race caught fire again as St. Louis and Brooklyn faced each other head-on in a four-game series. The Dodgers lost a heartbreaker, 1–0, to the Cardinals on June 13 at night in Ebbets Field. On June 14 the Dodgers got back within two of the Cards by outslugging them 12–5. A seven-run outburst in the sixth inning paced by Dolf Camilli's home run ruined St. Louis, who couldn't touch Dodger relief pitcher Vito Tamulis for the last four innings. Tamulis, like the soon to be famous Rip Sewell, threw a blooper or floater. Watching him pitch, according to local wags, was like viewing a filmed game in slow motion.

Roosevelt this day made his first move in open retaliation for Germany's sinking of the *Robin Moor*. He froze all assets of the Axis powers in America, including the accounts of nearly 1 million resident aliens, mostly German and Italian. Mussolini was furious at the freezing of Italian funds. After all, *he* hadn't sunk the *Robin Moor*. Il duce countered by immediately freezing all American funds in Italy. For the next several weeks the cycle of deteriorating relations continued, affecting what few loose ties remained between the United States and war-torn Europe.

Abroad on June 14, British troops had by now squeezed the Vichy French forces tightly around the Syrian capital of Damascus. The U.S. secretary of state, Cordell Hull, rubbed salt in Pétain's wounds by telling him that the United States planned to take action if the French employed their colonies as Nazi bases. Since the Germans had virtually deserted Vichy forces in Syria, the point seemed painfully moot. The British made another point on June 14. They launched the heaviest aerial bombardment against Germany's industrial Ruhr Valley so far in the war. A message was clearly intended: England wished to remind Hitler that no matter what surprise he thought he had in store for Russia, he still had a two-front battle to wage in Europe.

Meanwhile, Charles Lindbergh and his America Firsters had not heard or seen the last of Larry MacPhail of the Dodgers. MacPhail said on June 14 that he simply didn't want Lindbergh in the Brooklyn ball park and that was why he had told the organization's representative what he thought of him and it. A Brooklyn lawyer and member of the America First Committee, George Dyson Friou, got into the fray. He threatened to sue not over MacPhail's refusal—the park was privately owned—but over the relatively new phenomenon of night baseball. Friou wanted the Dodgers in court for the insult to Lindbergh and would use any tactic he could. He pondered a class action suit on behalf of Brooklyn's elderly, who were denied necessary sleep because of the clamor at the ball park. America First officially disassociated themselves from Friou's suit but intended to go over MacPhail's head to the Dodger owners. MacPhail, of course, had already checked in. The Dodgers stood their ground and barred Lindbergh from occupying it. Friou never did bring suit on behalf of the sleepless elderly. In another insult the day after MacPhail shut the doors of Ebbets Field to Lindbergh, the city council of Charlotte, North Carolina, voted to change the name of Lindbergh Drive to Avon Avenue: "Judging from the man's stand in regard to his country, he doesn't deserve to have a street named after him." This was a far cry from the spirit of St. Louis.

In New York on June 14, British author and actor Noël Coward was in town to arrange for the production of his play *Blithe Spirit* later in the year. He wanted to send an actor acquaintance a gag telegram about seeing him perform in another play then running on Broadway. Coward asked the Western Union clerk to sign the telegram "Mayor La Guardia." The clerk looked up at him and said, "Can't do that, sir. It's not permitted to sign a false name to a telegram." "Oh, all right," said Coward, "then sign it Noël Coward." "Sorry, sir," said the operator, "you can't use his name either." "But I *am* Noël Coward." "Oh, all right," said the clerk, looking up with a flash of recognition, "then you can sign it Mayor La Guardia."

GAME 28: June 15

Another huge crowd poured into Yankee Stadium on Sunday, June 15, to witness the tightening pennant race and to cheer DiMaggio as he approached the individual Yankee hitting streak record. Attendance was up all around the majors, aided by a large St. Louis crowd at Sportsman's Park (34,543) for the Dodger doubleheader. The Cards and Brooklyn split, enabling St. Louis to cling to a two-game lead. Rudolf Hess, whose daring leap had made headlines the world over a month before when DiMaggio began his streak, was again in the news. He took another leap on June 15, this time without a parachute. Hess tried to kill himself by leaping over the third floor balcony of his prison at Mytchett Palace. When Hess hit the ground, he broke his leg and his pelvis but remained alive, much to his dismay and certainly to Hitler's. Hess had just written his wife that the Reich had a special medal for successful heroic acts, but failed actions that endangered the realm called for execution within Germany or suicide without.

Circumstances were far happier for the Yankees in the American League. In their last three actual playing dates (four games), the Yankees and Indians had drawn over 146,000 fans. This day's 3–2 win for the Yanks, their seventh in a row, placed them just two games behind Cleveland for first place. The Yankees managed the win against the same two Indian pitchers, Al Smith and Jim Bagby, who would appear in reverse order in a game on July 17 that would have a different outcome for DiMaggio. But the Yankee center fielder settled matters early this time when in the third inning he belted a Jim Bagby pitch into the upper tier of the left field balcony for his thirteenth home run of the year. The long blow extended both the hitting streak to 28 and the team home run streak to 11. It put DiMaggio in position to tie the Peckinpaugh and Combs streak record the next day.

Red Ruffing breezed along with a three-run lead until the

Indians put together a rally in the eighth that stalled after two runs. The Yankees held on to win. A souvenir hunter grabbed DiMaggio's streak bat after the day's game and headed for open spaces, but DiMaggio loped after him and wrested it back. Now that the streak had gone public, the public felt it had the right to help itself to bits and parts of the streak. DiMaggio would be plagued by equipment thieves from here on, though few of the pirated goods stayed pirated for long.

The *New York Daily News* contacted George Sisler in St. Louis on June 15 because its baseball correspondents sensed that Di-Maggio might be making a run at the modern major league hitting streak record that Sisler had set at 41 in 1922. No one had begun dusting off the 1897 records for Wee Willie Keeler's 44 yet. Sisler told the *Daily News:* "You can't imagine the strain. The newspapers keep mentioning the streak. Your teammates continually bring it up. You try to forget but it can't be done. It's in your head every time you step to the plate." Sisler said that Ty Cobb, who had had a 40-game streak in 1911, had done all he could as manager of the Tigers to keep Sisler in check when he neared 40 straight in 1922. Unfortunately for Cobb, Sisler came into Detroit red hot, and despite Cobb's long meetings with his pitching staff before the game, he fed gloriously on Tiger hurlers. "Cobb was blazing mad. I don't know what he said to his pitchers and I don't want to know."

In American League action on June 15, Ted Williams, with a spurt of 7 hits in 11 at bats against the Chicago White Sox, raised his league-leading average to .425. Another famous left-handed hitter, Babe Herman, was also leading a league this day at .412, but not a major league. The colorful ex-Dodger, who had broken in with Brooklyn in 1926, was playing for the minor league Hollywood Stars at the age of 38. The Stars' management cabled Larry MacPhail of the Dodgers and asked if he wanted another crack at the Babe's contract, insofar as the Stars would be happy to garner the premium befitting the Pacific Coast League's leading hitter. MacPhail cabled back that he would let the Stars know if he wanted Herman for a couple of innings on the day the old-timers game rolled around at Ebbets Field. Ironically, World War II would give the Babe his revenge; Herman got one more whack at the majors in 1945, when at the age of 42 he played in 37 games for Brooklyn and hit .265.

There was a wonderfully zany episode in the second game of a doubleheader between the Cubs and Phillies at Wrigley Field this Sunday. Johnny Podgajny was on the mound for the Phils. After he served up a triple and two singles in the fourth, the third baseman, Pinky May, came over and urged, "Don't give up." Podgajny was so furious he stalked May back to third and popped him one on the nose. Umpire Larry Goetz had to break up the ruckus between the two Phillies. Podgajny got back on the mound, didn't give up, and won the ball game 8–4. Pinky May played the rest of the game nursing his nose and his dignity but keeping all inspirational comments to himself.

The war crept closer and loomed larger in mid-June. Hitler and Stalin had by now massed over 100 divisions along the eastern Russian border, and these nations were still nominally allies. On the other side of the world in Hawaii on June 15, civil defense planners announced that they were building a huge air raid shelter on Oahu that would cost nearly a million dollars and that might be ready, if construction stayed on schedule, by January 1942. Even on schedule, the timing would prove just a touch off. But Roosevelt had more immediate concerns on June 15. He secretly gave the order for a plan he and Churchill had been conjuring for weeks, America's first overt military action in the Atlantic. The President would send Marines and part of the Atlantic fleet to Iceland to release British forces, currently protecting crucial Icelandic waters, for more direct action against the Nazis. By law Roosevelt could not send draftees for this duty, nor could he send even a tugboat until the Icelandic government requested it of him. But the British were working on the appropriate Icelandic officials. These moves so far were top secret; when the isolationists in America found out, the roar would be heard from the Azores to the Golden Gate.

A week had now passed since Roosevelt had ordered the Army out against the renegade strikers at North American Aviation, and some in the CIO began to reconsider their hasty support of the President at the expense of union workers. Philip Murray, president of the CIO, while he had not stood with the renegade strikes of the previous week, commented that traditional antilabor groups in the nation were using Roosevelt's defense emergency speech to confuse the distinction between fair wages and defense priorities. Murray begged for national sanity in these matters, whereby every threatened or actual strike would not be labeled traitorous, communist, or profascist. Roosevelt assured him that big business was on line for some sacrificing as well before the summer was out, perhaps a 50 percent cut in auto production or, even worse, gas rationing. When the Chrysler Corporation, less obligated to the national government in 1941 than in subsequent years, caught wind of these possibilities, there was hell to pay. The scrap between Chrysler Motors and the Roosevelt administration would prove one of the more colorful and abusive of the summer.

GAME 29: June 16

At the same time that the Nazi command in Berlin admitted on June 16 that they had sunk the *Robin Moor* because it carried contraband war matériel, news reached the United States that the remaining lifeboats were sighted and all survivors rescued after weeks at sea. A British steamer, the *Wellington,* sailing in the waters off Brazil, spotted the three lifeboats with everyone still in them and everyone still alive. The sighting had occurred on June 13, but the *Wellington,* for its own safety, could not radio until arriving in Capetown, South Africa, on June 16. The chief officer of the *Robin Moor,* Melvin Munday, filled in some of the details of the raid.

Munday had come to deck of his ship in his pajamas the morning of May 21 when a crew member told him they were being signaled by a German submarine. The chief officer quickly put on his trousers and took one of his vessel's lifeboats to row to the surfaced U-boat. The German captain told him that the cargo on the *Robin Moor* was intended for the Reich's enemies and that in a half hour the Germans would send the freighter to the bottom of the sea. Munday claimed this was an outrage but rowed back and delivered the doleful information to the passengers and crew. Then he launched the ship's three other lifeboats. The U-boat captain torpedoed the abandoned *Robin Moor,* and the freighter's crew and passengers, 35 unlikely adventurers, began a 2-week odyssey in the open seas of the Atlantic.

On one of the lifeboats was a 2-year-old child, Robin McCullogh, who behaved through the entire ordeal like an old salt. The tot became extremely fond of the hardtack rations, not exactly the favorite fare of the drifting adults, and entertained himself all day by looking at the pretty fishes (sharks) circling the boat. After 5 days at sea, one of the lifeboats (the one that had been discovered a few days before) separated from the rest. The three remaining boats stuck together during the searing heat of many days, the anxiety of many nights, and the ordeal of several storms with waves up to 13 feet. As the survivors pulled into Capetown on the *Wellington* after 26 days adrift at sea, they were received as war victims and celebrated as heroes and heroines. One opposition paper, however, *Die Burger,* whose leanings were distinctly pro-German, reacted to all the fuss in South Africa with the headline "TORPEDOED WITH GREAT GENTLEMANLINESS."

For his part, Roosevelt was not about to let the Germans off easy for the *Robin Moor* sinking, rescued survivors or no. He continued his provocative retaliations by ordering all German consulates and travel bureaus in America shut down. Those staffing the offices were ordered out of the country by July 10. We were very close to breaking diplomatic relations with the Axis powers, and for Roosevelt the issue of the *Robin Moor* was intimately related to our convoy policy, which was solidifying in his own mind as he contemplated more moves in defense of the Atlantic sea-lanes from Nova Scotia to Greenland to Ireland.

At the Stadium on June 16, Joe DiMaggio went after the Yankee individual hitting streak record. After a rain delay of an hour and a half, he came to the plate hitless in the fifth inning. With the crowd screaming its support, southpaw Al Milnar served him one and DiMaggio smashed it to left for a double, tying the Yank record at 29 straight. Roger Peckinpaugh had reached 29 in 1919, the season of the infamous Black Sox; Earl Combs, also in the ball park this day as the Yankee first base coach, had done it in 1931. In the fourth inning, before the rains, Joe Gordon hit one 420 feet to left and out of the park with Buddy Rosar on base to extend the Yankee consecutive-game home run streak to 12.

The Indians actually gave the game away on June 16. Lou Boudreau muffed a ball at short in the eighth, setting up a bases-loaded Bill Dickey pinch hit, and Ray Mack's error at second set up another run as the Yankees came from behind to win 6–4. The Yankee shortstop, Frankie Crosetti, had his right middle finger severely spiked on a Hal Trosky slide, and Phil Rizzuto, riding the bench since the day after DiMaggio's hitting streak began, came in to replace the veteran. In his column Dan Daniel predicted that "the Flea will not allow Frankie to reclaim the job for the rest of the season." Daniel was right, just as he had been right in his prediction that DiMaggio would break out of his slump back on May 15, the first day of the streak. Rizzuto returned to the lineup hot; he would never relinquish his position at short to Crosetti again, except during the war, when he served in the Navy.

There was an unusual play in the Indians' half of the fifth inning. Cleveland had two on and none out when their first baseman, Trosky, hit a short fly to Tommy Henrich in right. With the runners staying close to their respective bases, Henrich dropped the fly intentionally, hoping to fire to second for a force-out and then, with a relay to third, another tag for a double play. But Jeff Heath on second saw what Henrich had in mind and took off for third. The umps, of course, also saw Henrich's maneuver and immediately signaled an intentional drop, which had been established to prevent just such chicanery. The batter, Trosky, was automatically out; the runners could try to advance only at their own risk. Jeff Heath, moving off base, never did arrive at third, so Henrich's crafty play, just invalidated by the umpires as a force-out, became a tag out on Heath. Henrich had his double play. Heath took a seat on the bench, and the Yankees had a laugh, something they were well able to do after this Cleveland series, unlike a month before, when Cleveland had blown them away in New York. On that occasion the Yankees had been in despair, Joe McCarthy in a slow burn, and Joe DiMaggio unable to buy a hit from the peanut vendor. This time, the Yankees, by beating Cleveland, won their eighth in a row, swept the three-game set, and sent Peckinpaugh's Indians out of town with but a one-game hold on first place—they had entered New York with a four-game lead. Moreover, Peckinpaugh left the city when DiMaggio was about to wipe him off the books as holder and then coholder for 22 years of the Yankee hitting streak record. As Dizzy Dean was wont to say, Peckinpaugh "shoulda stood in bed."

GAME 30: June 17

The Chicago White Sox, the team against which DiMaggio had begun the streak at the Stadium, revisited New York for a return engagement. When DiMaggio grounded a ball to Luke Appling late in the game—the seventh inning—it took a horrible hop and bounced off the Chicago shortstop's shoulder, enabling DiMaggio to set the all-time Yankee hitting streak record at 30 straight. There was no way Appling could field the ball. The day's game was a close one until the Chicago half of the seventh, when the White Sox broke it open with four against Yankee rookie Steve Peek. John Rigney, nearing his scheduled Army induction day set for June 20, pitched for Chicago.

The Yankees almost came back, picking up three in the seventh and going for more when Johnny Sturm got caught in a rundown between first and second. Rizzuto broke for the plate from third, hoping the Sox would concentrate on Sturm. They didn't. Catcher Mike Tresh got the relay and put the tag on Rizzuto to end the inning. In the eighth, Keller tied the game with a monstrous home run into the upper tier in right field to extend the Yankee home run streak to 13 games, and the Yankees might have been able to score before the Keller drive had not White Sox right fielder, Taft Wright, made a brilliant catch of a DiMaggio line smash heading over the low barrier at the fence. A ninth inning rally on a bloop single by former Yankee Myril Hoag led to a White Sox victory, 8–7, stopping the Yankee winning streak at 8.

As World War II approached a momentous day and a momentous action along a second European front, the scale of which would put everything before it in a new perspective, Roosevelt continued to grind what few Axis interests remained in America into finer and finer dust. On June 17 he placed all German aliens in America under a kind of house arrest—they couldn't come and they couldn't go. But on this same day another new policy emerged from the White House, one that had devastating implications for the Jewish populations under German domination. The United States would accept no more Germans or German Jews if they still had family in Nazi-dominated areas of Europe. Ostensibly such admissions would pose a threat to America because of pressure the Nazis could exert on family members still living in German-occupied lands, but there were also tactical and cynical reasons. Some in the State Department worried that saboteurs and agents would slip into America disguised as refugees; others were alarmed at a new Jewish diaspora to American shores. As was the case in much of the western world in the early '40s, denial of the Jewish problem played as powerful a role as outrage at the German "solution" to it.

Roosevelt's refugee limitation had a disheartening and chilling effect on groups in America and in Europe working at extreme risk to their lives to move Jews out of Germany and German-controlled lands. A story in *The New York Times* this day told of the separation of one young Jewish girl from her family in 1939 and plotted her pathetic journey from country to country as she awaited entry into the United States via Portugal. She, like tens of thousands of others not exterminated by the Nazis, would now become citizens of a confused state of international limbo for the duration of the war.

Excitement began to build in New York City for the next day's heavyweight championship fight between Joe Louis and a converted light heavyweight, Billy Conn. By most accounts except Conn's, Louis figured to have an easy time of it. The fighters were well primed. Louis was 27 and Conn 23; the champ weighed in at 200 pounds, Conn at 175. Conn, who had been talking a terrific fight all week, insisted his speed would win it for him, but Louis looked as though he could put out Con Ed's lights, let alone Billy Conn's, with either hand. Conn added some spice to the act just before the fight by applying for a license to marry Mary Louise Smith, 18-year-old daughter of the former outfielder for the Cincinnati Reds and New York Giants, Jimmie Smith. Mary Louise's father declared himself dead set against his daughter's marriage. He said he would punch hell out of Conn if the fighter kept hanging around his kid, but he wished Billy well in his fight with Louis.

GAME 31: June 18

With the Polo Grounds across the river from Yankee Stadium receiving its final fitting out on June 18 for what turned out to be one of the finest heavyweight championship fights of the century, DiMaggio and the Yankees were only a preliminary to a New York City main event. Another prelim of sorts took place across the Hudson River in Newark. Ten Italian nationals were on trial for blowing up their freighter, the *Aussa,* after federal officials had impounded it earlier that spring in American waters. All were judged guilty, and as the convicted crew members marched out of court stone-faced, the owner of the former *Aussa* stood up and roused his crew to patriotic outbursts and fascist salutes in honor of Mussolini. The freak show appalled the spectators milling about, who hooted and jeered in return. Court officials acted with dispatch before they had a prelude to the Anzio beachhead on their hands.

At the Stadium, DiMaggio extended his hitting streak to 31 straight that afternoon with considerably more ease than Louis would display extending his title defense streak to 18 that night. Once again DiMaggio continued at the expense of Luke Appling, who could barely get his glove on a blooplike fluffer beyond short. It was senseless for Appling to throw to first since DiMaggio was already past the bag when he picked up the ball. For his part, DiMaggio helped the White Sox score their first run of the game they eventually won 3–2 when he overran a Luke Appling second inning fly to left center and saw the ball drop embarrassingly behind him. These two great ballplayers were helping each other out, or helping each other on, with consistency during the days of DiMaggio's streak.

Charlie Keller's two-run homer against Chicago lefty Thornton Lee in the second put the lid on the Yankee scoring for the day but kept the consecutive-game home run streak alive at 14. The Yankees were chasing the major league record of 17 straight home run games set the previous year during the Detroit Tigers' run for the 1940 pennant. Chicago moved ahead in this day's game when in the eighth Phil Rizzuto tried to get Joe Kuhel at third after fielding Myril Hoag's grounder. The entire Yankee bench, along with Rizzuto and Rolfe, swore they had nabbed Kuhel, but the umpire thought otherwise. Kuhel, who later became famous for his outburst when fired as manager of the Washington Senators—"You can't make chicken salad out of chicken feathers"—then scored on a single. Hoag soon crossed the plate on Skeets Dickey's sacrifice fly. Young Skeets was Bill Dickey's brother.

Red Ruffing smashed yet another pinch hit in the ninth, to no avail for the Yankees. If there were such a thing as a record for pinch hits achieved by a teammate during a 56-game hitting streak, the amazing Ruffing would certainly hold it. In 1941 he ended up with a .400 pinch-hitting average and a .303 season's average. For his career he had 58 pinch hits. Ruffing played 22 years with the Red Sox, Yanks, and White Sox and racked up a healthy .269 lifetime batting average. More significantly, in 7 of those years he hit over .300. Only such old-timers as pitcher-infielder Doc Crandall (.285 lifetime), Carl Mays (.268 lifetime), Ruffing's contemporary Schoolboy Rowe (.263 lifetime), and Don Newcombe (.271 lifetime) approached the skill of Ruffing as a hitting pitcher. Babe Ruth's .320 average in his 3 full-time pitching years for the Red Sox belongs in a somewhat different category.

On the night of June 18 in New York, promoters expected a gate of 40,000 for the Louis-Conn championship fight, but 58,487 fans jammed the Polo Grounds for the nighttime spectacle. Lefty Gomez and Joe DiMaggio were among the throng, and fight fans went slightly berserk at the sight of the great Yankee as he moved to his seat. DiMaggio got a rousing ovation without hitting anything that evening. The New York Giants, whose absence from town had freed the Polo Grounds, found themselves preempted by the fight at the very stadium they had vacated. Their game under the lights at Pittsburgh was held up while Don Dunphy's radio broadcast of the bout played over the loudspeakers. For the Giants this was the second time in 3 weeks a broadcast had interrupted their play; they were also on the field May 27 when their night game at the Polo Grounds was delayed by the broadcast of Roosevelt's "unlimited emergency" speech. Giant manager Bill Terry was more than willing to listen to the President during the ball game but balked at listening to Don Dunphy. His protests, however, fell on the deaf, or preoccupied, ears of the Pittsburgh Pirate front office.

From the opening round to the extraordinary conclusion in the thirteenth, the championship fight proved a spellbinding, classical, brilliant effort. Billy Conn began with a burst of embarrassing energy—he slipped untouched to the canvas shortly after the bell sounded to begin round 1. At first Conn appeared tentative, but through the middle rounds his confidence increased. His speed enabled him to move inside and crash Louis with accurate hooks and crosses before the champ could open up. Conn, with his hands held unusually high, then danced backward and clockwise, away from Louis's left.

Louis circled after him with the monotony of a second hand, but Conn consistently beat the champ to the punch in the middle rounds. And his punches were elegant, stinging, and accurate. By the twelfth round Conn commanded the action. Though his legs were wearying and were rooted more securely to the canvas, he hit Louis harder and more often than Louis hit him, landing one especially devastating hook that buckled the champ and made his eyeballs look as though they were attached to coiled springs.

By round 13 his corner men told the champ he was behind, as indeed he was on the scorecards of one judge and the referee (the other judge had it even). Conn, having outboxed Louis for 11 rounds and outslugged him in the twelfth, then made a tactical mistake bred from eagerness. Louis had begun a more menacing direct stalk that bore little resemblance to his earlier fruitless circling, and Conn took the bait. He moved in swinging to center ring to meet Louis head-on, but the champ's punches now reached their target first. Louis threw them short, from the shoulder, generating shock from a powerful, balanced stance. The alternation was textbook: head, midsection, head and hook, uppercut, hook, cross.

Near the end of the round, Conn seemed exhausted. Louis finally hit him with a right-hand blow square on the chin. Conn stopped and stood dazed in the middle of the ring. The next Louis blow, a left uppercut to the gut, made Conn dance half an Irish jig. A right hand to the side of the head put him away. Conn's spirit told him to get up, but his flesh just sat there. There were 2 seconds left in the round when the referee counted him out. Conn gave the ref a desperate, helpless look that measured eternities during the unhappy progress of the count.

Billy Conn this night made Joe Louis work harder than he had on any occasion since he had taken the crown from Jim Braddock 4 years before. And the young challenger certainly earned the tidy $77,202 he took home for getting in the ring with Louis, though nothing in the contract said he had to put up this kind of fight. Louis earned $154,404, and he would need all of it because his wife would soon sue him for divorce, claiming the champ found it easier to land punches with her as the target than he had in the ring with Billy Conn.

GAME 32: June 19

On June 19 at the Stadium, Joe DiMaggio faced Chicago left-hander Edgar Smith, the same pitcher against whom he had begun his streak with a single in the first inning on May 15. Now, 32 games later, he greeted Smith with another single in the first inning. The Yankees went on to a 7–2 win. DiMaggio had a perfect day at the plate. He singled in the fifth off Buck Ross, and in the eighth he drove one out of the park for his fourteenth home run of the year. His 3 for 3 began a streak within a streak, a sequence of at bats over two games in which American League pitchers not only couldn't get him out for an entire game but couldn't get him out at all.

The Yankee win, after two losses to the White Sox, came quickly and cleanly this day. Charlie Keller's grand slam home run in the fourth (he now had two grand slams during DiMaggio's streak to match his two inside-the-park home runs) virtually sewed up Chicago's seams. The big blow extended the Yankee home run binge to 15 straight games, the third in a row in which Keller powered the streak. So far DiMaggio led the sweepstakes since the beginning of the sequence on June 1 with 7 home runs; Keller followed with 6, and Henrich with 5. All the White Sox could manage off Marvin Breuer was a skimpy run in the fourth and a home run by Bill Dickey's brother, Skeets, the rookie's first in the major leagues.

Another rookie sensation hit the baseball world on June 19 and signed the largest bonus ever for a raw recruit in the major leagues. The path of gold was roundabout for Dick Wakefield, hot off the University of Michigan campus. Brooklyn got to him first when they were playing the Cubs in Chicago that past week. The Dodgers put the big, dashing fellow in a uniform and had him take his cuts during batting practice. Dodger player-manager Leo Durocher licked his chops. But before Larry MacPhail and Dodger Company could say Jack Robinson (indeed, before they even set sights on Jack Robinson, just out of UCLA early in 1941 and considering, among other things, a pro basketball career), the Detroit Tigers offered Wakefield $45,000. Dick signed. This was exceptional money for the era, and Wakefield was truly the first of the bonus babies.

Wakefield got in a few games in 1941 for Detroit but enjoyed his best years during the war, when big league pitching left much to be desired. He also gained a special kind of notoriety by being the first major leaguer to face Rip Sewell's famous eephus pitch in a 1943 exhibition game between Detroit and Pittsburgh in Muncie, Indiana. With two strikes on Wakefield, Al Lopez, catching for the Pirates, signaled for a change-up. Sewell improvised with the high-arching and achingly slow blooper. Wakefield started his swing, readjusted, started again, hitched, and finally went down from the force of his own roundhouse cut. Amid the laughter and the dust, a pitch was born.

The current issue of the *Sporting News* bannered a long feature article on Ted Williams and his torrid hitting in May and early June. "Hitting is the biggest thing in my life. I love it. And the next thing I like best is to hunt ducks." Short of ducks, pigeons would do. The year before he and Red Sox owner Tom Yawkey had gone out to an empty Fenway Park and killed 70 to 80 pigeons with 20-gauge shotguns. The now infamous Dave Winfield adventure with the sea gull in Toronto paled before this incident, which put the Boston Humane Society in deep mourning. Then the society consulted its lawyers.

Unlike DiMaggio's classical dignity and restraint, Williams behaved like a kid whose brashness would set him up for abuse all over the American League. Any bench jockey with imagination could get to him. In 1940, during a slump, Ted said in despair that maybe he should have been a firefighter like his uncle. From that point, wherever the Red Sox traveled, Williams had to deal with mock sirens, rival players wearing ridiculous-looking children's fire fighter's hats, and pleas for assistance during hot-foot sessions in the dugouts. Lefty Gomez got thrown out of one Yankee–Red Sox game by ump Bill Summers after he refused to stop ringing bells from the dugout and shouting "Fire!" whenever Williams appeared to take his cuts at the plate. A .400 hitter has one sure way of responding to all this, and Williams always had his sweet stroke to make up for his rabbit ears.

When asked in the profile about another part of his game, his marginal work in the Boston outfield, Williams insisted that he was a much better fielder than he was credited for being. In fact, he hadn't made an error yet this year. The *Sporting News* correspondent told him that one of his throws had hit a runner for an error in a game on May 28 against the A's, and Williams retorted: "What kind of scoring is that? Do you mean to tell me they give you an error for hitting a runner with a throw? Gosh, these newspapermen!"

On June 19 the United States made another crucial move toward funding a war that many throughout the land recognized as imminent. A plan came out of the House Ways and Means Committee that when voted into law later in the summer would change the structure of the income tax system and raise tremendous revenues for defense. In addition to almost doubling the tax obligation of middle-income citizens, the pending bill introduced the marriage tax, the notion that two incomes filed together ought to be more vulnerable than two incomes filed separately.

A family earning $5,000 a year would see its tax liability jump from $110 to $308; at $10,000 a year, taxes would leap from $526 to $1,166. An income of $20,000 moved one's tax liability from $2,336 to $4,338; $50,000 annually, from $14,128 to $20,002; and $100,000, from $43,476 to $53,310. As hefty a rise as the new bill projected, it came nowhere close to wartime England's tax structure. No one in that beleaguered land was permitted to earn more than £10,000 ($28,000) a year. The exchequer merely siphoned anything in excess of that amount into the war budget.

At no time during DiMaggio's streak had the world seemed so aware about what was fated to happen in the war before it actually happened. The "showdown" as *The New York Times* put it, was near. With Nazi Germany poised on Russia's borders, it was hard to imagine that Hitler would waste any of his ire against Roosevelt. But June 19 saw another tat in the tit for tat game going on over the last several days regarding Axis-American relations. Berlin announced that all U.S. officials in Axis territory would have just about the same amount of time to pack their belongings and clear out as Roosevelt had given to German consular officials in America. A deep diplomatic freeze set in at home just before a dramatic and massive outbreak of hostility abroad that would kick the entire war into another gear.

For the 2 years since the German-Soviet treaty of 1939, Hitler and Stalin had parceled out spheres of influence in eastern Europe. Now Hitler wanted his parcel to include Stalin's. Moreover, he wanted the rich Russian Ukraine region for the Reich's agricultural and industrial needs, and he wanted Leningrad just for spite. Moscow appeared calm, and there seemed to observers something surreal about the looming invasion. It was simply too enormous to gauge. What might two armies, each 3 million strong, each with air support, each with mobile auxiliaries, do to each other? No one in the world really knew. Hitler's intercepted and decoded plan, Operation Barbarosa, boasted that he could do fairly much what he wanted to do and could do it in 3 months, before the mud and snows of fall and winter. British intelligence sources came to the same conclusion, only they phrased it differently: Hitler would find himself in deep trouble if he failed to do what he hoped to do in 3 months, and his armies would suffer the same fate in the folds of Mother Russia's wintery midsection that Napoleon's had in 1812.

GAME 33: June 20

DiMaggio and the Yankees rolled over visiting Detroit at the Stadium on June 20, 14–4, to move within 1½ games of first place in the American League. That night in New York, an ex-vaudeville comic and former child star in the the Pearl White serial, *Perils of Pauline,* Milton Berle, celebrated his twenty-seventh year in show business. Some names—like Berle's, Bob Hope's, and in its way Joe DiMaggio's—seem always to be around to grace the century. Currently hosting a variety act at the Paramount between movie screenings, Berle and his on-stage shtick became a New York legend that stood him in good stead when television beckoned in the late '40s and early '50s.

The afternoon's onslaught at the Stadium was vaudevillian in its own right, with the Tiger's traveling clown, Bobo Newsom, heading the bill. Newsom hated to get hit hard, and he always showed the strain when balls were launched off him. This outing was particularly stressful for Newsom and delightful for Yankee fans. Tommy Henrich began the action in the first by driving one out with Johnny Sturm on base. The blast, whose parabolic flight over the right field fence Newsom balefully tracked, continued the Yankee home run streak, now at 16 games. DiMaggio followed with a single and an equally quick resolution of his hitting streak at 33 games. Charlie Keller then drove in DiMaggio with a mighty home run blast 430 feet to right center. He had been unstoppable in his last several games. Newsom looked ready to enlist in the Army on the spot and join his teammate Hank Greenberg at Camp Custer, Michigan.

Before either Newsom or McKain in relief could get DiMaggio out this day, he ripped four hits—three singles and a double—in four at bats. Counting his perfect day the previous game against the White Sox, DiMaggio had now chalked up seven straight hits, the last two coming in one inning, the fifth, as the Yankees sent

11 men to the plate and scored seven times. DiMaggio also enjoyed an interesting day in the outfield. Though his feet slipped out from under him as he manhandled Paddy Mullim's single in the first for an error, later in the game he made one of his best defensive plays during the streak. He glided, as only he could do, through the seemingly endless reaches of Yankee Stadium's center field to snare Rudy York's monumental drive some 450 feet from home plate.

DiMaggio still recalls this day as the first when he thought seriously about a shot at the major league streak record, which he assumed was Sisler's 41 straight. No one remembered anything at this point about Keeler's 44. Up till now DiMaggio had been aware of the streak but hadn't measured it against his own 61-game record with San Francisco in 1933 or against Sisler's modern-day major league record. After he passed both Sisler and Keeler, he would tell Dan Daniel: "I didn't get warm about this thing until the 33rd game. You may remember I got three singles and a double off Newsom and McKain. I hadn't made four hits in a game since the 12th against the Senators." This was DiMaggio's only detailed comparative assessment of his progress, and he made a mistake of over 2 weeks in recalling the four-hit day against the Senators. (Daniel put the correct date in brackets: not 3 days before the streak on May 12 but 12 days into it on May 27.) The error simply suggests that DiMaggio's substantial point was correct: He hadn't begun projecting beyond the day-by-day growth of the streak until the thirty-third game, when he felt so good that it seemed as if he might hit in 56 straight at bats.

DiMaggio's seven hits in a row brought his season's batting average up to .354 and placed him in the top five batters in the American League for the first time since the streak had begun. His average since May 15 soared to .395. In his next game he could set his short-range sights on George McQuinn's 34 straight for the Browns in 1938. Ted Williams still led the league at .420, and his .456 average during the span of DiMaggio's streak, even including another "ofer" on June 18 against Schoolboy Rowe and the Tigers, topped the Yankee center fielder by over 60 points.

Chicago White Sox right-hander John Rigney showed up at his Army induction physical at 7 A.M. on the morning of June 20. Before he left the medical offices, a team of four doctors consulted on his case for an hour. Rigney's own doctor claimed he had a punctured eardrum, and the Army doctors reluctantly agreed, declaring him unfit for service. The White Sox told Rigney to hop a plane and join them in Philadelphia. Rigney made no secret of the fact that given a choice of boot camp or Philadelphia, he'd rather be in Philadelphia. Big John enlisted in the service on his own after the 1942 season at a time when both he and the doctors were less punctilious about punctures.

On June 20 Roosevelt demanded what he knew he would not get: reparations from the Nazis for the sinking of the *Robin Moor*. This was a legal maneuver so that he could publicly call Germany an outlaw nation, which is precisely what he did. The term "outlaw" was well chosen. There were precedents in U.S. history when we did not wish to declare war formally but did wish to behave as if we were at war. Outlaw activity was often the specific charge and excuse. Obviously, Roosevelt wanted Germany to think we were on the verge of arming convoys to Great Britain, though he meant his remarks to justify what he had already agreed to do in Iceland: send troops and ships. The President also decided to wipe the Axis slate clean and boot the Italians out of their U.S. consulates as he had done to the Germans. The wife of our ambassador to Italy protested this day that Roosevelt misunderstood the Italians. There was no nation that Italy detested more than Germany and no national leader whom they held in greater contempt than Hitler. Italians may well have felt this way, but public broadcasts to that effect were rare in fascist Italy.

A disaster that could not be laid directly at the feet or down the torpedo tubes of the German Navy took place in the coastal waters off Portsmouth, New Hampshire, on June 20. An American sub with the inglorious name of *0–9* sank to a depth of 400 feet and was crushed like an eggshell with 33 sailors aboard. Because of the pressure at that depth, divers could not descend to the wreck to determine the cause of the disaster or even recover the bodies. In the protowar we were angling for and to some extent suffering from in the Atlantic, there were times when an accident was just an accident. In this instance sabotage was considered highly unlikely.

In Los Angeles on June 20, Charles Lindbergh and his America First cronies spoke before thousands at the Hollywood Bowl.

Actress Lillian Gish joined the America First tour, fresh from her starring role in the Chicago production of *Life with Father*. Lindbergh wrote in his journal for this day how struck he was at the beauty of the bowl under the stars. He also distinguished in his journal between the intelligent looks of the people who came to see him speak and the barbaric shrieks and hisses of crowds at movie theaters during the *Movietone News* whenever Hitler or Mussolini appeared on the screen. Because he did not enjoy or feel comfortable around those who idolized him, Lindbergh related in his diaries how he spent a good deal of spare time while touring America at the movies, where, if his luck held, he would not be recognized. There he would listen in the dark to what he called the bloodthirsty sounds of an unthinking, hysterical populace. Lindbergh was either hard on the typical American movie fan or hadn't yet gotten over the awful public spectacle surrounding the kidnapping and murder of his child nearly a decade before.

That night at the Hollywood Bowl, Lindbergh adjusted to Roosevelt's new belligerence by expanding his own defeatism. He told the crowd we were capable only of defending our natural borders—we would lose to the Nazis on the high seas. Considering the relatively small size of the German Navy, the recent sinking of the *Bismarck,* and the new technological advances against submarine warfare, even Lindbergh couldn't have really believed this claim. Like virtually all the aviator's wartime forecasts, this one turned out to be dolefully mistaken.

GAME 34: June 21

Europe on Saturday was strangely calm, even though a sense of apprehension hung like a thick fog all along the Soviet border. In America reality temporarily gave way to mythology as the *Saturday Evening Post* featured a story reviewing the creation and history of Superman, just 4 years old as a money-making venture but approaching 9 as the kryptonic brainchild of a young Cleveland lad by the name of Jerry Siegel. One day in 1932 Siegel dreamed up Superman and spent the next several hours conjuring powers for him. Siegel and Superman now were grossing about a million dollars a year, with Joe DiMaggio doing his bit as an avid reader. The Nazis, too, had gotten hold of America's *Übermensch* by 1941. The monthly magazine of Hitler's elite Schwarze Corps published an article attacking the anti-Nazi role Superman played so actively in the comics. The magazine labeled the Superman myth a product of Jewish dementia and its creator Siegel "a clever little beetle that stinks." So much for the Nazi perception of western truth, justice, and the American way at a time when they were about to try crushing a communist behemoth to the east.

Before a Saturday crowd of 20,067 on this first day of summer at the Stadium, the Yankees lost to Detroit 7–2, though for the third straight game DiMaggio ended any streak suspense early with a hit in the first inning, his eighth in a row over three games. His hit—a single—wasn't much: Dizzy Trout jammed DiMaggio, who then blooped a handle shot over Rudy York's head at first base. Even a more versatile fielder than York couldn't have snagged this one. DiMaggio had now equaled George McQuinn's 1938 streak of 34 games; Ty Cobb's run of 40 in 1911 was next.

Trout had the Yankees under control all day, and he even got his team ahead for good in the second inning with a two-run single. The Yankees scored only once more all day, but that run proved to be telling: Phil Rizzuto, a most unlikely long-ball threat, laid into a fat one tossed up by Trout and put it 400 feet out of the park to left for his second major league home run. As Rizzuto rounded third a smile wreathed his entire face. The Yankees had tied the record for consecutive-game home runs by a major league team at 17, which had been set by the 1940 version of the Detroit Tigers. During Detroit's long-ball binge the previous year, Greenberg, York, and company had hit 26 home runs in 17 games; this year the Yankees stroked 28. No other team hit so many home runs in so few games until the Cincinnati Reds of 1956, followed by the Maris-Mantle Yankees of 1961, who hold the current record at 32 home runs over a span of 17 straight games. Neither the 1956 Cincinnati powerhouse nor the 1961 Yankees, however, were able to match the full run of the 1941 Yankee consecutive-game home run streak. DiMaggio, Henrich, and

Keller were simply too hot and too powerful for most of June this year for their performances to be quickly or easily duplicated.

An article for the issue of *Esquire* just hitting the stands on June 21 advocated an idea that would in due time gain some currency: designated hitters. For good measure, the article threw in a designated fielder or two. "I Want a Change" was the name of the piece, and its author, Felix Mendelsohn, Jr., was fed up with "all field no hit" rummies and big hitters who could barely fit their gloves over five thumbs. His solution was a modified platoon system with two or three positions designated as purely offensive or purely defensive. In 1941 almost everyone found this notion purely offensive. Not until 1973 would the American League produce a minimalist version of the proposal and introduce the designated hitter rule.

GAME 35: June 22

At 3:30 A.M. Sunday, sunrise in the Baltic, German armies crossed into Russian territory. With the release of his mighty forces at daybreak, Hitler made Russia his supreme project and, like Napoleon before him, his supreme folly. The size of the invasion even startled the führer, who marveled as the day progressed that never in its history had the world known or seen anything on so grand a military scale. Sunday, June 22, remains as significant a date for a great expanse of the European continent as another Sunday, December 7, 1941, remains for America.

German aerial and artillery barrages began the attack during the night, and by dawn an awesome total of 146 infantry, Panzer, and motorized divisions began pouring into Russian territory. The Germans also had at their disposal the entire Finnish Army, still smarting from its 1939 war with Russia. The Finns fought fiercely and got better as the weather got colder. Surely the Russians did not want to face these forces again, especially allied with several million Germans. In addition, 14 Romanian divisions, 28 reserve divisions, and Italian reinforcement units were available for the Axis onslaught. To provide a comparative sense of what was now happening along the Russian border, Hitler's strength over the rest of the war zone consisted of but 38 divisions in all western Europe, 1 in Denmark, 7 in Norway, 7 in the Balkans, and 2 in North Africa.

According to the plan for the German attack, Hitler envisaged three thrusts into Russia: a northern one through the Baltic states and on to Leningrad, a central one through Smolensk and on to Moscow (or north to Leningrad as it turned out), and a southern one through the Ukraine to Kiev and Stalingrad. He intended a summer campaign of 10 weeks' duration and had made few plans beyond that. The führer told Field Marshal von Runstedt, the commander of his army group of the south, "You have only to kick in the door, and the whole rotten structure will come crashing down."

The Russians were not exactly defenseless. They had more infantry divisions than the huge Nazi Army on their borders, but their tank and motorized divisions were no match in quality for the German forces. Worse, Russian defense plans for the western borders were helter-skelter. What Hitler and the world did not know—because Stalin's police state kept Russia's preparations secret—was the precise reserve strength of the Russian Army and the Russian production capacity currently gearing up in the region of the Ural Mountains.

Before the first day of fighting had concluded, the front stretched over a thousand miles. The Russians had masses of men in all areas, and they were faring much better in the battle's early hours than the Germans had expected. The casualties on both sides were enormous. But the Russian commander of the central zone, General Pavlov, made the single greatest mistake of the day, and perhaps of the war, when he moved 50 Russian divisions in Belorussia smack into the middle of the German pincer advance. Over the next days these divisions virtually disappeared from the face of the earth. Pavlov found himself in irrevocable trouble, and before Joe DiMaggio's streak edged into July Joe Stalin would have his general executed for this day's tragic blunder.

The Nazi propaganda minister, Joseph Goebbels, wasted little time in reading Hitler's proclamation of war against Russia over national radio. The führer claimed that all efforts to ensure peace for the area had failed when he became convinced Russia sought to enter into a coalition with England to ruin Germany. Oddly enough, this is exactly what the deputy führer, Rudolf Hess, thought Hitler wanted to do with England to ruin Russia. The truth in 1941 was somewhat less complicated. England, especially Churchill, could stomach neither Hitler nor Stalin, though the prime minister pledged aid to Russia and responded to Hitler's proclamation of war by calling him a "bloodthirsty guttersnipe."

Germany's invasion of Russia, though expected, was troublesome for America. Given the enormous anti-Soviet sentiment in this country, especially after the disgust with which even the extreme left had greeted the Stalin-Hitler nonaggression pact of 1939, Roosevelt did not know quite what to do on invasion day. As for America's isolationists, they now had some powerful new arguments against war, arguments more convincing than those they had been enlisting. Did we really want to waste the lives of our youth by thrusting them into the maw of a monstrous conflagration on a scale never before witnessed, contested by two nations we could not abide? Roosevelt asked himself the same questions, and after June 22 he began looking a bit less eagerly for a technical act of naval hostility to get us into the fray. On the other hand, two fronts in Europe gave the British what they thought they needed, a fighting chance, with Stalin's armies doing the bulk of the fighting and taking the bulk of the chances.

Amid all the excitement surrounding the invasion of Russia, the world barely noticed either the fall of Damascus to the British hours before Germany attacked Stalin or the RAF's most sustained attack of the war against targets in Vichy France and the German Ruhr Valley. England now had the absolute upper hand in the middle east as Vichy officers and officials began to secrete themselves out of the area any way they could before the British attacked Beirut. And in the long run the saturation bombing of Germany would prove disastrous for Hitler with his supply lines stretched over the entire European continent.

The final game of the Detroit series at the Stadium on this dramatic Sunday, June 22, began as news just started arriving over the wires detailing the massive German assault across the Russian border. Nothing that happened at Yankee Stadium could rival the initiatory shock of the invasion, yet the Tigers and Yankees did what they could. The ball game proved a thriller for the 27,072 fans who arrived in the searing 94-degree heat, the hottest June 22 on record for the city. DiMaggio waited a few innings longer than he had in the previous three games to continue the streak. But in the sixth he slammed an outside pitch from Hal Newhouser 370 feet over the right field fence to keep the streak alive and help his team set a new consecutive-game home run record at 18. At the time DiMaggio's home run put the Yankees up a run, 3–2, but Detroit came back in the eighth to chase Red Ruffing when the big fellow got himself in trouble by failing to cover first base on a grounder. The Tigers ended up with two runs in the inning and a 4–3 lead.

In the bottom of the ninth the Yanks looked completely wilted in the day's heat. With no one on and two out, the bat boys began to collect the lumber. But Red Rolfe connected with one of reliever Bobo Newsom's offerings and put it over the porch in right to tie the game. A rattled Newsom then hit Tommy Henrich with a pitch. After DiMaggio blasted a double to the corner in left, Dickey was intentionally walked to set up an easier force-out. But Bobo fritzed the Tiger strategy by walking in the winning run with no intent whatever. Already in a bit of trouble with Tiger management for his erratic behavior, Newsom was not a happy pitcher on June 22. The Yankees ought to have been kinder to him. A few years before, when he was pitching for the Browns, the Cleveland Indians arrived in St. Louis in a tight race for the pennant with the Yankees. The Indians razzed Newsom mercilessly, but Bobo walked to the front of the pitching mound and scratched one word in the dirt with his spikes: "YANKS." He then looked toward the Cleveland dugout and chortled, "I hope you bums can read."

Lefty Gomez left the clubhouse this day with a brand-new straw hat. A fan had tossed it onto the field after Rolfe's home run. This was long before the days of million dollar baseball salaries; Gomez perched the hat on top of his head and wore it home even though it was about a size too small. In the National League on June 22, the St. Louis Cardinals went to bed that night with a headache worse than Bobo Newsom's. Both the Cardinals and the Dodgers played doubleheaders, and a margin of four runs, one for each game, separated the winners and losers. Brooklyn won two in Cincinnati before a packed house at Crosley Field, taking the first 2–1 in 16 innings as Dixie Walker squeezed in Pete Reiser, and just managing to win the second game 3–2. Meanwhile, St. Louis lost two to the Giants. The Cards took a 3–1 lead into the ninth inning of the first game, but the Giants came up with three runs and a gift victory for their veteran lefty, Carl Hubbell. The Giants then won the second game 3–2, and the Cardinals' lead over the Dodgers drifted back to one game. Although the Giants didn't do much in 1941, playing under .500 ball, this day's double win over St. Louis matched the same feat back on June 8, when they had beaten the Cards twice at the Polo Grounds. Mr. Durocher, managing the Dodgers, must have felt well disposed to Mr. Terry, managing the Giants, for these two black holes in the Cardinals' firmament.

GAME 36: June 24

The Yankees did not play on Monday, June 23, as the world absorbed the full shock of the previous day's invasion of Russia. The Germans advanced with blitzlike quickness through East Prussia into Latvia in the northern push. Even so, there appeared indications that the Germans themselves, in gauging the scale of the Russian defense, had miscalculated the time it would take to complete their massive operation. Stalin had not been idle in the months when the world thought Hitler was his ally. On June 24 he began sending messages to Roosevelt that served as a kind of collateral for the secret requests he now put to America for immediate aid. Stalin wanted $2 billion, plus 3,000 fighter planes and 3,000 bombers. The President was stunned, but he listened carefully as Stalin's message also revealed that the Russians were currently training nearly 200 divisions in the hinterlands and gearing up to produce 1,800 planes and a thousand T34 tanks (perhaps the finest in any of the world's armies) per month. If Hitler had any notion of Stalin's plans, he might have provided his armies with more than a 10-week supply of gas—at the very least he might have supplied his troops with winter coats.

Roosevelt now had to begin the difficult public relations task of readying America to aid Russia, something the nation appeared less than willing to do. America's usual policy was to aid any nation that asked for help in opposing Hitler's forces, though Roosevelt quickly added that our immediate funds were all earmarked for Great Britain and that aid to Russia would have to be long-range. All we would do at this early juncture was declare publicly that the portions of our 1937 Neutrality Act forbidding trade with a warring nation were waived in regard to Russia. A White House directive this day authorized future arms shipments to Vladivostok under lend-lease.

In the middle of what seemed horrifying and destabilizing increments of modern warfare, the excitingly bad St. Louis Browns came back to New York City on June 24 to see if they could help the Yankees' pursuit of the Indians for the league lead. Lefty Gomez had an easy time of it, coasting to a 9–1 win. Red Rolfe extended the Yankee consecutive-game home run record to 19 with a two-run blast in the second inning, but DiMaggio and his streak had a closer call. In the first inning, he tapped out on a grounder to Clift near third base; in the third inning, he fouled out to the catcher Ferrell; in the fifth, with Tommy Henrich on first, he put one of Bob Muncrief's pitches into the open pastures of left center, with Roy Cullenbine drifting to a spot 457 feet from home to make the catch. Henrich, thinking DiMaggio's blast was by that time somewhere near the Bronx Botanical Gardens, got doubled off first as Cullenbine relayed the ball back into the infield.

Only during a five-run Yankee rally in the eighth did DiMaggio get his first and lone hit of the game. He came up against Muncrief after Tommy Henrich had just cleared the right field fence with a two-run home run. Muncrief worked inside to DiMaggio, who fouled off the first pitch; then DiMaggio took a ball that backed him off the plate. With the crowd chanting "We want a hit" (nothing subtle), Joe finally rammed a curve on the inside part of the plate over Johnny Berardino's head at short.

When asked in an interview after the game by Dick McGann of the *New York Daily News* whether he felt it jinxed him to talk about the streak, DiMaggio answered: "Heck, no. Voodoo isn't going stop me. A pitcher will." The Yankees' win placed them a mere game behind Cleveland and into second place. With 12 wins in the last 15 games, the Yankees had the staid *New York Times* leading the cheering in the aisles: "Those Yanks are rolling." This was a far cry from the derision of other New York papers the day DiMaggio's streak began. Cleveland helped the surging Yankee cause by getting themselves shellacked in Boston on June 24, 13–2. The Red Sox blasted the Indians with 18 hits on the day, and no matter how much his teammates softened up Cleveland's pitching staff, Ted Williams got none of them, taking the collar for the second game in a row and for the third time in the last four games. His average dipped, if that's the word, to .403.

Dan Daniel caught up with Ty Cobb, who was on his way to play Babe Ruth in a Boston charity golf tournament, and asked him his opinion of DiMaggio. He framed the question for his *New York World-Telegram* column: Would he rather have Feller or DiMaggio on his club? Cobb dodged it with typical dexterity: "That is much too tough a question to reply to offhand. Feller certainly is the pitcher of the day. DiMaggio is the No. 1 outfielder, though I will admit I have seen this new sensation, Ted Williams, play only one game of ball. I would hate to be placed in the predicament of deciding to give up one for the other." I showed Feller Cobb's quote and asked him the same question. He dodged it too: "There's good reason to have a pitcher who can give you a shot at winning every fourth day, but there's also good reason to have a center fielder who can give you a shot at winning every day." Feller said that Cobb saw him pitch in 1937 and told him: "You're very good, son, but I would have hit you— I would have taken you to left field." In another bit of baseball news, a young executive, the treasurer of the Chicago Cubs, had gotten wind that the Milwaukee Brewers of the American Association were in danger of folding. He and several other entrepreneurs rounded up $100,000 and cut a deal to buy the club. The young man asked the Wrigleys whether he could depart with their blessings. They blessed him. His name: Bill Veeck. This was Veeck's first foray into the realm of baseball ownership in a long career that would produce wonders.

GAME 37: June 25

Joe DiMaggio extended his hitting streak to 37 straight against the Browns on June 25, and baseball fans began to murmur about his challenge to George Sisler's modern-day record of 41 straight. DiMaggio settled things early with a two-run home run on a line into the seats in left in the fourth inning. The blast extended the Yankee home run streak to 20 games and knocked the Browns' ace, Dennis Galehouse, out of the box. In the second inning of the game DiMaggio had hit one to the same spot over 450 feet to left center where Roy Cullenbine had snagged one on him the previous day. Cullenbine got this one as well. With two swings of the bat on different days DiMaggio hit drives totaling over 900 feet, and he had nothing to show for them but outs. Enough of his blows were clearing the fences in recent days, however, for him to take over the American League home run lead from Rudy York at 16. On his streak he had now hit 11 home runs, 9 of them in the last 20 games. St. Louis did much better before a small Wednesday afternoon Stadium crowd than they had the day before, but the Yankees scored three in the bottom of the eighth when Keller doubled and Gordon, Rizzuto, and Sturm followed with singles. Final score: 7–5. The win moved the Yankees into a virtual tie with Cleveland for first place, since the Indians were losing to the Red Sox and Lefty Grove, 7–2. Grove chalked up his 298th career win this day.

On the night of June 25 at the Polo Grounds in New York, the world welterweight champion, Fritzie Zivic, smashed Al "Bummy" Davis to a pulp in a nontitle fight. The past November Davis had been suspended for life for kicking the referee during his first fight with Zivic, and he fought again this night only through the good graces of a reprieve earned by a tour of duty in the Army. When he took his bruised body home on Wednesday night he no doubt felt the justice of his original suspension—the old kick delivered might well have prevented the new blows received. A prelim on the night's card featured a young lightweight named Ray Robinson, Sugar Ray to his friends, against a New Yorker, Pete Lello. Robinson knocked his opponent all over the ring before the bout ended in the fourth. In November Ray would welter up, as it were, and smash hell out of the same Fritzie Zivic now celebrating victory in the main event.

While DiMaggio played long ball at the Stadium on June 25 and Zivic and Robinson played hard hit at the Polo Grounds, another mighty slugger was putting little round balls into orbit at the Commonwealth Golf Club in Massachusetts. Babe Ruth turned up for a challenge round with Tyrus Raymond Cobb. Though the Babe outdistanced Cobb off the tees, the lifetime major league batting average leader finessed the big fellow around the greens. Cobb came out on top, scoring 81 to the Babe's 83.

In war news, the British had the Vichy forces in dead retreat in the middle east. The rout was complete as French generals tried to cut special deals for surrender. Along the Russian front, the awesome German blitz met head-on with masses of Russian troops and motorized divisions, but the Nazis took their first town in Russian-occupied Poland, Brest-Litovsk. German Panzer and motorized divisions pushed forward on a two-pronged attack toward Minsk in the central front. Tens of thousands of Russian troops found themselves trapped in a swiftly closing pincer move. To the south, the Germans advanced across the Dniester River into the region known as Bessarabia, bordering the Black Sea and the Ukraine. The Russians cleverly pulled back the bulk of their troops in this minerally and agriculturally rich region, a tactic that was to serve them well in their later heroic defense of Stalingrad.

America First officials all over the country screamed outrage when it began to sink in that the hated Soviets were about to become recipients of Roosevelt's lend-lease largesse. From the isolationists' point of view, the President's directive had enmeshed us with an ally much worse than Hitler's Germany. Former President Herbert Hoover, quiet by nature and even quieter during the depression of the 1930s in America, saw the German invasion of Russia as cause to come out of his isolationist closet and speak loudly against throwing our might against Germany. Hoover pinned his case on the recent Rudolf Hess escapade, claiming the Russian invasion had revealed the urgency of Hess's guessed-at terms of peace for England. Friends in England told Hoover that the Hess proposals were reasonable and that it was irresponsible of Churchill to suppress them, especially now that Russia would prove an inescapable diversion for Hitler. The former President would have been less pleased, or at least less proud, to know that in his discussions with the Duke of Hamilton the day after his capture, Hess had dismissed the United States as a negligible British ally, no threat whatever to German military dominance.

Despite the new apprehensiveness in America about the widening scope of the war after the invasion of Russia, Lindbergh and Wheeler still found it difficult to get their rallies booked. The America's Hall Association of San Francisco this day refused to allow the use of its auditorium for the America First Committee's swing up the west coast from Los Angeles. A spokesman for the organization knew what was coming from Lindbergh, Wheeler, Lillian Gish, and company and stifled it with a simple "We don't approve of your policies." The country's other famous aviator, Eddie Rickenbacker, back at his Eastern Airlines post after his terrible plane crash in February, picked this day to meet Lindbergh's position head-on: "We are in the war and the sooner everybody knows it the better."

The Chrysler Motor Corporation of America, stewing for several days about a Roosevelt request that they cut production and refit for defense, protested on June 25 that it had no intention of voluntarily cutting back on quotas in order to retool for war production. Leon Henderson of the Federal Price Control Administration threatened to fix the prices of all autos if Chrysler continued to refuse government requests under emergency powers for cutbacks. Chrysler officials responded that Henderson was simply a tedious meddler. Henderson claimed that never had he or his agency been treated so rudely and that Roosevelt would immediately receive a report on the entire matter. The very next day the President stood squarely behind Henderson and told Chrysler executives that they would have to do what they had no wish to do in this time of near war: bite the bullet. Having a couple of weeks earlier won a round against American labor, Roosevelt won another this day against American business. No special interest in the land was going to stand in the way of his defense plans in the summer of 1941.

GAME 38: June 26

The ball game at Yankee Stadium on June 26 provided the most exciting, electric moment of DiMaggio's hitting streak so far and marked the day radio announcers all over the country began to bulletin streak news in earnest. St. Louis submariner Eldon Auker had not allowed the Yankee center fielder much all day. In the second he took a cut at an Auker 3–0 cripple and flied to left, and in the fourth he bounced one right at shortstop Johnny Berardino, who muffed it for an obvious error. Dan Daniel, who was the official scorer for the game, wrote about this play: "The Yankees themselves dramatized the DiMaggio effect. When he bounced a hot grounder to John Berardino they rushed out of the dugout to watch the official scorer. When that worthy held up the error sign, Joe Gordon acted as the semaphore man for the club and signalled violent displeasure and vehement disagreement." That worthy, Daniel himself, had no choice. Any other call would have been a travesty.

In the sixth DiMaggio grounded out routinely to third, and never had the pressure mounted to the degree it had now. For one thing, it was not certain that DiMaggio would get another at bat; for another, Tommy Henrich and Joe McCarthy made the first strategic move of the streak calculated solely for DiMaggio's benefit. The Yankees were ahead 3–1 in the eighth when they prepared for what seemed likely to be their final cuts at the plate. Sturm opened with a pop out. Red Rolfe, with the crowd screaming for him to do something just to get DiMaggio another chance at Auker, worked the Brown pitcher for a walk. DiMaggio appeared on deck to the relief of everyone in the park but Henrich, then stepping in to hit. Henrich first took a stroll over to the dugout for a chat with Joe McCarthy. What if the unthinkable happened and he hit into a double play? Maybe he ought to bunt. This seemed an odd bit of baseball strategy with his team two up in the last of the eighth, but McCarthy went along with it; he wanted to assure another shot for his great center fielder. Henrich bunted to perfection, and when the roars subsided, Rolfe stood securely on second and DiMaggio came to the plate for a last whack at Eldon Auker.

Auker had already thrown him a lot of bad pitches, and the only visible sign of DiMaggio's nervousness at this stage of the streak appeared in his eagerness to swing at anything around the plate near the beginning of the count. This was not an uncontrollable urge; DiMaggio knew what he was doing. A walk was no longer a free base but a missed opportunity. So Joe tried to swing with dispatch and avoid the kind of inevitable tension that would plague him if a pitcher worked the count to 2–2 or 3–2.

The submarining Auker took a look at DiMaggio in the box, swiveled for a glimpse at Rolfe on second, set, stretched, and delivered. DiMaggio's left leg moved almost imperceptibly from his wide stance, his bat whipped ahead of a low inside strike, and he drove Auker's first pitch on a line past Clift's outstretched glove at third and into the left field corner for a double. The crowd cheered for minutes on end, and even the Yankees in the dugout joined the excitement by pounding their bats on the stone steps. Dan Daniel wrote: "When DiMag finally got his hit the Yankees rushed out on the field and put on a bigger demonstration than their 1927 predecessors did when Babe Ruth hit his sixtieth homer and the all-time mark." For 3 weeks now the streak had been a recognized baseball event; now it began to edge toward permanent status as baseball legend. Marius Russo, who was working the game for the Yankees and also working on a potential no-hitter into the seventh, told me recently that this game had made him aware for the first time how riveting DiMaggio's streak was for player and fan alike. Here he was throwing a no-hitter, and not a soul in the ball park gave a damn.

The tension surrounding DiMaggio's final appearance at the plate this day even obscured the by now commonplace Yankee home run power. But Tommy Henrich, helping DiMaggio with a gentle sacrifice in the eighth, had already helped his team's consecutive-game home run streak with a none too gentle shot out of the park in the sixth. That record stood at 21. The Yankee win against St. Louis ended a successful 12-game home stand that pushed the club into a 1-percentage-point lead for first in the pennant race. Cleveland kept pace by beating Boston in an 11–8 slugfest behind Bobby Feller's sixteenth win of the year. Ted Williams fired out of his brief slump with five hits in eight at bats in his last two games and raised his league-leading average back to .412. During the run of DiMaggio's streak, Williams logged in at .441 (63 for 143). DiMaggio's 38-game average stood at .380 (57 for 150). In the National League, the Dodgers and Cards sat on top of each other and on top of the pack with identical 45–21 records. On June 26 the pennant races in both leagues were virtually dead even.

If all the tensions generated by DiMaggio's streak, by the tight pennant races, and even by the new scope of hostilities in the war proved too much for the New York fan, he or she could perhaps gain some relief by dropping by the Café Pierre, where the extraordinary "Lu Cellia" opened as headliner on the night of June 26, billed as "the most primitive dancer in America, beating out savage jungle rhythms atop a giant native drum." DiMaggio himself may well have reached the point where such a resource could have helped him shift the burden of anxiety. He began complaining that the streak was having an effect on the interior lining of his stomach.

With the Browns in the Bronx and with the Cards and Dodgers sharing the lead for the National League pennant this day, an item contoured for the St. Louis–New York rivalry appeared in the *St. Louis Post-Dispatch*. One William McChesney Martin, Jr., a Missouri draftee at 33 years of age, told the story of his attempts in basic training to do a "right about-face." He just couldn't get the moves down. The sergeant drill instructor told him, "You're the stupidest man I've ever met. You're lucky to be in the Army. You couldn't make a living anywhere else. Where did you live? What in the world did you do before you were drafted?" Martin told his superior that at the time of his induction he had held a $48,000 job as president of the New York Stock Exchange.

From Hollywood on June 26 came an array of lesser known names that were destined for luminosity in later years. The *Motion Picture Herald* ran a list of 60 minor stars and starlets and asked its readers to pick 10 most likely to achieve fame and glory. Among the names from which readers had to choose—including Desi Arnaz, Lucille Ball, Victor Mature, Robert Stack, and Ronald Reagan—was a young actor, William Holden, who had just experienced an interesting week in Hollywood. Holden was known to take a nip on the set now and again, but his difficulties assumed a more bizarre shape when he accidentally shot himself in the hand with a blank while filming the western *Texas*. On June 26, he collapsed on the set from the effects of a tetanus shot for his gunshot wound; at least such was the version released by the studio for public consumption.

GAME 39: June 27

As the Germans continued to push toward Minsk this day, trapping entire Soviet armies en route, the Yankees left New York for what W. C. Fields might have thought just as reckless a venture: They headed for Philadelphia. From the way the A's whined and brawled this day, and from the way their fans abused ump Bill Summers after a couple of close calls, Fields might have been right. The Yankees lost this hostile ball game—Yankee catcher Buddy Rosar at one point got into a fight with a contingent of Athletics' coaches converging on the plate to protest a tag play—to Connie Mack's club 7–6. DiMaggio, however, advanced the streak to 39 games without breaking a sweat, singling sharply to center in the first, opening up on the first pitch delivered to him by lefty Chubby Dean. In the seventh inning DiMaggio kept the team consecutive-game homer streak alive at 22 by unloading a drive deep to left that ricocheted far back in the bleacher seats. The blast moved him back into the American League home run lead with 17, just ahead of the A's Indian Bob Johnson at 16, who himself had crept ahead of Rudy York with two home runs the day before.

From beginning to end, the game in Philadelphia proved a riot, capped off after a fashion when Yankee irregular Frenchy Bordagaray stopped a ball with his ear in the ninth, running smack into a relay throw after trying to score on yet another pinch hit by Yankee pitcher Red Ruffing. Frenchy staggered home in a state of semiconsciousness and fainted cold as he crossed the plate. All in all, the lead changed hands or the score was tied nine different times. Philadelphia finally won in the ninth when Dick Siebert doubled in Bob Johnson, who scored on another close, contested play at the plate. The Yankee loss, coupled with Cleveland's 3–1 win over the White Sox, put the Indians back in first place. In the National League, the Cardinals took a half-game lead over the idle Dodgers by beating the Reds 5–3. Joe DiMaggio's brother Dominic threw two runners out on the bases in Boston's night game loss to the Senators and smashed a single as well, even though his draft board earlier in the day had declared him unfit for service because of poor eyesight. With the aid of glasses he was batting .318. Dominic, of course, would later join the armed forces for the bulk of the war when the need was desperate and the standards less severe.

On this day in June, with Joe DiMaggio's streak in high gear, the United States Senate, after debating for less than an hour, passed a military appropriations bill of $10,384,821,624. This was the largest single money bill ever to enter and exit the halls of either house of Congress, surpassing a 1918 World War I appropriations measure by $153 million. To provide a sense of the scope of the bill and the increment of our forces, the appropriation contained a single line item of $3 billion for the construction of over 12,000 military aircraft, including the largest plane in the world, the B-19 bomber. The huge wingspan of this giant graced the front pages of newspapers all over America on June 27 as the plane flew its maiden flight for the benefit of photographers and aviation aficionados.

After another delay, *Life* magazine printed in its current issue the second installment of John Cudahy's interview with Hitler at his Berghof. Since the gist of Cudahy's argument was that Hitler really wasn't trying to worsen world affairs, *Life* threw another barb at its own correspondent by holding the piece until just after the Russian invasion. Cudahy's version of Hitler betrays a strange mixture of awe and patrician contempt. He wasn't about to praise the man, but he wanted to show Hitler's scorn of Roosevelt's notion that Nazi Germany's policies were a threat to the western hemisphere. Here's what *Life*'s readers saw of Hitler refracted through a weakening but still sizable isolationist lens in the summer of 1941.

> His hair was a plastered mouse-brown mop, the mustache showing a few gray hairs and also there was a hint of gray commencing at the temple and back of the ears. The forehead showed a remarkable protuberance above the eyebrows, which the phre-

nologists call the perceptive cranial area. The upper forehead receded and did not indicate great contemplative capacity. The nose was thick and heavy, without clean-cut lines, and the lower face, although not heavily boned or projected, gave an impression of great energy and aggressiveness. When I spoke about the German menace to the Western Hemisphere, he laughed a harsh, strident laugh, disagreeable as a rasping automobile gear. His face looked as if spontaneous mirthful laughter had taken a long holiday.

A local story began in New York City on June 27 that would soon sound another sort of discordant note through the land. A group called the Grand Central Red Caps won the statewide barber shop quartet contest sponsored by the Parks Commission in New York. The group was black, but in New York at least, the competition was open and immensely good spirited. All who participated, including the former governor of the state and former presidential candidate, Alfred E. Smith, the contest judge, joined in a rousing finale chorus of "Take Me Out to the Ball Game" that rocked the concert hall. Next day the Grand Central Red Caps packed their bags for the national competition in St. Louis and a bitter taste of what it was like to be black in America in 1941. Second class was their only class, even for great black entertainers and legendary baseball stars such as Satchel Paige, Buck Leonard, and Josh Gibson, then in their prime, and youngsters on the way up such as Monte Irvin and Roy Campanella. So with the strains of "I don't care if I never get back" still in their ears, the Grand Central Red Cap Barber Shop Quartet was about to meet something in St. Louis they wouldn't like.

GAME 40: June 28

Baseballs bounced around old Shibe Park like billiard shots in Saturday's game as the Yanks amassed 14 hits, 6 of them for extra bases, to take back first place with a 7–4 win over the A's. The White Sox helped them do so when their rookie second baseman, Don Kolloway, struggling along at a meager .168 average, hit two home runs and stole home in the ninth to ensure a 6–4 Sox victory over Cleveland. At Shibe Park in the Yankee game, Philadelphia muscled a couple of doubles and a big three-run homer by Bennie McCoy but couldn't recover from the damage inflicted by Charlie Keller's home run in the seventh, a blow that extended the Yankee streak to 23 games. Of course, everyone's focus remained on DiMaggio as he crept within one of George Sisler's modern-day streak record of 41 straight. DiMaggio told reporters after the game that the pressure had now mounted for him more than he would have liked. He felt it each time at bat, though he was in no way volunteering to call it quits. The major league record was too close, and he still had his Pacific Coast League record of 61 in the back of his mind. When DiMaggio doubled in the third inning off right-hander Johnny Babich, one of the toughest and stingiest pitchers in the league against the Yankees, even the notoriously hostile Philadelphia fans demonstrated their raucous approval.

Babich had beaten the Yanks five times in 1940 and had made it known that he intended to give DiMaggio garbage to hit at the plate whether ahead or behind in the count. Indeed, the count was 3–0 on DiMaggio in the fourth inning when coach Art Fletcher at third relayed the hit sign from McCarthy. Babich delivered what he thought was ball 4 outside, and DiMaggio reached out over the plate and slammed it on a line within inches of Babich's crotch and on into right center for a double. Legend has it that Babich's face was white as a sheet when DiMaggio rounded first base and kept going before the relay reached second; much more likely he was red as a beet. No pitcher likes to get hit 3–0, especially when the pitch is out of the strike zone. Whit Wyatt of the Dodgers this day, when asked to comment on Babich's tactics, had a better idea. DiMaggio wouldn't even get a chance to swing against him unless he could hit from a spread-eagle position in the batter's box. The fruit sown by this interview would be reaped in the second game of the 1941 World Series, when Wyatt would put two balls under DiMaggio's chin and the usually constrained Yankee center fielder would charge the Dodger pitcher after an exchange of insults. Baseball chroniclers have written a good deal about this abortive fight, but none have traced its origins to the famous hitting streak.

DiMaggio's hit off Babich this day and one a few days later

off Dick Newsome of the Red Sox while going for the Keeler record pleased him more than any others. DiMaggio was genuinely miffed at Babich's tactics because his experience around the league had shown him that most pitchers wanted to get him out with their best stuff, not walk him with their worst. The strain, at least on Babich's side, might have gone back to 1933, though he never said so. Johnny Babich that year had been traded from the San Francisco Seals to their crosstown rivals, the Missions, just before a young Joe DiMaggio began his Pacific Coast League hitting streak. Babich was always especially keyed up when he pitched against the Seals during DiMaggio's 1933 streak; the local papers at the time were filled with mutterings about what he intended to do to his former mates. He wanted to beat them badly, and DiMaggio, who was hotter than a pistol, made that difficult. Whatever Babich thought about DiMaggio's current hitting streak, the days surrounding the earlier one had left a sour taste.

After the game on June 28 the Yankees were getting ready to catch a train for Washington, D.C., when an official from Jefferson Hospital in Philadelphia called the clubhouse and asked to speak to DiMaggio. He got a message through that a young boy, 10-year-old Tony Norella, who worshiped DiMaggio and was following the streak daily, had an incurable spleen ailment and only a day or two to live. Could DiMaggio pay him a visit at the hospital before leaving town? This is one of those stories which are often the stuff of press releases rather than genuine human impulses, but Lefty Gomez and DiMaggio ducked out of the clubhouse without any word to reporters and swung by the hospital in a cab before joining the team at the train station. DiMaggio told the boy to listen to the radio for bulletins on the streak—by now a summer feature—and promised that if he broke Sisler's record in Washington, he would think of the lad. The bulletin, when it came, came too late: The boy died early next morning. DiMaggio's gesture remained a private one until the boy's doctor called a local Philadelphia radio station, at which time a predictable river of sentimentality gushed in full flow.

In the wider world this day, the Germans continued to crush Russian resistance in the central sector of the invasion, while Stalin conducted the kind of ritual for which he was infamous. He purged his commanding general, Pavlov, and the bulk of Pavlov's staff, setting up a trial date at which a conviction was a foregone conclusion. In a few days' time a small squad of Russian soldiers would get the chance to do what an entire army would no doubt have liked to do: shoot its officers. The reorganization of the Russian defense lines that followed this brutal sequence allowed civilian provincial commissars to rise to prominence, among them one shrewd peasant-like Stalin crony by the name of Nikita Khrushchev.

In America on June 28, another soon to be famous name, that of a shrewd, provincial Roosevelt protégé, made national news. The people of Texas were voting in a special runoff election for a vacated United States Senate seat. Twenty-four candidates were battling for the office. One, "Cyclone" Davis, lived under a viaduct and was against "Hitler, Hannibals, and corporation cannibals." Another, Big Joe Thompson, favored awarding an automatic $50 a month to all old folks and $5 a month to every man, woman, and child in the country. The favorites were the governor of Texas, "Pass the Biscuits Pappy" O'Daniel, and a young politician, not so lean or lanky as when a raw New Deal member of Congress but just as hungry, Lyndon Baines Johnson. At the end of the day's tally, it looked as if Johnson had brought home the Texas bacon with a 5,000-vote plurality. But no one would yet declare the count official; the next 4 days taught Lyndon Johnson a lesson he would never forget and gave him a grounding in political reality that he later turned to his own advantage.

GAMES 41 and 42: June 29

It was a sizzling but active day in the nation's capital on June 29 as Joe DiMaggio went after George Sisler's record. *The Washington Post* ran a front-page leader: "DiMaggio's Drawing Power Packs in 31,000 in D.C." The streak vied for space with other front-page stories: Roosevelt still brooding over Stalin's enormous lend-lease request while dedicating the brand-new Hyde Park Presidential Library; a new draft call-up of 900,000 men; plans for massive increases in fighter and bomber airplane production;

astonishing casualty reports from the Russian front; the death of the former premier of Poland and world-renowned concert pianist, Ignace Jan Paderewski; the arrest of 29 suspected Nazi fifth columnists in American cities; and a broadcast on the war by Pope Pius XII from Vatican City ("the war is punishment for man's sins") in which he also attacked women's short skirts.

The large crowd that jammed Griffith Stadium did not come out in the hundred-degree heat for a suntan. They came to watch DiMaggio go after George Sisler's record. In fact, one fan came all the way from Newark, New Jersey, for the spectacle; while on hand he stole DiMaggio's streak bat. The saga of the crime and of the efforts by others to get the bat back for DiMaggio would take some elaborate turns in the next several days. Before the first game DiMaggio could barely reach the batting cage because of the crush of reporters and well-wishers on the field. He was clearly tense and showed his nerves early in the first game by questioning, if ever so slightly, a strike called on him as Dutch Leonard's dancing knuckleball did its tricks. "Sorry, Joe," said the ump, "it was right over." DiMaggio was having his troubles with Leonard's knuckler on his early at bats, but so was Leonard. His pitch was live this game, which meant that Leonard wasn't certain where it was going to go. He threw it in such a way that he almost completely stopped the rotation; the dips and twists could be brutal.

In his first at bat in the second inning, DiMaggio looked uncomfortable but finally got pretty good wood on a knuckler. He hit it on a line to Cramer in center, about shoulder high and right at him. In the fourth Leonard couldn't get his knuckler over, though he thought he had, and the count went to 3–0. DiMaggio wouldn't nibble, but he got the hit sign from Art Fletcher at third; if Leonard threw a straight ball, DiMaggio would whack it. Leonard did, a tough pitch on the inside, and DiMaggio popped it to George Archie at third. On a 1–1 count in the sixth Leonard tried to slip a fastball by DiMaggio on the outside corner, figuring the Yankee slugger would be guessing knuckler. Whether he figured right or wrong, a line drive rifled off DiMaggio's bat into left center between Cramer and George Case. Case stabbed at it on the run, but the ball was by him, rolling 422 feet to the bleacher fence. The big crowd and the Yankees erupted as DiMaggio stood at second base, tied with George Sisler at 41 straight. In his dispatch to the *New York World-Telegram* Dan Daniel was ecstatic, even redundant, in his enthusiasm about the reaction of the Washington fans to DiMaggio's hit off Leonard: "When Joe belted it mad bedlam broke loose." In most instances, bedlam alone would have been enough. The eventual 9–4 loss to the Yankees meant much less to the fans than DiMaggio's hit had, and his work in the first game gave the huge crowd more than enough reason to stick around in the devastating heat for the second.

During the run of George Sisler's 41-game streak in 1922, the Brown first baseman had hit .459, more impressive so far than DiMaggio's .383 for the same number of games. Of course, Sisler went on to hit .420 for the season, but he didn't go on to hit in game 42. When DiMaggio came out of the steaming clubhouse onto the steaming field for the second game to try doing what Sisler couldn't, he discovered that he had been robbed. Ballplayers are by nature a superstitious lot—DiMaggio would always touch second base on his way to and from his position in center—but he lost more than a good luck charm when the streak thief made off with his bat, which had been slotted in a rack along the dugout box seat railings at Griffith Stadium. DiMaggio had his bat distinctively marked on the bottom of the knob with indelible ink for ease of recognition, and it was in the fourth position in the rack because the bat boys matched them to the order of the Yankee lineup.

A bat is to ballplayer what sword is to samurai, a weapon of choice. Players have as many names for the bat—from simple stick to ethnic shillelagh—as a Trobriander has for coconuts. The merest of millimeters determines the difference between a bat's sweet and sour spots, between drives and dribblers, shots and shanks. Though bats can crack, chip, splinter, and shiver with unsettling dispatch, no ballplayer likes to imagine anyone stealing them. But someone stole the streak bat. This did not make Joe DiMaggio a happy man. He tried to be philosophic when he talked about the bat later: "It was just a piece of wood, but the bench was like a funeral parlor." The bench was right. DiMaggio had already told a few of the Yankees the story of his 61-game streak in San Francisco, when he had had a small bandage over a stone bruise on his hand the day the streak began. He made the trainer keep bandaging the hand in the same manner, even long after the bruise had healed, and didn't cease the ritual until the streak had run its course. To break routine during a streak, even when one has to struggle to find a routine to break, is to tempt the imps of the gods.

Tommy Henrich had a hunch. Back on June 10, Jack Smith's column in the *New York Daily News* had told the story of how Henrich had borrowed a few of DiMaggio's heavier bats, model D29 (36 ounces), for a May 21 game against the Tigers. He had been slumping and wanted a change. One of those he borrowed "had a good feel to it," and Tommy now told DiMaggio to take his bat back. This was not so simple a matter. DiMaggio used to sand down the handles of his bats to his own specifications. In taking the same model from Henrich, he did not take a bat customized to his specs. Nonetheless, if Henrich had a hunch, DiMaggio was going to go along with it. Besides, Tommy was about to marry a girl named Eileen O'Reilly, and maybe Joe sensed the luck of the Irish lurking in the shillelagh.

For a good while in this eventual 7–5 Yankee win behind rookie Steve Peek the bat did nothing for DiMaggio or his streak. He had everyone in the sweltering park on edge by going hitless in his first three at bats. He looped one to Lewis in right in the first inning off pitcher Sid Hudson, lined out to Travis at short in the third, and popped a harmless handle-hit weak fly to Cramer in center in the fifth. When DiMaggio came to the plate in the seventh against the Senators' big right-hander Red Anderson, he didn't know whether he would get any more chances on the day with Henrich's bat or anyone else's. Anderson's first pitch was high and tight up around the chin, but DiMaggio, after leaning back from it, quickly jumped back in the box and set himself. He drilled Anderson's next pitch, a fastball out over the plate, to left on a line for an emphatic single to set the modern-day hitting streak record at 42. The crowd responded with a tremendous rafter-shattering roar and another a moment later when DiMaggio crossed the plate on Keller's triple. *The Washington Post* reported that the whole Yankee team leapt to the top step of the dugout doing "their version of a jig." This was a great moment for DiMaggio. Sisler's record streak meant more to him than that of Wee Willie Keeler, the very existence of which he had first heard about only a couple of days before.

DiMaggio's characteristic response to reporters after the game had an unspoiled, ingenuous ring to it: "Sure, I'm tickled. It's the most excitement I guess I've known since I came into the majors." The Yankee center fielder thanked McCarthy for giving the hit sign on almost every 3–0 pitch during the streak, including this day's when he popped out: "He's played tall with me all the way." George Sisler's comment on the day his record fell was succinct and sufficient: "I'm glad a real hitter broke it. Keep it up." With several rainouts in 1922, Sisler took 53 days, from July 27 to September 17, to set his 41-game record. With less respite from the weather, DiMaggio reached 42 straight in 46 days. Sisler began off Joe Bush of the Yankees after Waite Hoyt had collared him, zip for five, the day before, a day on which Babe Ruth had helped hang a defeat on the Browns with two home runs. Joe Bush also stopped Sisler's streak, holding him hitless in a game on September 18 before 32,000 who were in attendance at Sportsman's Park for Sisler's streak and for the red-hot pennant battle with the Yankees, who ended up taking the league championship from the Browns that year by a game. Sisler's comment on Bush the day he lost his streak was as succinct as his comment on DiMaggio the day he lost his record: "I couldn't touch him."

On the train from D.C. after the ball game, the mood was jubilant. DiMaggio went a round of beers for everyone. He was clearly satisfied: "I wanted that record." The team's pleasure over DiMaggio's new record was such that hardly anyone realized the Yanks had extended their consecutive-game home run streak to 25, though not without an anxious moment. Tommy Henrich waited until one was out in the ninth inning of the first game before hitting a home run with a man on base. That made it 24. In the second game Charlie Keller kept the streak going with a home run to right in the second inning. Their doubleheader win put the Yankees 1½ up over Cleveland, who lost to Chicago 9–2 this day. In the National League, the Cards held on to a one-game lead, splitting their doubleheader with the Reds as the Dodgers split theirs with the Braves.

Ty Cobb, fresh from his recent match play golf tournament with Babe Ruth, told the reporters covering the USO charity event that he still remembered Sisler's arrival in Detroit during his 1922 streak, when Cobb managed and played for the Tigers: "George blistered my pitching staff." Cobb was impressed with DiMaggio and happy for him; now Sisler knew how he, Cobb, felt when he lost his record of 40 straight set in 1911. Cobb got to chatting about his days as player-manager and told a wonderful story. Many years before, during a game between the Tigers and the Red Sox, Boston was threatening with runners on second and third and first base unoccupied. From center, Cobb signaled to his pitcher to walk the hitter intentionally. The pitcher nodded to Cobb and then blew a strike right past the startled batter. Cobb threw a fit in the field, kicking his hat, shaking his fist, and gesturing frantically to put the man on base. He then slapped his forehead in despair. His pitcher looked chagrined and nodded his head. The Tiger catcher stood at the plate with his glove extended. Whoosh! Strike 2 right down the middle of the plate. By this time all the fans in the park realized they had been witnessing a mime show in center field. The batter got back in the box, ready to swing at anything, and Cobb's well-rehearsed Tiger pitcher fanned him on a curve in the dirt. Cobb had worked out the routine with his pitcher before the ball game and waited for a spot to pull it off.

In a sports-related event in America on June 29, the former University of Kentucky and New York Giant football player Shipwreck Kelly married an equally famous "café society girl," former debutante Brenda Frazier. Brenda was the symbol of depression wealth, a lovely miss whose trademark strapless gowns appeared on the cover of *Life* magazine with her in them. In the late '30s she invited an intimate gathering of 1,400 friends to the Ritz for her coming-out party, and, still as a teenager, she dallied with the mysterious Howard Hughes before settling in with her colorful Shipwreck.

One of the lead stories that shared headlines with DiMaggio's streak this day in Washington, D.C., was of such a different dimension as to be almost beyond comprehension. The first official figures had come out of the Berlin command on the Nazi invasion of Russia. The carnage along the Russian front was surreal. More than 50 Soviet infantry and motorized divisions were completely annihilated, with nearly half a million men killed, wounded, or captured. What the Berlin command did not say was that the Germans were butchering whole towns, lining up and killing thousands in long burial ditches in the local woods. Columnist Walter Lippmann, who didn't know even a fraction of these horrors at the time, wrote that the world had never before seen savagery on such a scale. Had the Russians not been fighting with fortitude and tactical finesse in the crucial southern thrust of the front, Hitler might well have realized his dream and humbled Stalin's massive country and its millions of citizens within a few weeks. As it was, the invasion of Russia set in motion the extirpation by the Nazi SS forces of minority populations, primarily European Jewry, in the territories already possessed and those soon to be possessed by the Germans. What had been sporadic slaughter in the tens of thousands before June 1941 became a systematic slaughter of millions after this date.

GAMES 43 and 44: July 1

The Yankees had a travel day on the last day of June but picked up a half game on the Indians anyway when Bobby Feller got routed 12–6 by the lowly Browns. On Tuesday, July 1, the Yankees played a doubleheader against the Boston Red Sox before a huge midweek crowd at Yankee Stadium. The heat was still savage, hovering in the mid-90s as 52,832 trooped into the Stadium to watch DiMaggio go after Wee Willie Keeler's all-time major league hitting streak record of 44 in 1897. Dominic DiMaggio told me that he remembers joking with his brother before the games about where the writers had dug up this record: "Hell," said Dom, "I thought they made it up." He had been following Joe's pursuit of Sisler, and then when he arrived with the Red Sox in New York, he discovered that Wee Willie had a streak on the books from the time when foul balls didn't even count as strikes: "Well, maybe Joe would break that one too."

Artist and caricaturist Ed Laning was at the game this day, sitting near Mayor La Guardia; he made sketches for a large oil painting depicting the moment in the second game when DiMaggio tied Keeler's record. La Guardia is the one full-faced figure in the painting, and he looks ecstatic or sunstruck. When *Life* magazine later ran a story on the painting just before the World Series, Laning said that "nothing that happened during the season, and nothing that can happen in the Series," is apt to be remembered longer than this historic moment." Among these real and hypothetical "nothings" was Ted Williams's .406 season, but perhaps Laning was right then and still is. The thrill of DiMaggio's record was tangible for him.

The Red Sox played both games of the day's doubleheader against the Yankees in a muggy stupor, losing a replay of an earlier 9–9 tie (May 23) 7–2 and falling in the nightcap 9–2 when darkness and thunder-laden skies shortened the game. Both the earlier tie and the replay counted as part of DiMaggio's streak. The lapses of the Red Sox meant nothing to the huge crowd, for whom DiMaggio and the Yankee team home run streak were the only issues. Each time DiMaggio stepped to the plate in the first game the large crowd let go with tumultuous cheers and then, when he failed on his first two at bats against right-hander Mike Harris, groaned in despair. DiMaggio was an easy out in the opening inning on a foul pop to Lou Finney at first base and an equally easy out on a grounder to Jim Tabor at third base in the third inning. But on his next trip to the plate in the fifth off reliever Mike Ryba, he again grounded one to Tabor at third, who had considerable difficulty picking it up and even more woe trying to toss it to first. DiMaggio scampered into second as Tabor's hurried throw got away from Finney. The official scorer in the press box, Dan Daniel of the *New York World-Telegram,* held up one finger, signifying a hit, but only those in the huge crowd who could see him knew for sure, since the scoreboard in 1941 did not flash HIT or E and the public address system at the Stadium was used only for lineup and battery changes. The crowd seemed strangely quiet—a few cheers, some sighs, and a kind of communal puzzlement.

The hit was not a clean one. Writing later for the *Sporting News,* well before the conclusion of the streak, Daniel defended his call on Tabor's play, adding more zip to the grounder than it had at the time: "DiMaggio pasted that ball with every ounce of his strength. He stumbled a little as he dashed for first. Tabor is playing deep. The ball almost knocks him over. Jim has to make a hurried heave. Joe has it beaten. It's a HIT. The throw goes wild and Joe reaches second." Daniel claims he was absolutely certain of this call: "As the pitiless spotlight was trained on Joe, official scorers, too, found themselves in the limelight. Scoring standards became the most stringent, the most exacting, under which a big-league hitter has performed over a long stretch of games."

Daniel remembers that what was stringent to him was bunk to a colleague in the press box who held his nose between his fingers; at the same time several Yankees craned their necks out of the dugout and smiled with approval when they saw the hit signal. On his next trip to the plate DiMaggio made Daniel's call a moot issue by lining a smash to left off Ryba for a sure and pure base hit. The crowd this time roared without restraint, and as DiMaggio came back to the bag after rounding first, he too displayed a huge smile on his lean, distinctive face. He wanted his hits clean. The cheering went on a full 5 minutes.

Something important did not happen in the first game of the day's doubleheader. Though a man named DiMaggio hit a home run, the Yankee consecutive-game home run streak stalled at 25: The wrong DiMaggio hit it out, Dominic of the Red Sox. Only Phil Rizzuto's line drive triple off the wall in left field, 2 feet from clearing it, came close to extending the Yankee record in the first game. Rizzuto's unaccustomed long-ball power had enabled the Yankees to tie Detroit's record at 17 games, but his drive just didn't have enough mustard (or garlic) on it to clear the fence this time.

The remarkable Yankee power streak generously distributed the glory attached to it, from Johnny Sturm, whose first major league home run began the streak against Cleveland on June 1, to Joe DiMaggio, whose total of 10 during the 25 games led the onslaught. DiMaggio just edged Charlie Keller and Tommy Henrich, both with 9. The pitching staff of the hapless St. Louis Browns took the brunt of the Yankee attack during the record by offering up 13 of the 40 Yankee home runs. Brown submariner Eldon Auker won the dubious honor of coughing up the most gopher balls at five, with his teammate Bob Muncrief on his heels at four.

The Yankees' record still stands. In 1956 the Cincinnati Reds made a run at it from August 4 through August 24, hitting a higher total of 41 home runs in 21 games (with Wally Post, Ted Kluszewski, and the rookie Frank Robinson doing most of the damage) but coming up empty on August 25, the same day the Yankees released Phil Rizzuto from their active roster and the same day that during an old-timers game in Yankee Stadium Tommy Henrich, Charlie Keller, and Joe DiMaggio showed up to take a few futile swings for the fences. It was during the Cincinnati streak in 1956 that Ted Williams, on August 7, let go a volley of expectorations and a few choice gestures at Boston fans in left field, not to mention hurling his bat 35 feet in the air after a walk. Tom Yawkey, Red Sox owner, and Joe Cronin, general manager, fined him five grand. For the next Red Sox game that summer the first 18 rows of the left field seats at Fenway were roped off. In a sense Ted's fine bought out the section that was troubling him.

The only other threat to the 1941 Yankee team consecutive-game home run record came from the Yankees of 1961, the great Mantle and Maris year, when those sluggers were joined by Bill Skowron, Bob Cerv, Yogi Berra, Elston Howard, and Johnny Blanchard for a brief demolition job on the rest of the league, blasting 32 home runs in a run of 17 consecutive games. At the time, Nikita Khrushchev, having first been elevated to a position of importance by Stalin in early July 1941, met President Kennedy at the 1961 Paris summit, and Adolf Eichmann, factotum of the Nazi Jewish "solution" in Europe from those very same July days of DiMaggio's streak, was on trial in Israel for crimes against humanity.

Joe DiMaggio still had the second game of the doubleheader to go on July 1 and the ancient record of Wee Willie Keeler before him; he wasted little time settling his account. He came to the plate in the bottom of the first against hefty Boston right-hander Jack Wilson and lined an inside pitch over Joe Cronin's head at short into left center for a single. The big crowd erupted again. DiMaggio had now tied the all-time major league streak record set before the turn of the century, when the day's head-lines recounted the chicaneries of the shady entrepreneur and robber baron, Jay Gould, lambasted the volatile politics of an is-land we were about to invade, Cuba, and worried over the death throes of Ottoman empire in Europe. Playing for the old Balti-more Orioles of the National League, Keeler had begun his streak on April 22, the opening day of the baseball season, and contin-ued until June 17, when Pittsburgh left-hander Frank Killen col-lared him. At 5 feet 4 inches and 138 pounds, Keeler slapped the ball all over the place, though not very far: all but 21 of his 82 hits during the streak were singles. Of DiMaggio's 66 hits so far, there were 12 doubles, 3 triples, and 12 home runs. His streak average stood at .379; Keeler in his 44 games had hit .408, co-incidentally the same average DiMaggio would reach before his streak was over.

The second game lasted only a merciful five innings. The Red Sox were out of it as the result of powerful hitting by Charlie Keller and Bill Dickey and pitiful fielding by Ted Williams, who let the tricky Stadium left field befuddle him for two errors. De-spite his difficulties in the field, Williams picked up a hit in each game of the doubleheader, staying ahead of DiMaggio in com-parative average during the days of the streak, .423 to .379. In the pennant race, the Yankees picked up another half game on the Indians, who beat the Browns 10–6. New York led by 2½ games. In the National League on July 1, St. Louis held on to its slim one-game lead over the idle Dodgers by beating Pittsburgh 11–7.

DiMaggio tied Keeler on a day when the spirit of the upcom-ing Independence Day celebration in America began early on several fronts, not merely at Yankee Stadium in New York. Sec-retary of the Navy Knox announced in Boston that "the time to use our Navy to clear the Atlantic of the German menace is at hand." What he didn't say was still top secret. On July 1 Iceland had officially requested through British diplomatic channels that we send troops and ships to protect the sizable island and its sea-lanes from German U-boats and battleships. This would be the first active participation of U.S. forces in the war effort, though another unit of American fighters, the famous American Eagle pilots, were set on July 1 to fly their first sorties over Vichy France and Germany under the command of the RAF. The American Eagles' first venture would bag three German fighters in Axis airspace. The immense skill of these American fighter pilots produced impressive results for the British through the summer and fall of 1941.

Overseas on July 1, western correspondents found out that Stalin had executed General Pavlov, commander of the sector around Minsk in Belorussia, on June 30. The rhetoric of the dispatch coincided with the finality of the thing done. Pavlov was terminated before the west knew he had been tried. With Russian armies in the central region of the fighting deteriorating or disappearing, the Germans continued to attack along two salients, trying the same pincer tactics near Smolensk that had worked so well at Minsk. This time what was left of the Russian forces pulled back, as they had been doing tactically in the south, and the Germans walked into the heavily Jewish populated city of Lvov. The wholesale slaughter of thousands of the city's Jews began immediately as the German SS execution squads, the *Einsatzgruppen,* rounded up citizens, shot them, and dumped their bodies in ditches on the outskirts of town.

The British War Office in London on this day closed another chapter of the disastrous campaign on the island of Crete when it announced the removal of Major-General Archibald Wavell from the middle east command. With the British victorious in Syria, Churchill had the breather he needed to dump Wavell, a man who had bedeviled him for months, particularly during those trying days on Crete near the beginning of DiMaggio's streak. Churchill deposited Wavell in India and had a British knight, General Auchinleck, named to the middle east command. *The New York Times* guessed, somewhat tentatively: "On the surface it appears General Wavell is being shelved."

Charles Lindbergh finally said it straight out. Speaking in San Francisco for America First on July 1, he admitted that he preferred Hitler to Stalin as an ally, harping yet again on the sour geopolitical saw about superior and inferior races while echoing the Nazi position that the Europeans and Asians of the east were insidious by nature: "I would a hundred times rather my country ally herself with England, or even with Germany with all her faults, than with the cruelty, the godlessness, and the barbarism that exist in Soviet Russia."

GAME 45: July 2

The blistering heat continued in the east as the Yankees beat the Red Sox 8–4 before a crowd much smaller than the one that had shown up for the Tuesday doubleheader. Those on hand watched DiMaggio try to break the major league streak record he had tied the day before, a mark that had graced the books ever since the gay nineties when whoever "they" were weren't wherever "where" was when Wee Willie Keeler used to "hit 'em where they ain't."

Because of the extreme heat in New York, DiMaggio spent much time out of the sun before the game chatting with Pulitzer Prize–winning journalist Russell Owen, who was doing a profile on him for *The New York Times*. Owen had won for his brilliant work on the Admiral Byrd expedition to Antarctica. Tom Connolly, chief of American League umpires, spotted DiMaggio with Owen near the clubhouse. Connolly had known Keeler but wished DiMaggio the luck of the Irish nonetheless in his broadest brogue: "Boy, I hope you do it. If you do you're breaking the record of the foinest little fellow who ever walked and who never said a mean thing about anyone in his life. Good luck to you."

The few but noisy witnesses at Yankee Stadium on Wednesday afternoon had a great time of it. Lefty Grove was scratched because of the heat, and DiMaggio faced Dick Newsome instead. On his first time up he lined a ball hard and deep to right center. Stan Spence, who had taken a step in on the ball, turned to his right and raced back. Dom DiMaggio approached from center to back him up, but Spence speared the drive with a lunging desperate leap. It was a great catch. DiMaggio remembers the play so vividly, he added another like it with his brother Dominic making the catch on his second at bat. That play never happened. With any one of a dozen great catches on drives hit by Joe over the years to choose from, Dominic DiMaggio was ready enough to agree that he had speared this one as well, though he told me in a conversation that years later he and Joe kidded each other about whether he should have dropped it. In earnest or in jest, both DiMaggios have probably jumbled this play with an earlier one on May 24 when Dominic had dropped a fly at Yankee Stadium at the same spot deep in right center. "Please drop it" conspired with "I did drop it once" to bedevil the brothers DiMaggio. Over the years the phantom catch has become a family heirloom.

When DiMaggio came up for his second time in the ball game, the only fly ball he hit was off a Newsome pitch he slammed a mile foul into the left field stands. He then hammered a grounder to Tabor, who threw him out. On his next at bat in the fifth, he took two balls from Newsome outside and then drilled a high fastball on a straight line over the left field fence. Williams turned his back to the diamond to play the ball on the carom, but it shot over the wall. The liner was an arrow, out of the park so fast that DiMaggio had precious little time to admire his record-breaking streak hit and his eighteenth home run of the year. All the writers in the press box leapt up and joined the small crowd in a sustained ovation as DiMaggio trotted around the bases. After the game Lefty Gomez mimicked the famous sobriquet attached to pesky punch hitter Wee Willie Keeler: "Joe hit one today where they ain't." From here on all was gravy for DiMaggio, though fan interest in the streak kept growing through July as record crowds turned up in ball parks all over the American League whenever the Yankees were in town.

Manager Joe McCarthy, who had been keeping his own counsel about the streak before DiMaggio broke the record, spoke this day in full unchecked admiration of his great center fielder: "I don't believe anybody but a ballplayer is in a position to appreciate just what it means to hit safely in forty-five straight games." Ted Williams made the same point. A streak allows for no intermittencies of mind or heart—there are no resting points, no breathers, no off days. The variables are just not visible to the fan in the stands. On this sweltering day especially, Williams marveled at the way DiMaggio not only beat the pressure of the streak but beat the heat. Williams told the writers covering the game: "I really wish I could hit like that guy Joe DiMaggio. I'm being honest. Joe's big and strong and he can club that ball without any effort. These hot days I wear myself out laying into it, and I lose seven or eight pounds out there. When it's hot, I lose my snap or something."

It might have been hard to tell from Williams's .401 average, but he was actually right in terms of his performance during the earlier part of DiMaggio's streak in contrast to its summer segment. DiMaggio would continue to blister the ball into and through July and raise his average as the thermometer rose. The two halves of DiMaggio's streak tell the story. In springtime, from May 15 through June 17, he hit .364 and Williams hit .466. As the weather heated up, from June 18 through July 17, DiMaggio hit .444 and Williams hit .324.

The Yankees' sixth win in a row put them three up over Cleveland. Lefty Gomez helped his cause in the wild fifth inning, when the Yanks scored six runs to go ahead 8–0, by singling in two after an embarrassing sequence of Red Sox errors and passed balls. DiMaggio almost lost his streak cap this day. A fan lunged for the cap and tore off in the direction of the exit, but Boston pitcher Mike Ryba and a security guard cornered the thief and returned the Yankee cap. Meanwhile, a friend of DiMaggio's from Newark, Joe Ceres, heard talk in local taverns about a fan boasting that he had DiMaggio's streak bat. With the instincts of a bloodhound, Ceres went to work.

Two preludes of a sort took place on July 2, one in Texas and another in New York. Franklin Roosevelt sent a congratulatory telegram to a gangling, drawling New Dealer, Lyndon Baines Johnson, who had just won, so he thought, a special run-off election to the United States Senate. But the plurality young Lyndon had accumulated a few days before dwindled away as the experienced incumbent, Governor Pappy O'Daniel, garnered the recounted rural vote and edged ahead in the total count by 1,113. Roosevelt told his raw friend from Texas that "real" politicians do not lose by such slippery counts, leaving Johnson to draw what conclusions he would. The next time he ran for the Senate, in 1948, Johnson won an election in which over 1 million ballots were cast by a mere 87-vote margin. Either Johnson was extremely lucky or he took more than careful heed of Roosevelt's counsel from early July 1941.

The other prelude, eventually more colorful than even Lyndon Baines Johnson, appeared as a note in the entertainment section of *The New York Times:* Commercial television would begin its first broadcast in the metropolitan area on July 2. Transmitters atop the Empire State Building were set to broadcast sponsored programs to 3,000 or 4,000 private receivers within a radius of 50 miles. Allen Du Mont Labs was rapidly manufacturing television sets to retail for $300 to $400 each. The sets came with a choice of three screen sizes, 8-, 10-, or 12-inch. Of course, World War II pulled the plug on home front television, and the medium that would change the cultural face of the nation had to wait a decade for its true commercial renaissance.

The Columbia Broadcasting System planned to begin with 15 hours of still shots of masterpieces from the Metropolitan Museum of Art. The National Broadcasting Company hoped to get into the picture more ambitiously with Bulova Watch paying $4 at 2:30 P.M. and $8 at 8 P.M. on July 2 to broadcast an on-screen video image of a clock. Sunoco Oil paid somewhat more for a Lowell Thomas evening news broadcast, and Lever Brothers and Procter & Gamble sponsored two evening shows, *Uncle Jim's Question Bee* and *Truth or Consequences*. NBC later planned to televise a Philly-Dodger game from Ebbets Field, an undertaking that would prove pretty much a disaster, with reception murky and the stationary cameras unable to follow the ball, the fielders, or the runners.

Orson Welles's *Citizen Kane* closed its immensely successful first run at the RKO Palace in New York on July 2, and Frank Buck's *Jungle Cavalcade* moved into the theater. Two other movies opened in New York and around the country on July 2: Clark Gable and Rosalind Russell's *They Met in Bombay,* and the more subtle and moving Howard Hawks film, *Sergeant York,* with Gary Cooper. The advertising blitz for *Sergeant York* was extraordinary. Earlier in the spring the distributors of *That Hamilton Lady,* with Laurence Olivier and Vivian Leigh, had displayed an original Gainsborough portrait of Lady Hamilton in the lobby of Radio City Music Hall, shipping it all the way from England and insuring it for half a million dollars. But *Sergeant York* produced for its ad campaign a portrait that dwarfed Gainsborough's Lady Hamilton. The largest sign ever constructed for a movie went up on Broadway, fully four stories high with nearly 15,000 neon bulbs and half a million feet of wiring, depicting Cooper as the Tennessee hillbilly topped off by the huge letters "Y-O-R-K."

Citizen Kane, among many other things, had touched on the power of the media in America to shape attitudes toward national events and, more important, toward international events in regard to war—the Spanish-American War of 1898 served to make the general point. *Sergeant York* reversed one of the perspectives of the Orson Welles masterpiece and showed the way opinion formed as a matter of conscience from the inside out. The time was World War I, and the story involved a backwoods dirt farmer, Alvin C. York, a conscientious objector from Three Forks of the Wolf near the Cumberland River in Tennessee. A growing sense of obligation worked on a pacifist conscience, en route to York's winning the Congressional Medal of Honor for an exploit in France on October 6, 1918, in which he killed a score of Germans and arrested over a hundred others single-handedly.

The interventionist theme of *Sergeant York* was not lost on the summertime audience of 1941. York himself, now district director of the Selective Service System in his home area, was on hand for the opening of the film, along with one of the stronger voices in support of Roosevelt's prewar policies, Wendell Willkie, the very man the President had run against in 1940. Cooper was also on hand for the premiere, quietly negotiating at the time for the role of Lou Gehrig in the upcoming *Pride of the Yankees.* Secretary of State Cordell Hull sent Cooper a congratulatory telegram on his performance in *Sergeant York,* and when the film opened the next week in Washington, D.C., Roosevelt himself was at the premiere. The quiet, dignified, and finally devastating image of American heroism on the screen, a role that won Cooper the Academy Award, was too pertinent for the President to resist.

A festive and seemingly minor story that had begun a few days before took a sour turn this day, symptomatic of a strain in this country from its origins. The National Barber Shop Quartet finals were held on July 2 in St. Louis, but officials disallowed the winning entry from the state of New York, the Grand Central Red Caps, because the four crooners were black. Al Smith, former governor of New York and the most famous member of the National Barber Shop Quartet Organization, resigned his membership in protest over this mean-spirited incident. The commissioner of city parks, Robert Moses, under whose auspices New York City's winners had traveled to St. Louis, fumed that New York would never again participate in such a travesty. In a still heavily segregated land, the problem had less to do with crooners in St. Louis than with racial inequality on a national scale.

With all the activity in the area of national defense in 1941, whether in the draft army or in the armament industries, Roosevelt began to worry seriously about America's discriminatory racial customs and practices. During the days of DiMaggio's streak he issued a series of policy proclamations to counter the more obvious and more telling civil rights violations that could hamper the productive and defensive capacities of the country. There were instances of defense workers refusing to share shifts with black employees. Roosevelt oiled the machinery in the Justice Department to handle such matters.

Though none of Roosevelt's concerns had to do with integrating baseball in 1941, some of the shrewder major league executives, sensing a change down the line, if not in the deeper veins of the land's racial prejudices at least in the legal ramifications of barring black talent, began to think about shaping custom into new opportunity. One executive in particular, Branch Rickey, then of the Cardinals and later of the Dodgers, thought harder than anyone else. Rickey, who by adjusting his travel schedule earlier in the spring had set a personal (and perhaps world) record of viewing 11 complete ball games within a 2-day span, was always on the lookout for new talent. He would be the first to draw on the black athlete as a baseball resource after the war.

GAME 46: July 5

As DiMaggio surged beyond Keeler's record, the hitting streak entered a less intense though no less wondrous phase. Awe replaced anticipation, and the issue was no longer whether DiMaggio would challenge a preexisting record each day but how often he would set a new one. The continuing ballyhoo, inspired by lead stories in newspapers, familiar radio bulletins, and hyperactive public relations employees throughout the American

League corridor, made the streak into a truly national resource. The Yankees had a couple of more games at home before heading west, and the franchises fortunate enough to be en route intended to put fans in their seats and money in their purses on the strength of the DiMaggio phenomenon and the great drawing power of the Yankees. In New York, only rain and the postponement of a big July 4 doubleheader at the Stadium honoring the memory of Lou Gehrig put a damper on the streak's newest phase.

DiMaggio earned a brief holiday respite from the pressure as President Roosevelt took over the spotlight on Independence Day, July 4, 1941. With the Germans temporarily bogged down at Berezina near the Dnieper River in their push toward Smolensk about 300 miles from Moscow, and with the British mopping up in Syria and Lebanon in the other major theater of World War II, Roosevelt addressed millions via radio and urged all citizens of all nations to work for human freedom everywhere. The President insisted that appeasement of the Nazis represented a greater threat than arming to face them down, a "deeper sabotage," as he put it. His remarks were clearly aimed at figures such as Lindbergh, now parading through the country hinting at the possible virtues of a German peace alignment. For Roosevelt, the famous aviator had become more than a nuisance during the weeks of DiMaggio's streak—he had become the bane of a forming western alliance. And before DiMaggio's streak ran its course the President would unleash his personal hound dog, Secretary of the Interior Harold Ickes, on Lindbergh. Ickes's acid tongue could take anyone's measure, and in 2 weeks he would have Lindbergh writhing.

The holiday deluge brought relief from the relentless heat wave in New York and the rest of the east, not only forcing postponement of the memorial doubleheader planned for Gehrig but also forcing the Dodgers to scratch a big doubleheader at Ebbets Field. The Dodgers had reason to celebrate anyway when the Cubs took two from the Cardinals on Independence Day. Brooklyn moved a full game in front simply by watching Chicago's fireworks from afar.

During the lull in New York and with all the recent fuss over Joe DiMaggio, it occurred to a reporter for *Baseball* magazine to ask a San Francisco Sicilian immigrant fisherman, Giuseppe Di-Maggio of North Beach, which of his sons was the best ballplayer. The elder Mr. DiMaggio did not hesitate. "Joe." "Why is that?" the reporter asked. "Because he makes the most money." If Joe DiMaggio's father judged the cause by the effect, the Hillerich and Bradsby Company judged the effect by the cause. They took out a full-page ad in the current edition of the *Sporting News* that week complimenting DiMaggio on breaking Sisler's record with a Louisville Slugger. The company would take out another the next week complimenting him again on breaking Keeler's record.

With the Yankees, DiMaggio, and the streak postponed by rain, the Cleveland Indians edged back into the thick of things with a doubleheader win over the Browns. Their first game win was marked by an unusual play. In the ninth inning Jeff Heath, heavily muscled but fleet on the bases, was standing on third with two out. The Browns' third baseman, Harland Clift, told pitcher Jack Kramer to get the hitter, Hal Trosky, and forget about Heath. Clift then moved away off the line at third for the left-handed-hitting Trosky. Kramer looked at Heath's long lead and appealed to Clift almost plaintively to hold him a little closer. "Don't worry," said Clift, "he ain't goin' nowhere." As Kramer began to wind up, Heath faked a dash for home, and Clift calmed Kramer on the next pitch: "Just forget him, get Trosky." Kramer looked back at the plate, wound up slowly, and Heath, already about 30 feet down the line, broke for home. The big fellow slid across the plate an instant before Kramer's hurried toss arrived. It must have been a pleasure for Clift and Kramer to chat about their mutual interests in the clubhouse after the game.

When the Yankees retook the home field on July 5, they mauled the visiting Philadelphia A's 10–5. Before the day at the Stadium was over, the Yankees had blasted five home runs. Connie Mack of the A's began managing in the days when the quick hook for starting pitchers didn't exist, and in a nostalgic mood he left poor right-hander Phil Marchildon on the mound the entire game to take whatever the Yankees dished out. DiMaggio served up the hors d'oeuvres with a mighty first-inning home run to extend the hitting streak to 46; Sturm and Rolfe followed with solo home runs, and Charlie Keller hit two. Only Dick Siebert's two home runs for the A's made the day respectable. The Yankees had now won 7 in a row, 11 of their last 12, and 21 of 25 to sustain a building lead in the American League pennant race.

Prior to the game DiMaggio got a fine surprise. His acquaintance and admirer James Ceres had been doing some sleuthing for the past several days in Newark and managed to coax the bat out of the hands of its pilferer with the lure of reward money. A courier showed up at the Stadium with the package. DiMaggio's relief was such that he donated the bat he used to break Wee Willie Keeler's record to a USO support raffle at a San Francisco Seals ball game in his hometown. At a quarter a shot, the bat collected $1,678, DiMaggio's first direct contribution to the war effort. Former Yankee Tony Lazzeri, who had driven Joe Di-Maggio to his first major league spring training back in 1936, was then playing for the Seals in the twilight of his long career. On the day DiMaggio's bat was raffled, Lazzeri hit one out of the park for San Francisco. Time seemed to be going backward in this small generational tribute.

Chicago White Sox manager Jimmy Dykes, whose playing days had come to an end on the first game of DiMaggio's streak, reappeared in the baseball news with a flourish on July 5. He protested to umpire Steve Basil that Cleveland's bull pen corps had interfered with right fielder Taffy Wright's attempt to pick off a foul fly during his team's 5–3 loss to the Indians. Dykes's tantrum was so severe that even he marveled at his resourceful and colorful use of the English tongue: "All I called him was a liar and he threw me out for that. Of course after he had given me the bounce I really opened up with some choice language." The tirade not only appalled the umps, but according to the league office, Dykes's foul language in fair territory upset some of the fairer fans sitting in foul territory. Dykes was suspended indefinitely, with American League president William Harridge's explanation striking the decorous, slightly paternal tone characteristic of life in the '40s and baseball in particular: "Dykes's tactics in delaying our games, attempting to bulldoze and browbeat the umpires while filing protests, which have no basis in fact nor justification in the rules, have become very offensive not only to the spectators in other cities throughout the circuit but to our entire organization."

Another story that touched on the decorum of the early '40s

hit the national news this day. Just before the Fourth of July holiday, the U.S. Army completed an extensive series of war games near a military complex in Memphis, Tennessee. Relaxing from the effects of several grueling days, a company of soldiers from the 110th Quartermaster Regiment at Camp Robinson spotted two young women in golfing shorts playing with two more mature gentlemen on a Memphis course abutting the Army campgrounds on the Tennessee-Arkansas border. They greeted the ladies with good-natured but clearly libidinous glee: "Yoo-hoo" was the witticism of choice. What the soldiers didn't know was that one of the older gentlemen, wearing civvies on the golf course, was their commanding officer, Lieutenant General Ben Lear. Lear was a tough old nut, and when he heard the appreciative chorus for the young ladies, he bagged his mashie and ordered a 15-mile march in full battle regalia for the offenders. They could run up and down Highway 70 to cool their spirits.

Lear suspected what was probably true: It wasn't so much the soldiers' libido that was at issue as the mockery directed at the older men, an irrepressible comic situation going all the way back to ancient Greece. The come-hither cheers to ladies Lear could bear; the insult to him was actionable. If ever there was a hoot and a holler that the 110th wished it could have back, "yoo-hoo" was it. There would be hell to pay for the soldiers, but after the story got out, several members of the United States Congress, prodded by the mother of one of the disciplined lads, were furious at Lear's reaction and let him know about it. The "yoo-hoo" incident shortly came to symbolize the spirit of the entire draft army, and there were many in a land readying for war who were prepared to capitalize on that spirit.

The holiday accident toll included nearly 600 fatalities, mostly on the nation's highways, but there was a near accident in San Diego, California, that involved two famous Hollywood names. Pat O'Brien invited his good friend Ronald Reagan for a family picnic at his beachside home in San Diego, and the two actors were swimming in the Pacific when O'Brien's small children, 6-year-old Mavoureen and 5-year-old Shawn, got caught in the pull of an ocean current caused by a recess in the sea floor. O'Brien and a lifeguard swam out immediately to the flailing kids for the rescue, while former lifeguard Ronald Reagan surged in from farther beyond the breakwaters, arriving too late to help but just in time to console. There's a lesson here somewhere.

During the Fourth of July holiday festivities Billy Conn snuck off to marry his young sweetheart, Mary Louise Smith, a love affair that had caused some consternation before the brilliant Joe Louis fight a few weeks earlier. Mary Louise's father, a former major league ballplayer, at last report had threatened to punch Conn out if he refused to leave his daughter alone. Reporters tracked the newlyweds down as Billy and wife were about to skip to Hollywood, where the fighter had a bit part in a movie, *The Pittsburgh Kid.* When asked whether he had told Mr. Smith about the marriage, Billy gave the questioner his new father-in-law's phone number and said, "Here, you tell him."

GAMES 47 and 48: July 6

There were 60,948 fans jammed into Yankee Stadium on July 6 for Sunday's unveiling of the center field monument to Lou Gehrig. Joe DiMaggio picked the occasion for one of the best days of his streak. As the Yankees beat the A's twice, 8–4 and 3–1, to extend their current winning streak to 9 in a row while posting wins in 23 of their last 27 games, DiMaggio collected three singles and a double in the opener. He quickly canceled any potential second installment of the Johnny Babich story with a sharp single in the first inning. Babich had no chance to finesse Di-Maggio into swinging at bad pitches because the Yankees knocked him off the mound before Babich got anybody out in the second inning. On his first at bat in the nightcap, DiMaggio jolted one deep to center off right-hander Jack Knott that landed over Sam Chapman's head for a triple. Joe then doubled in the third inning for his sixth hit of the day.

DiMaggio reserved his tributes to Gehrig for the games. In the pregame unveiling of the monument that still graces the center field region of the Stadium, Gehrig's former Yankee manager, Joe McCarthy; Lou's roommate, Bill Dickey; Fiorello La Guardia, mayor of New York City; the A's manager, Connie Mack; and Mrs. Eleanor Gehrig participated in the ceremony.

La Guardia said of Gehrig that he "will be remembered as long as baseball remains. Lou Gehrig will be appreciated as long as good government exists." By good government La Guardia might have meant his own city regime, since Gehrig had served in it as a member of the New York City Parole Commission, or more generally the mayor might have had in mind the light that shone so steadfastly in the presence and in the memory of the German-speaking Lou Gehrig in a world darkened by the dictatorial shadow cast by the Nazis at the time of his death.

As a warm-up for the all-star game scheduled in Detroit for July 7, Ted Williams raised his league-leading average to .405 with four hits in eight tries in Boston's doubleheader against the Senators. During the span of DiMaggio's streak Williams was hitting .425; DiMaggio had pushed his streak average up to .385 and his league average to .357. In the National League, St. Louis dropped another to the Cubs, 3–0, and their fifth loss in a row put the Cardinals three games behind the Dodgers in the pennant race.

A Hollywood movie about high-wire telephone repairmen, *Manpower,* opened in New York this holiday week. In the movie, Edward G. Robinson and George Raft did some fighting over Marlene Dietrich, but nothing like the real scrap that broke out during the filming when Raft and Robinson, failing to see eye to eye, squared off jaw to jaw. Film technicians had to separate the boys. Tough guy Raft was just warming up with Robinson; he also took a poke at Marlene Dietrich (this one scripted) and inadvertently knocked her down a flight of stairs, where she ended up in a heap with a broken ankle. Later in the production, Raft fell 30 feet off a telephone pole. This was war. Raoul Walsh, who directed *Manpower,* wanted to add his own touch of reality to the film's dialogue, so he hired a waitress from Chicago as a consultant for a hash house scene. Fricasseed oysters were "angels on horseback," a bottle of sherry turned into "grapes of wrath in a sports jacket," eggs and bacon were "cackleberries and grunts," a glass of water was "one on the city," and a simple sugar bowl became "a gravel train." Popular culture and the idioms of trade in America have always flung those words around like hash.

GAME 49: July 10

After the big Lou Gehrig Day doubleheader on July 6, the Yankees took a breather for the all-star game on Tuesday at Briggs Stadium in Detroit. Commissioners Harridge and Frick announced that the proceeds from the game this year would benefit the USO, as had the take from the auction of DiMaggio's streak bat. The USO earned just under $1,700 from DiMaggio and just over $70,000 from the all-star game. On the first day of the break, Monday, July 7, President Roosevelt made a historic announcement. He informed Congress that he had, at Iceland's request and with continuing assurances about the sovereignty of Iceland's government, sent marines to take up positions on the large, strategic island. He also had instructed the Navy to protect with force the sea-lanes around Iceland.

In addition, the President sent troops to bases in Trinidad and British Guiana that had been secured in a swap agreement with the British back in April involving 50 of our supposedly old, surplus destroyers. Roosevelt informed Congress that he would in the near future request that the length of service for draftees be extended beyond a year and that the draftees be allowed to serve in any location outside the country deemed essential for defense. Furthermore, he intended to request a $5 billion increase in the national defense budget and a $7 billion increment for lend-lease. The President had reached a new wartime plateau.

These announcements were electric, and hard-line isolationists found themselves in a state of shock. Burton Wheeler screamed to reporters: "What next? The Azores? Cape Verde Islands?" The senator demanded an investigation into other charges, circulating for weeks now in Washington, that we were already in the thick of it with German U-boats and had been engaging them since April 1941. Secretary Knox admitted that there had been an incident in which the destroyer *Niblack* had dropped a depth charge while picking up survivors from a sunken British merchant ship, but the *Niblack* had done so only to ensure the safety of the victims afloat in dangerous waters.

Lindbergh wrote in his journal the day after Roosevelt's message to Congress: "The morning papers announce that American forces have occupied Iceland. This is, I think, the most serious step we have yet taken. It may mean war. Iceland is in the German war zone, and, in my opinion, it is definitely a European island" (July 8, 1941). For Roosevelt, Iceland's longitude registered Anglo-American; for Lindbergh, European. Nothing could more emphatically demonstrate the kinds of thinking that divided the nation in the summer of 1941. Two days later Lindbergh steadfastly disavowed Roosevelt's wider line of defense in a journal entry: "The President has very cleverly maneuvered us into a position where he can create incidents of war and then claim we have been attacked." This was only slightly more circumspect than the senior Charles Lindbergh's notorious remark back in 1918 that we had been "buncoed" into World War I by the sinking of the *Lusitania,* in which the undersecretary of the Navy at the time, young Franklin Delano Roosevelt, and the first lord of the British Admiralty, Winston Churchill, had, according to Lindbergh's father, conspired to ship explosive armaments in the *Lusitania's* hold.

Befitting the dramatic year and the dramatic season in which it took place, the all-star game on July 8 proved a thriller. With Bobby Feller tabbed to start against Brooklyn's Whit Wyatt and with DiMaggio and Ted Williams burning up the circuit, the American League hoped to avenge the previous year's 4–0 loss to the Nationals. Before the game a rumor circulated that DiMaggio had hurt himself in an auto accident in the Motor City, and the big Detroit crowd of 54,674 shouted itself hoarse when DiMaggio was introduced. The fans not only were happy to see DiMaggio ready to perform, they were delighted to see him in one piece.

Led by Arky Vaughan's two home runs, the National League took what looked like a workable 5–2 lead into the ninth. Vaughan, by the way, started at short for the Nationals after having warmed the bench for his current team, the Pittsburgh Pirates. Manager Frankie Frisch had found himself a rookie shortstop named Alf Anderson, and the Pirates had won a few with Anderson playing and Vaughan sitting. Vaughan's all-star performance didn't help him when official league play resumed. Pittsburgh was going nowhere, and he continued to sit while the rookie played.

Down by four runs at 5–1, the American League began to edge back into the game in its half of the eighth. Joe DiMaggio doubled off Cub right-hander Claude Passeau and scored on his brother Dominic's hit. In the ninth the American League loaded the bases against Passeau, and DiMaggio came to the plate again. He bounced what appeared to be a perfect double play ball to the Boston Braves' shortstop, Eddie Miller. Miller grabbed it and threw slightly wide to the Dodgers' Billy Herman at second. Herman got the force, but Cecil Travis tangled him up so that he couldn't double DiMaggio at first. With a run in and two on, Williams stepped up. In the previous inning he had argued briefly with umpire Babe Pinelli after being called out on a savage Passeau third strike. Passeau was a fine pitcher but also a bundle of nerves. He was so high-strung, he had permission from the Cubs, especially after winning 20 games for them in 1940, to skip curfew on days when he pitched because the only way he could work off the tension of the game was by wandering the streets late at night.

Passeau fidgeted, and Williams wanted another shot at him. This time he would not get behind in the count or let Pinelli have the last word on a called third strike. According to Williams, Passeau had great stuff; his ball had a way of breaking into left-handed hitters and clipping the corners. Ted cranked up a bit earlier than usual, but not so much that he'd swing at a bad pitch. He was ahead in the count 2–1 before taking a button-popping, uninhibited cut at a Passeau waist-high delivery. Ted crushed the ball, hitting it off the overhang of the right field roof, a glorious three-run homer. The pure joy of Williams's home run trot told everyone in the park what a tremendous thrill the game winner was for this superb young power hitter.

After celebrating the 6–5 last-inning win with his American League mates, officials, and reporters in the clubhouse, Williams wanted to escape the ball park without getting mobbed by Detroit's fans. He slipped out from the clubhouse through a side door and tried to hail a cab on the street. No empty ones passed, but a man with a kid in his car pulled up and asked Williams if he wanted a lift. As the three drove toward midtown, the sparse conversation did not touch on baseball. Williams assumed the man and his boy were merely being tactful. When the car pulled right up to his hotel curb, Ted offered his thanks for the ride and then couldn't bear it any longer—he burst out with the news that the American League had just won the all-star game. "Is zat so?" said the man. "I don't follow baseball."

The regular season resumed on July 10, and the Yankees were in St. Louis to play the Browns. Tommy Henrich joined the team after a brief honeymoon following his marriage to the attractive and wonderfully Irish Eileen O'Reilly. The streak had become an advertising bonanza for the teams along the circuit when the Yankees came to town. As Dan Daniel wrote in the *Sporting News:* "DiMaggio's batting streak certainly captured the fans and fired their imaginations. Joe always is skillful and colorful. Dramatize a player like that with a streak like his and you have a superb, turnstile-clicking, electrifying situation." For this Thursday's game, scheduled under the lights, the Browns placed ads in all the local papers making it sound as if DiMaggio were coming into town not with the Yankees but with the Ringling Brothers Circus: "THE SENSATIONAL JOE DIMAGGIO WILL ATTEMPT TO HIT SAFELY IN HIS 49TH CONSECUTIVE GAME." In tribute to the ad campaign and to DiMaggio, 12,682 showed up at the ball park. Five of the seven major league games on July 10 were at night, and the Browns added their share to the largest combined major league night-time attendance of all time as 102,930 fans around the leagues watched the sun go down and the lights go on.

Former Browns' star George Sisler participated in the pre-game ceremonies and congratulated DiMaggio on breaking his own modern streak record and Wee Willie Keeler's ancient one. Dizzy Dean, announcing his first game for Falstaff Beer on St. Louis radio station KWK, was also supposed to speak on the field and on the air in honor of DiMaggio, but Dizzy got to rambling about this and that and forgot to say a word about DiMaggio or the streak. No one seemed to mind.

Once again DiMaggio settled the streak early. He came to the plate in the first against Johnny Niggeling and bounced a slow grounder wide of Alan Strange at short, who approached it at an angle, just managing to knock it down. He obviously had no play, and the brand-new Sportsman's Park electronic scoreboard flashed HIT. This was the fourth game in a row that DiMaggio resolved the hitting streak in the first inning. In the sixth, the rains came and the umpires called it a night. Not much happened after DiMaggio's hit. Joe Gordon's home run in the second was all the Yankees and Lefty Gomez needed to win the abbreviated but official game 1–0 and stay 3½ games ahead of Cleveland. The Indians won their game against the A's 3–2 behind Bobby Feller's seventeenth win of the season, a win made possible when Feller tripled and scored the deciding run.

As a relief from the strains of war and the bleakness of European civilization in the summer of 1941, the great Benny Goodman went classical on a memorable July 10 in Philadelphia. Goodman played a Mozart clarinet concerto with the Philadelphia Philharmonic in an outdoor concert at Robin Hood Dell before a delighted audience of 10,000. On that same afternoon, along a boiling Highway 70, the forced march of the "yoo-hoo" company took place. The troops tried to make the best of their run-in with the golfing general by singing, "General Lear, he missed his putt, *Parlez-vous*," to the tune of "Mademoiselle from Armentières." The next day Everett Dirksen of the House of Representatives harangued Lear and reminded him that Congress paid not only the enlisted men but the generals, too: "They work for us, and for all taxpayers." Dirksen wondered: "Who wouldn't whistle at the girls? Imagine a contingent so devoid of the buoyancy and effervescence that makes the young American a great soldier." For his part, Dirksen could do without an Army run "by golfing old generals and sourpuss soldiers." Undersecretary of Defense Robert Patterson leapt to the general's defense: "We always support our generals. Where would discipline be otherwise?" Where indeed? Surely not on Highway 70.

GAME 50: July 11

The Yankees continued to inch farther ahead of an idle Cleveland in the American League pennant race on July 11 by easily beating the Browns 6–2 behind their hot young lefty, Marius Russo. Now the Yankees sat on top of the league by 4 games, having won 11 in a row. All streak long DiMaggio thrived on St. Louis pitching, and this was no different. He singled three times off Bob Harris and then parked one off Jack Kramer in the ninth inning for his league-leading twentieth home run. DiMaggio's single to center in the first continued the streak at 50, the fifth straight game in which he had settled matters on his initial trip to the plate. Phil Rizzuto, who had reentered the Yankee starting lineup when Frankie Crosetti was spiked, had now hit in each of his 14 games since returning at shortstop. The newspapers picked up Rizzuto's streak and began charting it—the rookie was a mere 36 behind DiMaggio. Ted Williams took an "ofer" against Detroit in his team's 2–0 loss, with Lefty Grove failing to win his 300th game. Next game Williams would twist his ankle, and Joe Cronin would relegate him to pinch hitting for several days. He dipped beneath .400 for the first time in weeks at .398, though he was still outhitting DiMaggio during the streak .416 (77 for 185) to .397 (79 for 199). DiMaggio's four-hit day against St. Louis brought his season's average up to .365. In the National League, the Dodgers pounded the Reds 12–2 and moved 3½ games in front of the Cardinals.

The last installment of the "yoo-hoo" story wrote itself into the *Congressional Record* on June 11. With all the punished soldiers national celebrities of a sort, the mother of one of the exhausted yoo-hooers wrote to her member of Congress about the incident, saying she would like to slap General Lear's face. About the raucous reaction to the general's golfing party she wrote that "anything that makes a soldier smile is not a bad thing." This was not too far from the nationally sanctioned philosophy of frontline entertainers such as Bob Hope during the war years. Hope's movie, *Caught in the Draft*, had just opened all over the country, a comedy not quite as funny as the Abbott and Costello screamer earlier in the year, *Buck Privates*.

A very odd incident, probably so bizarre that only the likes of Abbott and Costello could have done it justice, took place this day in Belleville, Illinois. America was faced in 1941 with the task of training thousands of pilots to minister to the controls of the thousands of planes coming off wartime assembly lines. But romancing the skies too quickly had its problems, one of which—the midair rescue of a dangling paratrooper—had occurred the day DiMaggio's streak began. On July 11 an even zanier if less heroic aerial spectacle took place. An Army cadet, Victor Woodrick, just learning to fly, sat peacefully in the backseat of a PT-19 Fairchild trainer with his civilian instructor in the cockpit. The plane was cruising between 500 and 1,000 feet above the ground when it hit a patch of turbulence, and Woodrick, who apparently had failed to latch his shoulder harness correctly, vaulted out of his seat and did a complete somersault, finding himself perched on his back on the tail assembly of the fuselage. He had nothing to grab on to but the taut canvas covering of the trainer's frame. The civilian pilot in front couldn't believe his eyes, but in a near panic he brought the plane down for a landing as gently as he could. The trainer taxied to a stop with the young cadet still splayed out on the fuselage. His knees and ankles made a permanent impression in the fabric covering, though the total damage for this escapade turned out to be a torn sock and the prospect of recurring nightmares for Woodrick.

GAME 51: July 12

DiMaggio did not get a hit on his first at bat this day. He waited until the fourth inning to extend his streak to 51 straight by doubling to center against Eldon Auker, the same submarining right-hander who had held him hitless until his tense last at bat in game 38. In the middle of the Yankees' 7–5 victory over the Browns, the team's twelfth in a row, Phil Rizzuto, with a single in the fourth, extended his hitting streak to 15 straight; the *New York Herald Tribune* noted that the rookie shortstop had attained DiMaggio's figures in reverse. The Browns as usual were sitting ducks for the Yankees. A five-run fourth, aided by DiMaggio's and Rizzuto's streak hits, plus Bill Dickey's two-run homer, broke the game open. The Yankees added two in the sixth, and only a three-run pinch home run by Chet Laabs made the game look more respectable than it was. With the Indians dropping one 4–2 to Philadelphia, the Yankees increased their league lead to five games. Things had changed so radically since the days of dolor near the beginning of DiMaggio's streak in mid-May that for their last 30 games the Yankees were clipping along at a winning percentage of .867.

For several days now along the Soviet front the clashing armies had been consolidating their positions; the Germans those they had taken, and the Russians those they had remaining. On July 12 the Germans broke the momentary lull in the fighting with another devastating blitz. Nazi forces crashed through what was known as the Stalin line running north and south and connecting key positions from Leningrad to Smolensk, Kiev, and Odessa. The most severe German thrust occurred in the northern sector through Estonia to a position about 125 miles from Leningrad. In the central sector the Germans were now rapidly on the move beyond Minsk, pounding Russian positions on the Dnieper River near the Moscow road. In the south, the Germans and Romanians moved toward Kiev across the Dniester River. The only bad news Hitler received came from Vichy French military analysts who now believed they had hard information that Axis intelligence had underestimated Stalin's reserve strength by as much as 6 million. Oops! Hitler was informed that Stalin had plans to put every available inhabitant of the Soviet hinterlands in a soldier's uniform, even the Abominable Snowman if he could find him. He wanted to lure the Nazi armies into spending more time than they might have liked as guests of the Russian winter.

GAMES 52 and 53: July 13

As the Yankees left St. Louis for Chicago, Roosevelt launched a howitzer at Charles Lindbergh: He let his Secretary of the Interior, Harold Ickes, loose against the famous aviator. Ickes always got his man. He called Lindbergh a fellow traveler in the fascist cause, claiming he "never heard this Knight of the German Eagle denounce Hitler or Nazism or Mussolini or Fascism." Ickes was no kinder to Mrs. Anne Morrow Lindbergh, whose 1940 book, *The Wave of the Future,* seemed to him "the bible of every Nazi, Fascist, and appeaser" in America.

Ickes was a jingoist, but he'd had a belly full of Lindbergh's defeatism. The secretary's none too kind reference recalled the medal presented by Göring to Lindbergh in 1938 on Hitler's behalf. The precise name of the medal, which now hung like an albatross around Lindbergh's neck, was the Service Cross of the Order of the German Eagle. Ickes savagely derided the image of the famous aviator as a Teutonic knight flying in the wrong cause, comparing him with the heroic volunteers of the American Eagle Squadron now flying missions over Germany for the RAF. Lindbergh stewed silently for the time being at the abuse dispensed by Roosevelt's point man, but he would not be silent for long.

The largest White Sox crowd—50,387—since the all-star game of 1933 filled Comiskey Park on Sunday, July 13, for the return of manager Jimmy Dykes after a short suspension for foul language, eager to see the doubleheader against the streaking Yankees and their streaking center fielder. DiMaggio's hit in the opening game, which the Yankees went on to win 8–1, came in the second inning off Ted Lyons. He bounced one that Luke Appling muffed at short; the hit call by the official scorer was debatable. Appling was the closest thing in spikes to DiMaggio's streak cousin. Several balls hit in his direction began as potential outs and ended up marginal hits. In this game DiMaggio took Luke off the hook for the gift hit by ramming a clean single to center on his next turn at bat in the fourth. The two hits, cheap and dear, were the first he had gotten off Ted Lyons during the streak, and the White Sox workhorse became the second pitcher to give up both a home run to Babe Ruth during his record 1927 season and a hit to DiMaggio during his record 56-game hitting streak in 1941. Lefty Grove had completed the trick at Yankee Stadium back on May 25.

The veteran Ted Lyons was among the most durable pitchers ever to rub in the liniment and toe the rubber. He broke in with the White Sox in 1923, he took off a few years to serve a stint as a U.S. Marine during World War II, and then he returned to the White Sox and pitched a few more games as player-manager in 1946. The sixth inning of this day's game might well have done something to prepare Lyons for the rigor of the Marines; the Yankees jumped all over him and his reliever Jack Hallett by sending 12 men to the plate and scoring 6 of them. Spud Chandler had no difficulty holding the lead his mates had given him for the easy win.

In the second game, a much tighter and grittier 1–0 extra-inning affair won by the Yankees, DiMaggio sliced a single to right center in the sixth off a Thornton Lee curveball for the streak hit and then waited out the tense game as the left-handed Lee dueled with Red Ruffing. Ruffing ended up winning his seventh straight, but it took a scratch Yankee run in the eleventh inning to earn it as Sturm doubled, Rolfe bunted him to third, and Henrich punched a sacrifice fly to bring Sturm home. Phil Rizzuto could do little in the second game with Chicago's Lee, and his ministreak ended at 16 games, though in those games he had hit a healthy .491 (28 for 57). Rizzuto was by far the most productive hitter for average at .368, aside from DiMaggio, during the Yankee center fielder's streak.

By taking the doubleheader, their sixth sweep in a row, the Yankees also won their fourteenth straight game, a new high for manager Joe McCarthy. In another baseball sequence, picked up in the back pages of the week's *Sporting News*, the fans of Evansville in the Three-I League raved about the pitching of a 19-year-old lefty phenom. The kid had just pitched his fourth shutout in a row, and from June 23 to the present he hadn't allowed a run in 40 innings. Maybe the lefty, by the name of Warren Spahn, had a future. Indeed, Spahn pitched in a couple of games for the Boston Braves in 1942 and after the war came back for 20 major league seasons in which he won more than 20 games 13 times.

The weekly magazine section of the Sunday *New York Times* on July 13 ran its long profile on Joe DiMaggio by Pulitzer Prize–winning author Russell Owen. Owen had gotten close to DiMaggio and his loquacious roommate, Lefty Gomez. For the most part DiMaggio liked to listen to Owen and Gomez kibitz before and after the games. Gomez chatted away as if DiMaggio, head and ear cocked right beside him, were somewhere in another universe. He told Owen that when the team traveled, DiMaggio sent him to hotel lobbies to buy reading material—mostly adventure comics—because it would look perfectly natural for Gomez to be reading such stuff and perfectly ridiculous for DiMaggio. "'Know what he reads?' asked Lefty, with an impish look. 'We go into a hotel, and get to the newsstand, and he whispers to me, "Hey, there's a new Superman. Get it for me." He doesn't dare buy it himself, they all know him, you know. So he gets me to buy it for him. Superman and the Bat Man. That's his favorite reading.'" Perhaps sensing that the comic book caper was too good a bit to keep out of the profile, DiMaggio turned to Owen and protested: "I like westerns too."

In his article Owen also revealed something of DiMaggio's habits around the ball park, a combination of ritual and nervous energy. The general factotum of the Yankee clubhouse, Pete Sheehy, made sure that DiMaggio's coffee cup was always half filled. No matter how much he drank, it was half a cup at a time. What the caffeine didn't do, the nicotine did—DiMaggio was never far from his pack of Camels before the game and sometimes in the runway during it. After a game DiMaggio would take his sweet time before leaving, waiting for the fans to weary of hanging out around the clubhouse exit. He was always quiet, listening to the radio, perusing the papers that Sheehy got for him, and doing a bit of light reading: "Westerns, Mr. Owen, westerns."

This day in the world at war, Stalin brought the British beyond the point he had brought America. Of course, the British were declared combatants. On July 13, 1941, England and Russia signed a mutual aid accord with key provisions for the exchange of military personnel and equipment. More important, the accord contained stipulations barring a separate peace with the Nazis, a different version of the enticing prospect that had made Rudolf Hess fly to Scotland to see if he could make just such an arrangement against Russia on Germany's behalf with the king of England. The signer of the pact for the Soviets was Stalin's foreign commissar, Vyacheslav M. Molotov, of "cocktail" fame. Perhaps to prop himself and his nation in the glow of a new alliance, Stalin boasted that the German advance, particularly in the central region along the road to Moscow via Smolensk, was being rebuffed with huge Nazi losses. The German communiqués presented an entirely different picture, much closer to the truth. Panzer divisions had by now penetrated way behind the Stalin line and were engaged in the same tactics that had overwhelmed Minsk, moving in pincer formation behind Russian columns. Smolensk would soon face a difficult siege.

GAME 54: July 14

The Yankee winning streak came to an end at 14 this day against White Sox ace John Rigney, relaxed and at ease 3 weeks after dodging his June 20 induction date into the U.S. Army. Rigney held New York to eight hits and one run, with Chicago scoring a comfortable seven. The punctured eardrum that had gained Rigney his 4F didn't seem to affect the quality of his pitching on July 14. The *New York Herald Tribune,* still on Rigney for his induction day shenanigans, wondered if he hadn't punctured the drum by sitting next to his loudmouthed manager, Jimmy Dykes, in the White Sox dugout.

DiMaggio had a time of it with Rigney on this day. A lazy pop fly in the second flopped out of Bill Knickerbocker's glove behind second for an error, but it also broke Joe's bat, the one returned to him after a ransom was paid to its kidnapper. Breaking a bat is hors de combat—nothing like getting it swiped. In the fourth DiMaggio walked, and in the sixth he took a big swing with another of his bats and topped a 2–0 pitch in the dirt toward third. By the time third baseman Bob Kennedy arrived to pick it up, DiMaggio had arrived at first. Rigney got him again in the Yankees' lost cause, and DiMaggio's streak average dropped a point from the previous day to an even .400 (86 for 215).

The Yankee loss coupled with Cleveland's and Bobby Feller's 4–1 win over the Red Sox, his eighteenth win of the season and his hundredth career victory, allowed the Indians to pick up a game and come within four of first place. They had beaten Boston twice the day before to keep pace. In 2 days the Yankees would arrive in Cleveland for a crucial showdown, one that would in a sense determine the course of a pennant drive and a hitting streak. In the National League this day, Leo Durocher snuck a win for the team on which he sometimes played and for which he always managed. The Dodgers and the Cubs were scoreless in the ninth, when Durocher, with Ducky Medwick on third, pinch-hit himself for his pitcher. The Lip layed down a perfect squeeze bunt, and Medwick flew home with the winning and only run of the game. With the Cards losing to the Phillies, the Dodger lead popped back to 3½ games.

Hollywood had baseball on its mind this July 14. Samuel

Goldwyn outbid David Selznick for the rights to the Eleanor and Lou Gehrig story, eventually called *The Pride of the Yankees*. Mrs. Gehrig had agreed to the deal with Metro-Goldwyn-Mayer, naming her choice for the lead: Gary Cooper. Samuel Goldwyn had already been dealing with Cooper for the role, though he kept all negotiations secret because the *Sporting News* was running a national poll to pick the best actor (or any facsimile thereof) to play Lou Gehrig; Metro-Goldwyn-Mayer didn't want to squelch the chance for a run of free publicity. The *Sporting News*'s list so far was fascinating. Near the top were Babe Dahlgren, now with the Boston Braves, who had taken over at first for Gehrig in 1939; Babe Ruth, who ended up playing himself in the movie; Hank Greenberg, the Detroit slugger currently playing for the U.S. Army Tank Corps; Ronald Reagan, who as a former sportscaster could call them better than he could hit them; newcomer Robert Stack; Eddie Albert; and an ex-minor league ballplayer, Dennis Morgan.

By fall this list would grow to nearly 60 possibilities, with Samuel Goldwyn keeping his mouth shut and Cooper's contract in his pocket. Given Cooper's earnings during 1941, partially for his work on two roles, one an ex-bush league hobo in the Capra film *Meet John Doe* and another for his upcoming stint as Gehrig, he would garner $460,000 more as a celluloid ballplayer than the highest paid major leaguer did on the diamond. Of course, Cooper also earned the gratitude of the nation by winning a celluloid Congressional Medal of Honor in his role as Sergeant Alvin York.

Winston Churchill spoke to England and to the world on July 14 and for the first time appeared convinced that Germany had made a devastating tactical mistake in invading Russia. Churchill sounded jubilant in claiming that the war effort had turned a corner, that England had staunched its losses at sea, that it was now in position to pound the Axis mainland with bombs day and night, and that Mussolini's Italy was next on the agenda for saturation bombing. Bastille Day, July 14, was usually France's most celebrated holiday, but this year it proved a grim affair. The Germans allowed the Vichy regime few patriotic displays and no Parisian parades. The French could contemplate what liberation might mean for their nation in the privacy of their homes or in the gloom of a quiet bistro.

But America was under no Nazi constraints. Bastille Day became a kind of surrogate holiday here for what it was not allowed to be over there. Secretary of the Interior Harold Ickes, addressing a Bastille Day rally of the organization France Forever in New York, continued hounding Charles Lindbergh. Ickes claimed that the flier's "passionate words are to encourage Hitler and to break down the will of his own fellow citizens to resist Hitler and Nazism." Warming to his subject, Ickes referred again to the "Knight of the German Eagle" and said of Lindbergh starkly, "He's a menace." Lindbergh and Ickes would crash into each other soon, the climax occurring on a crucial day for Joe DiMaggio's streak, a fitting coincidence given the intermittent presence of Lindbergh throughout its many days.

GAME 55: July 15

In the first inning of the game on July 15, in which the Yanks edged Chicago 5–4, Luke Appling booted a DiMaggio double play ground ball. In the third inning DiMaggio, as if recognizing the contribution Appling had made all streak long to the record's longevity, set his sights and drilled one in the direction of the White Sox shortstop, far enough to his left that second baseman Bill Knickerbocker also moved for it instinctively. Sure enough, it worked. Appling didn't muff it; he dove for it and ended up splayed on the turf without the ball, looking Knickerbocker, who had also given it a lunging try, in the eye. Base hit. The streak moved to 55 straight.

DiMaggio's hit in the third came off lefty Edgar Smith, the same pitcher against whom he had begun it all 2 months before on May 15. For good measure, he added a double against Smith later in the game. The Yankees won on the strength of a four-run fourth inning and some clutch late inning pitching by Norman Branch in relief of Steve Peek. Chicago made it close on home runs by Moose Solters in the fourth and Joe Kuhel in the fifth. Cleveland's 6–2 loss to Boston put the Yankees out in front by five again. In the National League, the Dodgers took a pair from the Cubs at Ebbets Field before 33,247 and the Cards outmarathoned the Phils 3–2 in a 16-inning game. St. Louis was headed for Brooklyn the next day for a showdown with the Dodgers, just as the Yankees were headed for Cleveland for what turned out to be the last really serious bit of pennant match play in the American League for the season.

With all the action on the Russian front during June and July, the world had almost forgotten that English forces had driven the Vichy mandates in the middle east into a position where they had to negotiate surrender terms. On this day, British officials threatened to light a fire under the stalled negotiations in Syria by arresting the commander of all French forces, General Dentz. If Vichy balked at terms, the surrender would be treated as unconditional. In regard to Syria and Lebanon, a correspondent for the *New York Herald Tribune* wired home a story whose observations on the area echo back through the centuries and reverberate to the present: "The area is a babel of thirty rabid sects where a thousand years of chaos promise little peace to any conqueror."

In America on July 15, the housecleaning operations against Axis interests that Roosevelt had begun in retaliation for the Nazi sinking of the merchant ship *Robin Moor* were concluded. A Navy vessel steamed out of New York with 450 ousted German and Italian consular officials and various other deported Axis citizens on board. Meanwhile, federal prosecutors proceeded against another group of 33 purported Nazi conspirators in an indictment handed down in Brooklyn. Curiously, a holdover case from before the time of the Russian invasion put 29 "Trotskyites" on trial in St. Paul, Minnesota, for conspiring to instigate an armed revolution in America when the time was propitious. One thing was certain about America on July 15, 1941: The time was not propitious.

GAME 56: *July 16*

The daily DiMaggio streak bulletins on radio had become by now a national rhythmic fix. How long could he go on? Who might stop him? The answers were not yet available on this day, July

16, though DiMaggio made the number of this streak game—
56—more famous in baseball annals than he could have guessed
at the time or would have wanted to. Millions remember exactly
what he didn't do in game 57, yet only a few remember what he
did do in game 56. He took his cuts this soon to be famous day
within the comfy precincts of old League Park, where the Indians
scheduled many of their home contests. DiMaggio settled things
early. On his first at bat he singled sharply to center off lefty Al
Milnar. In the third he looped a short fly to center off Milnar
for another hit, and after a base on balls and a ground-out, he
finished the day with a long double in the gap off Joe Krakauskas.
DiMaggio's three hits were representative of the range of the
streak as a whole: one clean, one a little lucky, and one driven
hard and far. Charlie Keller, breaking out of a brief slump, provided some additional Yankee muscle, homering and tripling in
New York's 10–3 romp over Cleveland. Reserve catcher Buddy
Rosar provided the rest, slamming two doubles and a single to
drive in half the Yankee runs for the day. In addition to his three
hits, DiMaggio also scored three runs, including a mad dash from
second base on an infield hit, sliding home ahead of shortstop
Ray Mack's throw.

In an interview about the streak with the *Cleveland Plain Dealer,*
DiMaggio compared the games around the time of his pursuit
of the Sisler and Keeler records with the open-ended nature of
his record-a-day pace now. He still felt pressure each game, but
not each at bat. The distinction may seem a fine one, but it had
tactical repercussions. When he was shooting for the Sisler
record—the one he had had in his sights for a couple of weeks—
he got edgy about walks and consequently became a less patient
hitter; now on almost every trip to the plate he waited for a pitch
he felt he could drive. As much as he still wanted to beat his own
minor league record of 61 straight, set for the San Francisco Seals
in 1933, he openly admitted that he had another goal: to catch
"that Williams" for the batting title by the homestretch of the
season. After this day, DiMaggio was at .375 for the year and
Williams was at .395. The prospect of catching Williams was not
improbable under these circumstances. DiMaggio had after all
outhit him for average during the previous two seasons. The com-

petition between these extraordinary hitters was as intense as it was professional.

At the end of 56 games DiMaggio's streak average moved up to .408 (91 for 223). Moreover, in the 11 games to date since breaking Keeler's record, DiMaggio was hitting .545 (24 for 44). He had been driving in runs so consistently that he now led the major leagues with 76, and his 20 home runs tied him with teammate Charlie Keller for the major league high. Williams, at present nursing a sore ankle, ended up 4 points ahead of DiMaggio at .412 for the span of the streak games. During one run of 21 games within the streak (May 17 to June 7) Williams hit .506, and this yeoman work helped carry him to his .406 overall season's average.

DiMaggio's torrid pace near the end of his record was in marked contrast not only to Williams's brief fade-out but to his own Pacific Coast League record of 61 with the Seals. In the last several games of that streak the young DiMaggio had been so exhausted that he could barely hit the ball beyond the infield. Perhaps this is the place for a bit of comparative streak morphology. The result says something about the way the younger DiMaggio and the more mature one carried themselves under the pressures of record hitting streaks.

In a doubleheader victory for San Francisco over Portland on May 28, 1933, a rookie Seal right fielder with just a couple of months' experience under his belt banged a double in the nightcap after going hitless in the first game. The *San Francisco Chronicle* couldn't decide whether they wished to spell the fellow's name DiMaggio, de Maggio, or De Maggio, and it seemed the mere whim of the day's copy editor how the name actually showed up in the daily sports section. The day DiMaggio's minor league streak began, Babe Ruth hit three home runs and went 5 for 7 in a doubleheader win against the White Sox as the Yankees went a game up over the Senators in the American League race. Al Simmons lead the league in hitting at .361; Jimmy Foxx, then playing for the Philadelphia A's, was second at .354.

In May 1933 Roosevelt's brain trusters had brewed up the National Recovery Act as a depression-era potion. During the course of DiMaggio's 61 games Mahatma Gandhi ended a hunger strike on behalf of India's untouchables; California became one of the many states to vote "wet" and align itself with others for the override of the Prohibition amendment to the Constitution; San Franciscans watched in awe as construction proceeded on two massive projects, the Golden Gate Bridge and the Bay Bridge; aviator Wiley Post broke the record for around-the-world flight, despite crashing in Russia and Alaska; the marriage of Douglas Fairbanks and Mary Pickford went belly up; and Clark Gable and Norma Shearer starred in *Strange Interlude,* Edward G. Robinson in *The Little Giant,* and Ruby Keeler and Joan Blondell in *Gold Diggers of 1933.* The first all-star game would be played at Comiskey Park on July 6, and Babe Ruth would hit one out in the American League's 4–2 win. Barney Ross took the lightweight title on June 23, and Primo Carnera, to the delight of Mussolini, won the heavyweight title on June 29 by knocking Jack Sharkey silly in the sixth; after the fight the newly appointed prizefight commissioner personally jumped into the ring to examine Carnera's gloves for lead pipes or slugs.

DiMaggio's hitting streak did almost nothing for the Seals in 1933. San Francisco was in last place when it began and was still in the cellar 34 games later when the *Chronicle* first noticed that "Joe de Maggio, the San Francisco right fielder, hit safely in his thirty-fourth game, beating a close throw to first on his fourth trip." By game 40 the streak story had reached boldface print status in the sports section, and by game 49, with the challenge to the old Pacific Coast League record set by Jack Ness in 1915, the streak became headline news in the sports pages.

Dominic DiMaggio remembers what it was like for his brother during the increasingly tense and exhausting days of the streak. The DiMaggio boys still lived at home on Taylor Street near Fisherman's Wharf. Even with the headlines in the papers every day as the streak hit 50 straight, the talk at the dinner table was not about the ball games. "Joe was just off the sandlots," Dominic recalled, "and the streak was a strain on him. Toward the end he needed some rest. The Seals played so many games—way over two hundred a year counting spring training. Nobody at home wanted to make the strain any worse by talking about it. Anyway, my father got his biggest kick out of the streak when it was over—he got his picture taken with the mayor. That really meant something to him."

The last several days of DiMaggio's streak were sheer torture, very different from the 1941 streak, during which he grew stronger toward the end. Most of his hits were infield singles, including a solo hit to Ray French at deep short against Sacramento in game 57, another just off French's glove in game 58, and two more scratch hits, again involving French, in both ends of a doubleheader in games 59 and 60. These last games were strange phenomena. The first was played the morning of July 26 in Stockton, and DiMaggio dribbled one past the pitcher in the ninth inning that French couldn't play. The official scorer was roundly booed. In the afternoon game, played 40 miles up the road in Sacramento, with talk still fresh about the suspect call in the ninth to preserve the streak, DiMaggio again hit one right at a charging French on his last at bat of the game. French grabbed it and juggled it, not bothering to throw to first. When the hit signal went up in the press box, the Sacramento crowd screamed at the call, with several of them frantically charging the official scorer. A police escort was necessary to steer the stunned newspaperman through the mob to a private room off the clubhouse.

DiMaggio appeared about ready to fall from weariness. A staff writer for the *Chronicle*, Ed Hughes, wrote, "Joe De Maggio is only a kid, playing his first year in professional baseball, and he plainly shows the strain." The next day, back home, DiMaggio struggled with no hits until a strong rally by the Seals in the eighth got him another at bat. He lined one over the second baseman's head for what was to be his last hit during the record streak of 61 straight. In his shot at 62, pitcher Ed Walsh for Oakland, son of Ed Walsh, the great Chicago White Sox knuckleballer, retired him on routine plays, one of which was a force to Cookie Lavagetto, with whom an older Joe DiMaggio would again hook up when the Yankees played the Dodgers in the 1941 and 1947 World Series. DiMaggio came up for his last at bat in the bottom of the ninth with one out, the game tied at 3–3, and runners on first and third. The man before him, Jimmy Zinn, had been intentionally walked to set up a double play. DiMaggio swung at a high outside pitch and connected soundly to send a long fly to right, sufficient to drive in the game-winning run on the tag-up but not sufficient to continue his streak. In all this time the Seals had edged up to seventh place, two games out of the league cellar.

During DiMaggio's 1933 streak reporters went scurrying for information on Joe Wilhoit's all-time record 69-game streak for Wichita of the Western Association in 1919, though there seemed to be considerable dispute about whether 69 was the correct number rather than 67 or even 65. In any event, Wilhoit had accomplished his feat from June 14 to August 20, 1919, during the time when the Chicago White Sox—later that year besmirched to black—were inching their way to the American League pennant. When Wilhoit's streak began, Ty Cobb was leading the American League at .377, with Joe Jackson comfortably behind at .338. The American cavalry at the time was chasing Mexican bandits over the Texas border, occupational therapy for some hundred years by that time, and Woodrow Wilson was fighting Congress tooth and nail over specific covenants and articles for the proposed League of Nations. Wilhoit hit a remarkable .505 during the run of 69 games (151 for 299), which says something about the pitching in that circuit, not to mention the fielding. For the entire 1919 season he hit .422; the next year he was slated to move up to the Boston Red Sox, but he never made their roster.

Both DiMaggio's own 61-game streak in 1933 and Wilhoit's 69-game record were still live issues after the Yankee game with Cleveland on July 16, 1941. As hot as DiMaggio was, writers had reason to think that with continued luck he might well mount a challenge not only to his Seal record but to Wilhoit's as well. That possibility shared space in the day's sports pages with a sadder piece of news, devastating in its way, having to do with a former big leaguer for the Giants and Braves, Eddie Mayo, who would later pull it together and return to the majors with the A's and the Tigers. Mayo was then playing for the Pacific Coast League's Los Angeles Angels, and news came from the commissioner's office that he was banned from baseball for a year, pending appeal, for an incident in which he had walked up to a surprised Pacific Coast League umpire and spit in his face. Mayo said at his hearing that he hadn't known what he was doing—akin to pleading temporary insanity. His plea didn't wash, if that's the right phrase. For the moment, he packed his spikes and went home.

Around the majors on the last day of DiMaggio's streak, the Cards faced the Dodgers in an Ebbets Field showdown. St. Louis spotted the Dodgers four runs and came back to beat them anyway, 7–4. The Cards were now three out of first and closing, while the Yankees were six in front of the Indians in the American League and coasting. New York had won 20 of the last 22 and for the past month was playing over .850 ball. The next night DiMaggio and the Yankees would join the Indians in the cavernous Municipal Stadium for a historically dramatic game under the lights. The big stadium would be filled nearly to capacity for the occasion.

If July 16, 1941, turned out to be a day of great consequence for DiMaggio without his knowing it at the time, it was also of great consequence for America without its government at the time knowing exactly why either. The cabinet of Prince Fumimaro Konoye resigned in Japan, and a heavily militarist regime formed a new cabinet. Intelligence and State Department analysts expected a major move in the Pacific theater but were unaware of the detailed plans for attacking Pearl Harbor that now moved to the top of the Japanese cabinet's agenda. On the floor of Congress this day, elected officials began voicing their first public and serious concern about an imminent threat in the Pacific. Representative Vinson, chairman of the Naval Affairs Committee in the House of Representatives, said in response to military testimony on the adequacy of our defenses on Pearl Harbor, "If we have a powder keg there, maybe there is something we can do about it." The matter escaped direct attention until December 7, 1941.

There is one more item, elegiac in its way, that marks the last day of DiMaggio's streak in the summer of a year at once energized and daunted by world war. On July 16 the *New York World-Telegram* ran a photo of Joseph Kennedy, Jr., in the cockpit of a Navy pilot trainer under the caption "A Kennedy Wants Wings." The picture of the intense young man, nearly DiMaggio's age, is tainted in retrospect only by what we know of Joe Kennedy's subsequent death as a World War II Navy pilot. In a time excited by flight as the new frontier of achievement, it is fitting that Di-Maggio's streak opened on a day featuring a daring midair rescue and closed on a day that ran a simple news photo which symbolized the spirit of the era's commitment—and, as it turned out, the immense toll that would be taken by our impending entry into World War II.

ENDGAME

July 17

On a day that saw the European war break forth from a temporary lull with an incredible 9 million men clashing furiously on all three salients along the Russian front, 67,468 jammed Cleveland's Municipal Stadium to cheer DiMaggio's effort to extend his streak and watch the Indians make what could be their last serious run at the league-leading Yankees. The hostilities in Russia constituted the largest single day's battle in the history of the world; the crowd in Cleveland that night was merely the largest of the 1941 baseball season.

The game was among the most memorable ever played. Millions know the name of the two Cleveland pitchers, Al Smith and Jim Bagby, who shut down DiMaggio that night. Sportswriter Dave Anderson pointed out that head shots of Smith and Bagby appeared in newspapers all over the country the next day as if they had assassinated a king. In many ways, aided by the skullduggery of Ken Keltner, the Indian third baseman, they had. DiMaggio's night at the plate in Cleveland remains one of those baseball moments that still fire the imagination; in recalling the two drives off his bat toward third, both potential hits converted into brilliant outs, one cherishes the hope that at least one will yet shoot past Keltner into the left field corner for a double. But neither did, and neither will.

Two left-handers were going at it in the night game before the huge, carnivalesque crowd: for the Yankees, DiMaggio's roommate, Lefty Gomez; for the Indians, Al Smith. Gomez remembers getting his shoes shined in the hotel lobby and the shoeshine man telling him that the Indians and Smith were going to hang the collar on DiMaggio that night. Lefty just stared unbelievingly at the voice before him uttering such doom. Though variants of this story placed DiMaggio and Gomez together in a cab with an irrepressible cabby putting on the hex, Gomez in truth suffered the "truth" all alone. DiMaggio later suffered the consequences.

On his first time at bat, DiMaggio pulled a low inside curve hard down the line at third and Keltner backhanded it deep behind the bag. When I recently asked DiMaggio how deep Keltner was playing him, he responded, "Deep? My God, he was standing in left field." DiMaggio also reminisced about the play on a tape recording now housed at the Hall of Fame Library in Cooperstown. He said he hit the ball on the nose right down the line, and Keltner stabbed it on the third or fourth hop, when it already appeared to be beyond him. His momentum carried him onto the grass well in foul territory. DiMaggio said, "I couldn't get out of the box quickly because of the rains the day before, and Ken's long throw just nipped me."

For the rest of the game DiMaggio noticed that Keltner's positioning behind third was even more exaggerated: "He gave me almost the whole left side between the line and Boudreau at short." When I asked Keltner recently how and why he had positioned himself as he had against DiMaggio, he responded that he figured to get an extra step's worth of time because of the damp field; he also wanted to hold any hit that got past him to a single. He wasn't thinking about DiMaggio's streak but about the Indians' attempt, perhaps their last serious one, to challenge the Yankees before New York made a mockery of the pennant race. Playing deep and near the line was in no way tentative; it was tactical. Keltner knew DiMaggio rarely if ever bunted, and he knew the Yankee slugger often hit shots right down the line when a lefty was on the mound. I asked Keltner what he thought generally when DiMaggio stepped up to the plate: "Joe was the greatest ballplayer I ever saw—the most complete ballplayer."

Al Smith walked DiMaggio his next at bat, and the big Cleveland crowd, pulling so hard for its team to make a run at the pennant, actually booed. If ever 67,468 people were confused, this was the night. The *Cleveland Plain Dealer* reported that Di-Maggio was taking it all gracefully, but the fans were deeply conflicted: "Only a psychologist could tell how they felt." First they cheered DiMaggio for what he had done already during the streak; then they cheered Keltner for preventing him from doing it again. The boos when Smith walked DiMaggio were deprivational.

In the seventh Smith came right at DiMaggio, who hit another hard grounder deep to Keltner. The great third baseman gloved it again, this time on a shorter hop and closer to him; the ball was in the same place, but Keltner was playing even closer to the line. The long throw to the bag beat Joe by a step. After the game Keltner was not happy about losing and snapped at reporters that DiMaggio hit 'em and he caught 'em, that's all. But then he unwound a bit and mentioned the incident he remembered from back on June 1, the last time the Yankees had been in Cleveland, when DiMaggio had hit one off his glove as he moved to his right toward the line. "DiMaggio said something when the inning was over as he was leaving the bases near the foul line. I couldn't hear what it was, but I remembered the ball he hit on the play. So I played him deep tonight, maybe a little closer to the line than usual."

Bobby Feller told me that "Keltner was simply the best in the American League. He could go to his right better than anyone and had a great, great arm." Every Yankee I asked about the last game of the streak concurred. Johnny Sturm was the most expansive on the subject. He said that Keltner was simply a "hell of a ballplayer, with tremendous confidence in his arm. He played as deep at third as the situation allowed, whatever the situation was. Joe would never bunt, and Kenny knew it. Once he grabbed those balls, he still had to throw ropes to first. Best arm at his position in baseball."

To this day Keltner's memory of the July 17 game is precise, though he has forgotten the earlier June 1 incident involving a similar smash to third entirely. When I asked him if it was true that of the streak-ending grounders the first was the tougher play, he said: "They were both pretty much in the same place. The throws were more difficult than the stops, and the throws were identical. I had to put something on them, and the plays at first were both very close." Keltner remembers that when he left the park he didn't want to run into any disgruntled fans, Yankee or Indian, so he had the police escort him to his car in the lot: "You know, Joe had lots of Italian friends in Ohio."

DiMaggio's last chance of the night came when he hit against reliever Jim Bagby in the eighth inning with one out and the bases loaded. The Yankees had already scored two in the inning to bounce Smith and go ahead of Cleveland 4–1. DiMaggio hit a fastball on a 2–1 count hard and deep to Lou Boudreau at short-stop. He might have been better off with his lucky charm, Luke Appling, at short, but the Yankees had just left Chicago. The ball took a nasty hop anyway—almost as if Appling were there—but not nasty enough to leave the scope of Boudreau's radar. In fact, the new trajectory was shoulder high, just right for the fast double play that ended up nipping DiMaggio at first on the relay from Mack to Grimes.

Boudreau's play looked like curtains for DiMaggio, but there might have been another chance, one the Indians would have been all too ready to extend to him. Cleveland had a shot at tying the game in the ninth, and if they did so, DiMaggio would bat in the tenth. The tying run was indeed sitting on third base with no one out after Larry Rosenthal tripled in two runs off fireman Johnny Murphy to shrink the score to 4–3. The huge crowd yelled itself silly at this quick turn of events. Not only were the Indians still in the game, DiMaggio would get another whack if only a simple run could be picked up from third. And Cleveland had three outs to play with.

Pinch hitter Hal Trosky was the first to try. He slammed a grounder to Sturm at first, but a hesitant Rosenthal remained on third. No sense taking a risk. Sturm made the play, keeping an eye cocked on Rosenthal. Next Soup Campbell, hitting for Bagby, bounced a shot back to Murphy that Murphy speared on a hard hop. No stopping Rosenthal this time; he was off for the plate. When he realized his folly, it was too late: Murphy had Rosenthal properly pickled between home and third. Campbell sat on first viewing the rundown, though he ought to have lit for second to get into scoring position. But Roy Weatherly made everyone else's poor baserunning moot by grounding out to end the game. The collective moan of the huge crowd when Murphy closed the door served both the hometown Indians and the streak-less DiMaggio.

Joe DiMaggio's brother Dominic, who had hit a home run at Yankee Stadium the day the Yankee team consecutive-game home run streak ended, homered, tripled, and drove in three runs for Boston on July 17 against Thornton Lee of the White Sox on the day his brother's hitting streak ended. Too bad family property is not transferrable in baseball. Phil Rizzuto remembers leaving the park with a pensive DiMaggio after the game. His *compare* asked him for a twenty—DiMaggio had left his wallet in the visiting team's clubhouse. Rizzuto complied silently, and DiMaggio veered off, alone, toward a local Cleveland watering hole to buy himself a drink, the streak's tribute and its epitaph. DiMaggio did not ask the rookie to keep him company, and the rookie never asked for his twenty back.

The Cleveland clubhouse was a tough place for an interview after the game as reporters crowded around the night's losers to ask about their combined efforts against DiMaggio. "I hate to lose," Keltner said. Right after the game, the visiting Yankee clubhouse was also strangely silent. The players were delighted with the tense, close win, but no one said a word until DiMaggio mumbled, "Well, I'm glad it's over. Keltner was a little rough on me tonight." Then the cheers and celebration began, partly for the win but mostly in honor of a great streak record now over and a great player whose performance made an impression on his teammates that they still marvel at half a century later. They remember the game that at once froze the legend preceding it and bore first witness to the excitement the legend has generated ever since.

DiMaggio spoke very carefully after the game. He said he was relieved the pressure was off, though he made it clear he would have liked to continue in pursuit of his own minor league record of 61. Relieved was not the same as happy. There was a way in which the major and minor league streaks shared something that made up for their five-game difference in duration. Ed Walsh, Jr., whose father's spitballs in the early decades of the century got him into the Hall of Fame, ended DiMaggio's 1933 streak;

Jim Bagby, Jr., whose father pitched for Cleveland in the 1920s, ended the 1941 streak. Generations of experience were dispensed against DiMaggio, which makes for a fine baseball trivia question: Which son of a major league pitcher stopped DiMaggio's record hitting streak? The answer: It depends.

Joe DiMaggio could hardly be expected to exit these days of his streak without Charles Lindbergh in some way or another entering them. True to form, Lindbergh's saga, forging itself through all of DiMaggio's streak, reached a climax on this July 17. Terribly upset at trying to put together the ruins after an encounter with Roosevelt's hit man, Secretary of the Interior Harold Ickes, Lindbergh wrote an open public letter to the President, releasing it to newspapers all over the country. He demanded that the President instruct his secretary to apologize for his vicious remarks about Lindbergh's general fondness for fascist causes and objects, especially the slander surrounding the infamous medal awarded him by Göring in 1938. Lindbergh was weary of being called the Knight of the German Eagle. He wanted it to stop. The President ignored Lindbergh's letter, and Harold Ickes immediately rattled the aviator again by refining most of the charges he had just leveled against him. No, he hadn't called the beleaguered Lindbergh a fascist, merely an appeaser of fascists. The secretary then challenged Lindbergh to quit preaching doom and give the notorious Knight of the German Eagle medal back to Hitler. That evening, while the Yankees played in Cleveland, Wendell Willkie tried to calm the crowd at a Manhattan "Beat Hitler" rally when it began booing and hissing at the mention of Lindbergh's name. Willkie said, "Let's not boo any American citizen. Let's save our boos for Hitler." DiMaggio's record topped out, and Lindbergh's stock bottomed out.

EPILOGUE

The brilliance of DiMaggio's record streak in 1941 is attested to by the intensity of interest and the sheer thrill attending any serious pursuit of it. Players approaching the streak, like Pete Rose in 1978 or Paul Molitor in 1987, with the concentration, the nerves, and the stamina to take the measure of its excellence, are nonetheless haunted by the fabled number 56 hovering somewhere in the middle distance. DiMaggio's great streak is not only a hitting marvel but a formidable obstacle, a record that by its very achievement adds pressure to those mounting a challenge to it.

Famous numbers are part of baseball's mythology, and they seem to stand guard at the larger statistical treasure trove so essential to those who follow and love the sport. Statistics are at once the stuff of baseball's memorial infrastructure and the provenance of the idiot savant; they mark the connections from at bat to at bat, game to game, season to season, decade to decade, and at the same time soothe the baseball insomniac. Here are some stats. From May 15, 1941, to July 17, 1941, DiMaggio fared as follows against the rest of the American League.

	G	AB	R	H	2B	3B	HR	AVG
Philadelphia Athletics	5	21	6	11	2	1	2	.524
St. Louis Browns	12	48	14	22	5	0	5	.458
Chicago White Sox	12	45	11	19	1	1	3	.422
Cleveland Indians	7	26	7	10	4	0	1	.385
Washington Senators	5	21	7	8	1	1	1	.381
Detroit Tigers	7	32	6	12	2	1	2	.375
Boston Red Sox	8	30	5	9	1	0	1	.300
Totals	56	223	56	91	16	4	15	.408

These are the nuts and bolts. For good measure, DiMaggio scored as many runs, 56, as he had streak games, just as he scored as many runs, 41, as he had streak games at the time he tied Sisler's modern-day record. He struck out only five times during the whole of the streak, walked 21 times, and was hit by two pitched balls. The pitching staffs of the Philadelphia A's and St. Louis Browns provided the most wholesome food for DiMaggio's feasts. Only head to head against the Boston Red Sox and Ted Williams did DiMaggio falter slightly, hitting .300 to Williams's robust .520 in those eight games. Williams outhit DiMaggio .412 to .408 for the games included in the streak, though DiMaggio had 36 more official at bats (he rarely walked and Williams rarely didn't), 14 more hits, 3 more home runs, 1 more double, 4 more triples, 5 more runs batted in, and a better slugging percentage, .717 to .684.

Chicago White Sox lefties Thornton Lee and Edgar Smith tossed DiMaggio the most balls that began as pitches and ended up as hits, six apiece. During the course of the streak DiMaggio faced three pitchers named Harris (Mickey for the Red Sox, Lum for the A's, and Bob for the Browns) who allowed him what seemed like a modest seven hits combined. But poor right-hander Bob Harris of St. Louis gave up five of those hits. He faced DiMaggio six times during the streak, and DiMaggio hit .833 off him, making Harris the sweepstakes winner for the 56 games.

He would get his revenge later in the season. As for DiMaggio's performance against the best pitcher in the league, he faced Bobby Feller in two games and stroked three hits off him in six at bats for an even .500 average.

For the entire 1941 season DiMaggio hit in 114 of the 139 games in which he played, impressive but not as impressive as the major league record held by Al Simmons while playing for the Philadelphia Athletics in 1925. Simmons hit in 133 of his 153 games that year, amassing 253 hits and a .384 average. The city of Philadelphia has a lock on this sort of consistency. Chuck Klein of the Phillies holds the National League record by hitting in 135 of his 156 games in 1930, with 250 hits and a .386 average.

During DiMaggio's streak the Yankee record was 41–13, but aside from DiMaggio only three Yankees averaged above .300 from May 15 to July 17: Phil Rizzuto at .368 (aided by his own 16-game hitting streak), Red Ruffing (including his phenomenal pinch hitting) at .351, and Red Rolfe at .305. Ted Williams still led the American League when DiMaggio's streak ended, hitting .395, though DiMaggio had snuck in behind him at .371, with Travis following at .370, Heath at .369, and Cullenbine at .362. Yankee pitching was superb all streak long, with the two staff veterans, Hall of Famers Lefty Gomez and Red Ruffing, winning six and seven games, respectively, while losing none. Johnny Sturm said that DiMaggio put out a little extra for the vets on the Yankee staff; it seemed as though they too put out a little extra for him during the days of his streak.

Hard upon losing his streak on July 17, DiMaggio gained a second wind. He hit in 16 straight games, beginning July 18 in Cleveland with a single and a double against Bobby Feller, who beat the Yankees 2–1 for his nineteenth win of the season en route to 25 for the year. On July 23, the next time DiMaggio faced Al Smith of Cleveland, he smashed a home run, just a reminder that though Smith might have gotten him twice on July 17, he hadn't put him in his hip pocket. On this same July 23, the rookie phenom who had received so much publicity during DiMaggio's streak, Dick Wakefield, fanned three times in his first game for the Winston-Salem Twins of the Piedmont League.

DiMaggio continued his new streak until an August 3 doubleheader against St. Louis. He came to the plate four times in each game without a hit. John Niggeling collared him in the opener, and Bob Harris, whom DiMaggio had slapped around unmercifully during the streak, hung him out in the nightcap. From August 3 on DiMaggio never hit in more than 7 straight games. On August 29, with DiMaggio out of the lineup recovering from a sprained ankle, the Yankee team planned an evening at the Shoreham Hotel in Washington in his honor. Lefty Gomez told DiMaggio that they were going to dinner that night where he, Gomez, wanted and then to a movie. Lefty was tired of all the glad-handed DiMaggio hangers-on at the usual American League watering holes. DiMaggio said fine but told Gomez to hurry; he was famished. Then he paced in annoyance as Gomez went through a complicated dressing ritual until Selkirk phoned him that all was ready. "Shake a leg, I'm hungry," said DiMaggio. Gomez complied, but on the way down the hallway he veered off toward Selkirk's room, and DiMaggio followed, rolling his eyes at yet another delay.

The door opened to the entire Yankee team. Pitcher Johnny Murphy and his wife had coaxed a craftsman at Tiffany's in New York to hurry a hand-tooled, elegant silver cigarette humidor with a detailed image on its lid of DiMaggio swinging a bat. Beneath a simple "56" the inscription ran "Presented to Joe DiMaggio by his fellow players on the New York Yankees to express their admiration for his consecutive-game hitting streak, 1941." Everything about this gesture pleased DiMaggio. The streak was in its way as handcrafted as the gift honoring it; the Yankees were eager even before the season ended to give DiMaggio a token of the excitement he had given them. DiMaggio could not say enough in thanks at the time or say it exactly right since, but he was deeply gratified.

After DiMaggio's streak ended in July, *Newsweek* magazine ran back-to-back profiles, the first honoring the Yankee center fielder and the second bemoaning the fact that the national attention paid to the progress of the hitting streak had all but obscured another legend in embryo, Ted Williams's mission to crack the .400 barrier for the season. With the streak now over, Williams made the last months of the season his own. He returned to the Red Sox lineup on a regular basis on July 22, after being consigned by a recurring foot injury to pinch-hitting service from

July 11. His slightly sagging average rose to exactly .400 against Cleveland on July 25; more important, Williams's bat helped Lefty Grove win his 300th major league game that afternoon. The score was a rather free 10–6, but Ted hit a two-run homer and Jimmie Foxx a two-run triple to break a late inning tie for Grove's long-awaited milestone victory.

Williams turned on what gas was left in his tank in early August (from August 7 through August 21 he hit .466), and that gave him the points he needed when he flagged toward the end of the year and precious decimals began dropping from his average. Before a final-day doubleheader against the Philadelphia A's, Williams was at .39955 (officially rounded off to .400), but he insisted on taking his cuts. He remembers umpire Bill McGowan dusting off home plate on his first at bat and telling him that a player has to be loose to hit .400. Loose he was. In the first game he chalked up four hits, including a single and a home run off Dick Fowler and singles off Porter Vaughan and Tex Shirley. Connie Mack, who usually stuck it out with his pitchers, gave Williams enough variety to spice up his life and average to .404. In the second game Mack gave Williams a gift of Fred Caliguiri, a rookie whose major league career was sensibly brief. Williams singled and slammed a gigantic shot off the speaker horn in right field for a double.

His six hits on this remarkable day buoyed Williams's average to .406 for the year. In addition, he had cranked up for 11 home runs in the last month of the season to take the major league lead that year at 37. No one but Williams in the American League ever hit over .400 and over 20 home runs in the same season, though Rogers Hornsby for the Cardinals in the National League took the home run crown with 42 during his .401 year of 1922. Hornsby's performance that year and the years surrounding it remains extraordinary. From 1921 through 1925 his five composite years averaged out to .402, and his home runs totaled 140. Even Ty Cobb paled before this feat.

While Williams slugged his way to the last .400 season by a major league ballplayer, the Yankees were making a travesty of the American League pennant race. On September 4 they clinched the pennant 20 games up over the then second place White Sox. This was the earliest ever in the majors, surpassing the 1904 Giants in the National League and the 1910 Philadelphia A's in the American, both of whom had clinched after 137 games, with the Giants playing a total of 153 games and the A's 150. The previous 154-game record was held by the 1936 Yankees, who clinched on September 9 after 137 games. At season's end the 1941 Yankees had won a total of 101 games, played .656 ball for the year, and held a 17-game lead over the Red Sox, who had sneaked past the White Sox for second. Chicago ended up in third, with Cleveland, having faded badly since the crucial July series with the Yankees, dropping to fourth.

The pennant race in the National League was an entirely different story, with the Dodgers scrapping and clawing to clinch a couple of days before the end of the season after a sequence of nail-biting extra-inning ball games that had the whole borough of Brooklyn in a cold sweat. In their own last-ditch efforts, the Cards brought up a minor leaguer on the roster expansion date, September 17. The young slugger, Stan Musial, had already moved to Rochester from Springfield late in July. He played in the first few Cardinal games after his elevation and hit .545 (12 for 22) until he cooled down later in September to a mere .426.

DiMaggio finished the year hitting .357, behind the league-leading .406 of Williams and the runner-up .359 of Cecil Travis, but he led the majors in runs batted in at 125 and registered 30 home runs. Later he won over Williams as American League MVP and as Associated Press Athlete of the Year for 1941. In the National League, Pete Reiser, at the age of 22, led the circuit in hitting with a .343 average, displacing Arky Vaughan as the youngest ever to do so. Vaughan had been 23 when he won the National League crown in 1935, hitting .385. Reiser was a superb ballplayer, and though he was hotter for most of the year than the proverbial pistol that gave him his nickname, he would just lose out to his teammate Dolf Camilli for the National League MVP in 1941. He won rookie of the year honors hands down, both hands in that he could hit from either side of the plate and throw with either arm; in the majors he threw with his right arm and hit from the left side. In center, he could catch anything that didn't have a rocket attached to it.

Reiser and Camilli, plus a tough pitching staff headed by Kirby Higbe and Whit Wyatt, led Brooklyn into their first World

Series ever against the Yankees. The Dodgers had won only two previous pennants, in 1916 and 1920, and had lost to the Red Sox and the Indians on those occasions. This year they had been bankrolled for another shot. Late in September the *Saturday Evening Post* ran a fascinating story about the tactics of Larry MacPhail during his time running the club, "Yes, You Can Buy a Pennant." The article pointed out what a crafty executive could do with $833,110, starting with as little as the $100 he shelled out for the near rookie, Pete Reiser. MacPhail's major deals included, among others, $80,000 in 1938 to the Phillies for Dolf Camilli; $25,000 for Whit Wyatt from Cleveland in 1939; $132,000 spent for Joe Medwick from the Cards in 1940; $42,500 for the minor leaguer Pee Wee Reese in 1940; $25,000 for Roy Cullenbine, whom he got from Detroit in 1940 and unloaded the same year to the St. Louis Browns; $100,000 for Kirby Higbe from the Phillies in 1941; and $50,000 to the Cards for Mickey Owen in 1941.

The 1941 World Series had its glories and legendary moments, but it also picked up one piece of unfinished business from DiMaggio's streak. Back at game 40 on June 28, Johnny Babich of the Philadelphia A's had said he intended to give DiMaggio slim pickin's to swing at that day. Dodger pitcher Whit Wyatt, when interviewed by reporters, thought Babich was overly charitable. He said that in the National League DiMaggio's strike zone would start at his Adam's apple. Apparently both DiMaggio and Wyatt remembered those gentle words in the second game of the series when Wyatt took the mound. DiMaggio flied out in the fifth inning after two rare strikeouts and two earlier pitches under his chin. As he passed the mound returning to the dugout, he shouted out, "This series isn't over yet." Wyatt responded, "If you can't take it, why don't you get out of the game?" DiMaggio's version of Wyatt's question had a racier second clause. Uncharacteristically, DiMaggio went after the Brooklyn pitcher, but no damage or even contact took place as both benches emptied, the players milled about, and the umpires settled things, which is what everyone seemed to want. Wyatt proved he was a man of his word, perverse as that word might have been, and DiMaggio proved he had read the local sports pages back in June.

In the series, the Yankees won the opener behind Red Ruffing, who defeated reliever Hugh Casey 3–2. Joe Gordon hit a two-run homer and a game-winning single. Whit Wyatt, while irritating DiMaggio, also stopped a 10-game Yankee consecutive win streak in the World Series by turning the previous day's score around in favor of the Dodgers. When the teams moved to Ebbets Field for the third game, the Yankee left-hander Marius Russo, suffering a miserable cold, held off the Dodgers 2–1 as Charlie Keller, not expected to play because of a badly sprained ankle, drove in DiMaggio with the game-winning run. Earlier in the day DiMaggio got his first hit of the series, a single.

Game 4 was perhaps the most famous in World Series history. Kirby Higbe of the Dodgers started against Ately Donald. A two-run homer by Pete Reiser had given the Dodgers a 4–3 lead into the top of the fabled Yankee ninth inning. With Hugh Casey working in relief, Johnny Sturm died on a full-count ground-out. Red Rolfe then tapped to Casey for an easy out number two. It looked like a wrap. But Tommy Henrich forced the count to 3–2 before taking an awkward cut at a slithering—some witnesses might have guessed slobbering—Casey pitch heading for the inside corner. Henrich was completely fooled, and his bat made no contact with Casey's savage and mysterious delivery. Mickey Owen's catcher's glove, to his utter dismay, made only slightly better contact with the pitch. Henrich flew to first base as the errant third strike rolled far behind the plate; half the Yankee team had to be summoned from an overly hasty retreat down the dugout runway toward the clubhouse. Poor Owen's surprise was greater than anyone's. The man was no slouch in back of the plate. From September 22, 1940, while with the Cards, to August 29, 1941, after his trade to the Dodgers, he had played flawlessly at catcher, amassing 508 putouts and assists without a single error. This play was a fluke, and the reputation earned by it was sadly unmerited.

Nevertheless, there stood a crestfallen Owen in foul territory, and there at first stood the ghost of Tommy Henrich's strikeout. All Dodger history passed before the Brooklynites' stunned eyes. DiMaggio followed with a line single to left. Keller, with the count 2–0, doubled high off the right field wall to drive in both Henrich and DiMaggio and put the Yankees a run ahead. Bill Dickey walked; Gordon doubled over Wasdell's head against the left field wall, driving in two more runs; Rizzuto walked; and finally, Johnny Murphy, Yankee relief pitcher, put Hugh Casey and the Dodgers out of their misery with a roller back to the box. The score: 7–4. Three Dodgers zombied up and out in order in their half of the ninth.

This had been a tight, gritty series until Casey's pitch and Owen's play loosened the Dodgers at the joints. In the final game, the series clincher, Tiny Bonham of the Yankees hurled a four-hitter against Whit Wyatt as Gordon, Keller, and Henrich combined to wreak significant enough havoc to sink the now subdued Dodgers 3–1. DiMaggio's series was mediocre at .263 and a mere one run driven in, but the series MVP, Joe Gordon, at .500 and Charlie Keller at .389, both with five runs knocked in, picked up the slack. Keller especially was remarkable. His ankle was so severely sprained shortly before the series that he sported a cast extending above his knee. I asked him recently how he had managed to ready himself for the series so quickly, and his answer was direct: "I ripped off the cast." Ducky Medwick took the Dodger team honors at the plate with a meager .235 average, and Brooklyn saw its fate reflected in the sad numbers of Pete Reiser at .200 and Dolf Camilli at .167. The Yankees in those days of modest earnings carried home $5,943.31 as their winning share; the Dodgers got $4,829.40 each for the solace of losing.

After the season and the series, DiMaggio and his wife, Dorothy Arnold, awaited the birth of their first child. Joe DiMaggio, Jr.'s, arrival on October 23 provided the great Yankee with his biggest thrill of a year in which thrills were many. DiMaggio sounded like every father when he told reporters the day after his son's birth: "You ought to see the little fellow, he has the most perfect nose. And I never saw such a pair of hands on a baby." Joe, Jr., grew up with the decade, and at 10 he figured in that memorable and poignant photograph taken in 1951 at the end of DiMaggio's career, with father and son walking into the gloom of the visitor's clubhouse corridor at the Polo Grounds during the World Series, a familiar number 5 hunched on DiMaggio's back and a tender arm drooped over his boy's shoulders.

The year ran its course. A crop of movies that made 1941 one of the most brilliant in the history of American film reaped more of its harvest in later summer and fall: *How Green Was My*

Valley, Here Comes Mr. Jordan, Hitchcock's *Suspicion* with Cary Grant and Joan Fontaine, even Disney's *Dumbo.* In his madcap comedy *1941,* director Steven Spielberg alluded to the currency of Disney's animated film when he had Robert Stack, as a commanding general, cry like a baby over *Dumbo* in a Hollywood movie house during an imagined Japanese invasion of Los Angeles. A much younger Robert Stack, coincidentally, was one of the rising stars in 1941; his name had even appeared on the *Sporting News's* list of potential candidates to play Lou Gehrig in *The Pride of the Yankees.*

After the World Series, the football season kicked into full swing with notables such as Frankie Albert, left-handed quarterback for Clark Shaughnessy's radical T formation at Stanford, and Otto Graham, exceptional sophomore passer for Northwestern. Navy beat Army in mid-November 1941, 14–6, before nearly 100,000 at Philadelphia's Municipal Stadium. The game was initiated as always by the on-field procession of midshipmen and cadets. On this November day the huge crowd cheered for minutes on end, seeming to sense that the pageant of American men in uniform would soon display itself less ceremoniously in a world perilously at war.

On the professional football circuit in 1941 George Halas's Chicago Bears, with Sid Luckman doing the passing and Joe Maniaci, Norm Standlee, and Ray Nolting most of the running, won their division in a rugged end of the season game with Green Bay and then coasted to a championship victory over the New York Giants, 37–9. The championship game, played a week after Pearl Harbor, drew only 13,000 disconcerted fans. A few days earlier Bruce Smith, tailback for the undefeated Big Ten champions, the University of Minnesota, had given his Heisman Trophy award acceptance speech. He cut his remarks short because President Roosevelt planned a radio address to the nation at the same time that afternoon to rally the land after the shock of Pearl Harbor. Smith's few words were in a language one now recognizes as prewar Americanese: "Those far eastern fellows may think American boys are soft, but I have had, and even now have, plenty of evidence in black and blue to show that they are making a big mistake."

There was no doubt at the end of the year that America was

a fighting nation. But even before Pearl Harbor and the declaration of war, the isolationist cause in America had begun to founder badly. This became more obvious as the months passed, and in an important editorial for *Life* Walter Lippmann called isolationism a "stupendous failure." By late summer and early fall Charles Lindbergh, whose appearances across the land had coincided with so many of the prominent days of DiMaggio's streak, spoke more desperately and more bitterly. Many in his own organization, America First, had deserted the troubled aviator. Things reached their sorriest level in a particularly vicious September rally in Des Moines, where Lindbergh blamed the Jews of Europe for bringing problems down upon their own heads. After Pearl Harbor, Lindbergh was a man without a cause and almost without a country. He had already quit his Army reserve rank of colonel, and Roosevelt not only refused to recommission him but withheld security clearance so that he could not work for the aircraft industry. The President finally relented when Henry Ford offered Lindbergh a job as consultant on the manufacture of the B-24 Liberator bomber. Even then Lindbergh could barely stifle his admiration for things German; he called the Ford plant at Rouge the highest creation of Faustian man.

The amazing flight of Rudolf Hess that had so startled the world near the beginning of DiMaggio's streak quieted as a story later in 1941, primarily because the British put a lid of absolute secrecy on the deputy führer's confinement. Churchill wished to keep Hitler off guard, and he also knew how furious the entire incident made Stalin. Hess's efforts to gain an English alliance against Russia rendered him a symbol of Nazi perfidy, and even if he were repentant—which he wasn't—the Russians would keep him locked up in Berlin's Spandau Castle until he died.

The military campaign along the huge Russian front in the latter half of 1941 remained the focus of the European war. Of the millions who fought, tens of thousands died; of the tens of millions who merely tried to live, hundreds of thousands were executed. Hitler's 10-week projection for taking Russia had not counted on the endless supply of manpower and the capacity of the Russian nation to endure the bitterest savagery the world had ever known. Soon the Nazi armies would find themselves bogged down in the mud and snows of the Russian plains and forests, facing the doomed prospect of having to lay in for a long siege of the two cities they had planned to capture weeks before: Leningrad in the north and Stalingrad in the south. These struggles would change the course of the European war.

It is sad testimony to the vigilance of the western democracies that the most extreme measures of the Nazi program, the murder of civilian populations and the full-scale siphoning off of European Jewry into SS detention and labor camps, were relegated to the back pages of the news late in 1941. Editors were reluctant to give prominent space to what they fervently hoped was just rumor. Civilized nations did not dematerialize populations. What no one knew at this time, however, proved even more appalling. Hitler's lieutenant, Reinhard Heydrich, had formed an addendum of sorts to the German plans for the invasion of Russia, plotting the elimination of so-called "racially inferior" populations of the captive nations. Göring put the second piece of the puzzle in place in regard to the final solution. He cabled Heydrich on July 31, 1941, "to carry out all the necessary preparations with regard to organizational and financial matters for bringing about a complete solution of the Jewish question in the German sphere of influence in Europe."

The world would all too soon see the undeniable result of Heydrich and Göring's newly conceived horror when 33,000 Ukrainian Jews were rounded up from the lovely city of Kiev and its environs and shot in an unspeakable series of mass executions at Babi Yar. Matters would get even worse through the bone-chilling Russian winter. By year's end the casualties for the campaign, including civilians and soldiers, reached close to 6 million. "Never before" is the only accurate way to describe what took place along the eastern front of the European war, and the experience inured Germany for a pan-European holocaust in regard to which much of the modern world has long intoned "Never again."

The emerging story of the war for America after DiMaggio's streak and into the fall and winter of 1941 concerns Japan, the far east, and the Pacific theater. There had been hints throughout 1941 of more than a mere tropical storm on this horizon, but Roosevelt's and the Defense Department's hearts and minds were forever at sea in the Atlantic. A week after DiMaggio's streak ended, Japan moved its armies into Indochina. In response, the United States froze Japanese assets, as we had done to the Germans and the Italians in June. Though months earlier the Japanese had worked out the full scenario for a sneak attack on the U.S. naval installation in Hawaii, diplomatically at least Japan wished to maintain contact with Washington. America offered a nonaggression pact in return for guarantees from the Japanese for a free China. A diplomatic stall set in, continuing to the very hour when the Japanese raided Pearl Harbor.

For its issue just after the attack on Pearl Harbor, as part of a story that had been prepared earlier, *Life* magazine hit the streets with a huge picture of a bucolic teenager, starlet Patricia Peardon, in the innocent Moss Hart Broadway musical *Junior Miss.* All was sweet innocence. The next week *Life* grew somber and tense. Its cover was an image of the American flag. The war raged with the United States fully in it when Hitler's Germany joined its Japanese ally by declaring war on us before the formality of our doing so on them.

Little in a culture as various as America's probably ever was as simple as many believed (and still do) before World War II, but that doesn't lessen the feeling for the last year before our full immersion into an awful conflict, a year that both forges and closes the myth of an epoch to which Joe DiMaggio's 56-game hitting streak contributes its bounty of energy, endurance, and grace.

AFTERWORD

When *Streak* first appeared in 1988, the Harvard polymath Stephen Jay Gould reviewed it in *The New York Review of Books*. What intrigued me was a statistical study Gould mentioned in which his colleague Ed Purcell, a Nobel laureate in physics, measured the comparative variables in baseball achievements. Purcell's conclusion was that "frequency" models for every important record but one fell within reasonable statistical probabilities. Joe DiMaggio's 56-game hitting streak, from May 15 to July 17, 1941, stood alone as a kind of freak of baseball nature.

Purcell's point is that the 56-game hitting streak was not only an extraordinary accomplishment for all the reasons usually adduced—DiMaggio's unique talent, concentration, consistency, and endurance—but because the closest competitors miss by so far. Given the profile of other baseball records, Wee Willie Keeler, George Sisler, Tommy Holmes, or Pete Rose should be closer to DiMaggio's 56-straight than they are. Therein lies the unique glory of DiMaggio's great record. Purcell frames it this way to make his comparison clear: There is a greater chance that the major leagues will be able to boast of four future lifetime .400 hitters, each of whom will play in at least a thousand games, than that one player will equal DiMaggio's hitting streak record.

Purcell drops down to .350 so that he might compare something that actually happened to DiMaggio's achievement. How many players would have to average .350 lifetime with a thousand games under their belts to equal the comparative odds of breaking DiMaggio's streak record? Fifty-two. How many have done so? Only three: Ty Cobb, Rogers Hornsby, and Shoeless Joe Jackson. Good for them. But math is unforgiving. Where are the forty-nine others whose presence would provide a statistical equivalent for the streak? Nowhere to be found. Even Ted Williams misses the list, with his .344 lifetime average.

Fifteen years have passed since I began working on *Streak*, reconstructing and recapturing its wonderful moments game by game, at bat by at bat. The question most often asked me by readers, interviewers, and friends bears on the observations by Stephen Jay Gould and Ed Purcell. How long do I think the streak record will stand? All I can say is, a long time. I am not even thinking about intangibles, such as improved relief pitching, better fielding, night baseball, and jet lag. Nor for me is it simply the statistical unlikelihood that anyone will soon or ever break the record, though that element does enter in. It is rather the mounting pressure of the enterprise. Fans over the last several decades have seen what the pressure of a streak does even to brilliant hitters like Pete Rose and Paul Molitor. Streaks are charted from their early games and become media frenzy by the time they reach the high 20s. DiMaggio had a run of only eight games when he said the pressure for him—beyond the normal desire to rip the ball as hard as he could on every at bat—was considerable. He claimed that his stomach began to knot up around game 38 when he was after George Sisler's modern-day record of 41, set in 1922, and did not relax until after he had surpassed Wee Willie Keeler's 1897 record of 44 straight.

The games after that were less intense, measured partly by DiMaggio's sheer doggedness at the plate under any conditions and by the public relations Juggernauts loosed in every visiting city as the Yanks and Joe came to town. DiMaggio told reporters that he felt fairly relaxed after he set the record. He was loose for the last twelve games, and even got a healthy percentage of his hits in early-inning at bats. Extending a streak is nothing like chasing down another. The gut-wrenching days for DiMaggio occurred when he was hard on Sisler's and then on Keeler's heels. (An oddity of streak lore is that DiMaggio was told of Keeler's record only when he was approaching Sisler's.) As for the pressure a ballplayer would face today if nearing DiMaggio's 56-game record, even Joe blanched at the thought when I asked him about it on the phone: "Oh, my!"

The last sentence in the preceding paragraph is blessed with a seemingly innocuous prepositional phrase: on the phone. Joe DiMaggio clearly did not like to talk to those writing books about him. I know. It took me six years to reach him, and I had to go through the good offices of A. Bartlett Giamatti, at that time president of the National League, to speak to DiMaggio at all. I knew Giamatti from my days at Yale University, and as a favor he convinced DiMaggio that I wasn't one of those New York intellectuals intent on ferreting out the personal secrets of his life. DiMaggio had an almost preternatural distrust of writers because he feared they wished to pry into matters best consigned to silence: his life with Marilyn Monroe; his emotional disconnect from his troubled son, Joe Jr.; favors that may have been done for him by Italian compatriots with all-too-predictable connections to the underworld; his cold-comfort friendships with hangers-on who wished to extract from him more than he was willing to give.

All these matters are charted without charity in a recent biographical work on DiMaggio, which tends to make this quiet, insecure, and somewhat sad man into a much worse human being than he was. I took away a very different impression of DiMaggio when I spoke to him. I found him quietly engaging, mostly on the subject of his hitting streak but also generally on his entire baseball career. He called from San Francisco. My young son took the call and his own words are forever etched in memory: "Dad, Joe DiMaggio is on the phone." DiMaggio told me that Giamatti had asked him to call because I wasn't a journalist after dirt—just an innocent-enough teacher at Columbia University—and because my work on the hitting streak was mostly about baseball. If I wanted to talk with him, well, then, maybe he could help, though "Please," he said, "nothing personal."

DiMaggio was unfailingly polite but clearly hesitant—even halting—for the first few moments he spoke to me. He truly thought I was after something, and he asked three or four times whether my interest was in baseball or in something else. He began by asking me what I taught at Columbia. Did I teach history? Are there courses in baseball history? He rambled for a moment about a writer in New York who said that because he, DiMaggio, was once seen having dinner at an Italian restaurant in Cleveland, he must have been a mobster. DiMaggio himself was steering the conversation toward dangerous territory.

Was this a test? I sensed that I had best turn the talk to baseball, to 1941, and to the hitting streak. So I asked DiMaggio when he first knew he had a streak going. He said ballplayers always remember when they take the collar, so he must have known from the beginning because for a fact he hadn't taken the collar since May 14, 1941. But he began thinking about the streak around games 15 and 16 when the Yanks were in Boston for a Memorial Day doubleheader. He had flu symptoms and his whole back and arm ached. McCarthy (the Yankees' manager) thought of scratching him from the lineup, but DiMaggio said he would play if Rizzuto would get his butt further out toward centerfield from shortstop to help with relay throws. Rizzuto or no, DiMaggio threw the ball every which way but straight in Fenway Park that day, committing three throwing errors. For good measure he muffed a ground-ball single. At the plate he managed to pop a wind-blown fly into right field for his only hit in game two. He recalls having barely kept the streak alive under miserable conditions, though at game 16 it mattered less to him than a cup of hot soup and getting into a warm bed.

I asked him when he really started caring about the streak. He said he was just glad the Yanks were winning some games at that point, but around games 32 and 33 against Detroit, when he got seven straight hits, he began to think he would go on for a good run: "I wasn't thinking consecutive streak games; I was thinking consecutive streak hits." (What was *that* record? Later I checked— Pinky Higgins's 12 straight hits.)

The legendarily silent DiMaggio was almost abuzz. He was chatting away about baseball, and he was wistful only that he couldn't remember things with the clarity he would have liked. There was but little of the DiMaggio whose reputation has been so tarnished of late, little of his glumness and reticence. And there were no mercenary moments at all. I heard not one ring of the cash register that was supposed to sound whenever DiMaggio opened his mouth. He asked for nothing, and he even told me that his first wife, Dorothy Arnold, had left him a collection of clippings from the early 1940s—maybe I would like to look at them. He warmed up more and more as I asked him questions about moments in the streak that the newspapers recorded but that still held some mystery for me—about tough grounders that might have been potential errors, about outfield catches, about the pressure that built during games in which he was hitless until later innings. Even when he had no recall of particular moments he talked fondly of the players involved, of what he thought of the pitchers in the American League, of how he changed his approach at the plate during the streak. For example, he hacked at pitches earlier in the count because bases on balls were what he feared most.

At the time we spoke my book was almost ready to go to press. To be honest, I already knew most of what he had told me, and I knew that he had misremembered some of it. But the talk I had with him struck another chord. DiMaggio probably spoke more animatedly than he had intended because he so clearly missed the era that he helped to define. It soothed him to remember the 1940s. He spoke about living in New York (I told him I taught just forty blocks up the street from his West End Avenue apartment), and he spoke about the ride to Yankee Stadium, often in Lefty Gomez's car up the West Side Highway (a portion of which now bears his name). He spoke of Bobby Feller, whom he said he could handle pretty well; of Ted Williams, who could hit the hell out of the ball; of Mickey Mantle, who was "just a kid." When I mentioned some particular moments during the hitting streak he sounded almost eager to take his cuts again: "Oh, Johnny Babich," he said about a Philadelphia A's pitcher, "he wouldn't throw me anything near the plate. I don't know why. Everyone else tried to get me out on pitches I could swing at." DiMaggio recalled how in game 40 of the streak he took one of Babich's hopelessly outside pitches, stepped nearly across the plate, and thrashed the ball midriff-high on a line right past the pitcher's mound and out into center field. Babich spun like a dervish dancer. It was one of the few times that the tone of DiMaggio's voice became almost boastful. Not a Ted Williams boast, mind you, but something camouflaged as a self-congratulatory chuckle.

After nearly an hour on the phone I asked DiMaggio whether playing for the Yanks in New York, especially in the year after Ruth departed and before Mantle came into his own, added to the mythology of his career. Silence. Then DiMaggio said, in an understatement that still registers for anyone who ever had the privilege of watching this wonderful athlete at bat or in the field, "Well, I think the way I played made my career."

Here is a man whose grace on the diamond and whose talismanic name embody the best of a game that is itself the best that sport has to offer. DiMaggio is now dead, but there is much that can be said on behalf of him and others who live on in our imaginations and who will continue to do so for as long as baseball lives on.

APPENDIX
Box Scores

GAME 1: MAY 15

CHICAGO	ab	r	h	po	a	e		NEW YORK	ab	r	h	po	a	e
Knick'ker, 2b	5	3	4	5	2	0		Rizzuto, ss	4	1	1	4	1	1
Appling, ss	4	2	1	1	6	0		Rolfe, 3b	4	0	1	0	1	0
Kuhel, 1b	4	2	1	8	1	0		Keller, lf	4	0	1	3	0	0
Wright, rf	5	2	2	4	0	0		DiMaggio, cf	4	0	1	4	0	1
Lodig'ni, 3b	5	0	0	1	4	0		Gordon, 1b	3	0	1	6	0	0
Kreevich, cf	5	0	0	2	0	0		Rosar, c	4	0	2	5	0	0
Hoag, lf	5	2	4	2	0	0		Bordagaray, rf	4	0	1	1	0	0
Tresh, c	5	0	1	4	0	0		Priddy, 2b	4	0	0	4	4	0
Smith, p	5	2	1	0	1	0		Bonham, p	1	0	1	0	1	0
								Stanceu, p	1	0	0	0	0	0
Total	43	13	14	27	14	0		aCrosetti	1	0	0	0	0	0
								Branch, p	0	0	0	0	1	0
								bRuffing	1	0	0	0	0	0
								Total	35	1	9	27	8	2

aBatted for Stanceu in seventh.
bBatted for Branch in ninth.

Chicago	2	0	1	1	1	0	4	2	2	—	13
New York	1	0	0	0	0	0	0	0	0	—	1

Runs batted in—Wright 4, DiMaggio, Kuhel 2, Knickerbocker 3, Kreevich, Hoag, Tresh.
Two-base hits—Rizzuto, Hoag, Smith. Home runs—Kuhel, Wright, Knickerbocker. Double play—Appling, Knickerbocker, and Kuhel. Bases on balls—off Smith 1, off Stanceu 2, off Branch 3, off Bonham 1. Struck out—by Smith 4, by Bonham 4, by Stanceu 1. Hits—off Bonham 7 in 4⅓ innings, off Stanceu 2, in 2⅔ innings. Wild pitch—Branch. Losing pitcher—Bonham. Umpires—Grieve, Ormsby, and Hubbard. Time of game—2:10. Attendance—9,040.

GAME 2: MAY 16

CHICAGO	ab	r	h	po	a	e		NEW YORK	ab	r	h	po	a	e
Knick'ker, 2b	4	1	1	0	3	0		Bordagaray, rf	4	0	0	2	0	0
Appling, ss	4	1	1	3	1	0		Rolfe, 3b	4	1	1	0	2	0
Kuhel, 1b	3	1	0	7	1	0		Keller, lf	4	1	1	4	0	0
Wright, rf	4	0	0	1	0	0		DiMaggio, cf	4	2	2	4	0	0
Lodig'ni, 3b	4	0	1	0	1	0		Gordon, 2b	3	1	1	3	3	0
Kreevich, cf	4	0	2	3	0	0		Rosar, c	3	1	2	4	0	0
Hoag, lf	4	0	1	3	1	0		Dickey, c	0	0	0	1	0	0
Tresh, c	4	1	1	7	0	0		Crosetti, ss	2	0	1	1	3	1
Lee, p	2	1	0	0	0	0		Sturm, 1b	3	0	0	8	0	0
								bRuffing	1	0	1	0	0	0
Total	33	5	7	a24	7	0		Breuer, p	2	0	0	0	0	0
								Murphy, p	1	0	0	0	0	0
								Total	31	6	9	27	8	1

aNone out when winning run scored.
bBatted for Sturm in ninth.

Chicago	0	0	0	0	5	0	0	0	0	—	5
New York	2	1	1	0	0	0	0	0	2	—	6

Runs batted in—Keller 2, Sturm, DiMaggio, Knickerbocker, Appling, Wright, Kreevich, Gordon, Ruffing. Two-base hits—Rosar, Knickerbocker. Three-base hits—DiMaggio, Gordon. Home runs—Keller, DiMaggio. Stolen base—Kreevich. Double plays—Gordon and Sturm; Crosetti, Gordon, and Sturm; Kuhel, Appling, and Kuhel. Bases on balls—off Lee 4, off Breuer 2. Struck out—by Lee 5, by Breuer 4, by Murphy 1. Hits—off Breuer 7 in 5⅔ innings. Wild pitch—Breuer. Winning pitcher—Murphy. Umpires—Ormsby, Hubbard, and Grieve. Time of game—1:52. Attendance—1,483. Ladies day.

STREAK

GAME 3: MAY 17

CHICAGO	ab	r	h	po	a	e
Knick'ker, 2b	4	1	1	1	2	0
Appling, ss	5	0	1	4	1	0
Kuhel, 1b	4	0	1	4	0	0
Wright, rf	5	1	0	2	0	0
Lodig'ni, 3b	3	1	1	2	2	0
Kreevich, cf	3	0	1	3	0	0
Hoag, lf	4	0	3	4	0	0
Tresh, c	4	0	1	7	2	0
Rigney, p	3	0	0	0	0	0
Total	35	3	9	27	7	0

NEW YORK	ab	r	h	po	a	e
Sturm, 1b	5	0	1	13	3	0
Rolfe, 3b	3	0	1	1	1	0
Henrich, rf	3	0	0	0	0	0
DiMaggio, cf	3	1	1	2	0	0
Keller, lf	4	0	0	1	0	0
Gordon, 2b	2	1	0	2	5	2
Dickey, c	3	0	2	3	1	0
aPriddy	0	0	0	0	0	0
Crosetti, ss	2	0	0	1	3	1
bSelkirk	0	0	0	0	0	0
Rizzuto, ss	1	0	0	1	1	0
Chandler, p	3	0	0	3	5	0
cRosar	1	0	0	0	0	0
Total	30	2	5	27	19	3

aBatted for Crosetti in seventh.
bRan for Dickey in ninth.
cBatted for Chandler in ninth.

```
Chicago .............................................  0 1 0   0 0 1   0 0 1   —  3
New York ...........................................  0 0 0   0 1 0   0 0 1   —  2
```

Runs batted in—Hoag 2, Dickey, Wright, Rosar.
Two-base hits—Dickey, Lodigiani, Knickerbocker. Three-base hit—Kreevich. Stolen base—Gordon. Double play—Crosetti and Sturm. Bases on balls—off Rigney 7, off Chandler 4. Struck out—by Rigney 5, by Chandler 2. Umpires—Hubbard, Grieve, and Ormsby. Time of game—2:18. Attendance—10,372.

GAME 4: MAY 18

ST. LOUIS	ab	r	h	po	a	e
Lucadello, ss	5	1	2	4	3	0
Estalella, lf	3	0	1	1	0	0
Laabs, rf	3	0	0	3	0	0
Judnich, cf	4	0	0	1	0	0
Cullenbine, 1b	3	0	1	9	1	0
Clift, 3b	4	1	1	0	0	0
Heffner, 2b	4	0	1	2	1	0
Grube, c	4	0	1	3	1	1
Harris, p	1	0	0	0	2	0
aFerrell	1	0	0	0	0	0
Niggeling, p	1	0	0	1	0	0
bSwift	0	0	0	0	0	0
Total	33	2	6	24	8	1

NEW YORK	ab	r	h	po	a	e
Sturm, 1b	5	2	1	9	0	0
Rolfe, 3b	4	3	2	0	2	0
Henrich, rf	5	1	1	2	0	0
DiMaggio, cf	3	3	3	5	0	0
Keller, lf	5	1	2	1	0	0
Gordon, 2b	3	2	2	4	1	0
Dickey, c	4	0	1	5	0	0
Crosetti, ss	5	0	2	1	3	0
Gomez, p	5	0	2	0	1	0
Total	39	12	16	27	7	0

aBatted for Harris in fifth.
bBatted for Niggeling in ninth.

```
St. Louis ...........................................  1 1 0   0 0 0   0 0 0   —   2
New York ..........................................  2 2 0   4 1 0   3 0 X   —  12
```

Runs batted in—Keller 2, Gordon 5, Clift, Rolfe, DiMaggio, Dickey, Crosetti 2.
Two-base hits—Lucadello, Henrich, Rolfe, DiMaggio, Keller. Home runs—Clift, Gordon. Stolen bases—Lucadello, Laabs. Double play—Lucadello and Cullenbine. Bases on balls—off Harris 4, off Niggeling 3, off Gomez 5. Struck out—by Harris 1, by Gomez 5, by Niggeling 2. Hits—off Harris 11 in 4 innings. Wild pitch—Niggeling. Losing pitcher—Harris. Umpires—Rue, Summers, and Stewart. Time of game—2:30. Attendance—30,109.

APPENDIX

GAME 5: MAY 19

ST. LOUIS	ab	r	h	po	a	e		NEW YORK	ab	r	h	po	a	e
Lucadello, ss	5	0	0	1	2	0		Sturm, 1b	4	0	1	13	1	0
Estalella, lf	4	2	2	2	0	0		Rolfe, 3b	4	0	0	0	6	0
Laabs, rf	4	1	1	2	0	0		Henrich, rf	4	0	0	2	0	0
Judnich, cf	4	1	0	3	0	0		DiMaggio, cf	3	0	1	4	1	0
Cullenbine, 1b	4	1	1	12	0	0		Keller, lf	4	0	0	1	0	0
Clift, 3b	3	0	1	2	1	0		Gordon, 2b	3	0	0	0	2	1
Heffner, 2b	4	0	1	3	7	0		Dickey, c	3	1	1	6	1	0
Ferrell, c	3	0	1	2	0	0		Crosetti, ss	3	0	1	1	3	1
Galehouse, p	4	0	1	0	1	0		Russo, p	1	0	0	0	0	0
								aSelkirk	1	0	0	0	0	0
Total	35	5	8	27	11	0		Peek, p	0	0	0	0	2	0
								bRizzuto	0	0	0	0	0	0
								Stanceu, p	0	0	0	0	0	0
								Total	30	1	4	27	16	2

aBatted for Russo in sixth.
bBatted for Peek in eighth.

St. Louis	3 0 0	2 0 0	0 0 0	—	5
New York	0 0 0	0 0 0	0 1 0	—	1

Runs batted in—Clift, Heffner 2, Cullenbine 2, Dickey. Two-base hits—Heffner, Ferrell, Cullenbine, DiMaggio, Sturm. Home run—Dickey. Double play—Galehouse, Lucadello, and Cullenbine. Bases on balls—off Galehouse 3, off Russo 5. Struck out—by Galehouse 2, by Russo 2, by Stanceu 2. Hits—off Russo 6 in 6 innings, off Peek 1 in 2 innings. Wild pitch—Russo. Losing pitcher—Russo. Umpires—Summers, Stewart, and Rue. Time of game—2:08. Attendance—5,388.

GAME 6: MAY 20

ST. LOUIS	ab	r	h	po	a	e		NEW YORK	ab	r	h	po	a	e
Lucadello, ss	5	1	3	5	2	3		Sturm, 1b	5	1	3	6	0	0
Estalella, lf	5	0	0	0	0	0		Rolfe, 3b	5	1	1	0	0	0
Laabs, rf	1	0	0	0	0	0		Henrich, rf	4	1	1	3	1	0
Grace, rf	4	0	1	4	0	0		DiMaggio, cf	5	1	1	5	0	0
Judnich, cf	5	1	1	0	1	0		Keller, lf	4	1	0	2	0	0
McQuinn, 1b	0	0	0	0	0	0		Gordon, 2b	3	1	0	1	1	1
Cull'bine, 1b-cf	3	3	3	9	3	1		Dickey, c	4	1	3	8	2	0
Clift, 3b	4	3	3	2	3	0		Crosetti, ss	3	1	1	2	3	0
Heffner, 2b	4	0	1	4	5	0		Ruffing, p	1	2	0	0	0	0
Ferrell, c	4	1	1	2	0	0		Murphy, p	1	0	0	0	0	0
Auker, p	3	0	0	0	0	0		Branch, p	0	0	0	0	0	0
Caster, p	0	0	0	0	1	1		Total	35	10	10	27	7	1
Total	38	9	13	a26	15	6								

aTwo out when winning run scored.

St. Louis	0 2 0	0 1 2	0 3 1	—	9
New York	0 0 1	0 4 1	0 3 1	—	10

Runs batted in—Cullenbine 2, Clift 4, Estalella, Sturm, Henrich 2, DiMaggio, Ferrell, Dickey 3. Two-base hit—Lucadello. Three-base hit—Judnich. Home runs—Cullenbine, Clift 2, Dickey. Double plays—Heffner, Lucadello, and Cullenbine; Heffner and Cullenbine; Clift, Heffner, and Cullenbine; Caster, Lucadello, and Heffner. Bases on balls—off Auker 4, off Murphy 1, off Caster 1, off Ruffing 1. Struck out—by Auker 1, by Ruffing 4, by Murphy 2. Hits—off Ruffing 7 in 6 innings, off Murphy 4 in 2 innings (none out in ninth), off Auker 8 in 7 innings (none out in eighth). Hit by pitcher—by Caster 1. Wild pitch—Murphy. Winning pitcher—Branch. Losing pitcher—Caster. Umpires—Stewart, Rue, and Summers. Time of game—2:30. Attendance—3,628.

GAME 7: MAY 21

DETROIT	ab	r	h	po	a	e
Mullin, cf	3	1	1	4	0	1
Gehr'ger, 2b	3	0	0	1	2	0
Radcliff, lf	4	1	2	2	0	0
York, 1b.................	4	0	0	9	0	0
Campbell, rf	4	0	1	6	0	0
Stainback, rf	0	0	0	1	0	1
McNair, 3b..............	5	1	2	0	2	0
Tebbetts, c	4	0	1	5	0	0
Croucher, ss............	3	1	0	0	2	0
Rowe, p	2	0	0	0	0	0
[a]Sullivan.................	1	0	0	0	0	0
Benton, p	1	0	0	0	1	0
Total	34	4	7	[d]28	7	2

NEW YORK	ab	r	h	po	a	e
Sturm, 1b	5	3	3	8	3	0
Rolfe, 3b	6	2	4	2	5	0
Henrich, rf..............	5	0	3	2	0	0
DiMaggio, cf	5	0	2	1	1	0
Keller, lf	2	0	0	2	1	0
Gordon, 2b..............	5	0	0	1	2	0
Dickey, c	4	0	0	11	0	0
Crosetti, ss	3	0	1	2	1	0
[b]Rosar....................	1	0	0	0	0	0
Rizzuto, ss..............	1	0	0	1	0	0
Donald, p	3	0	1	0	0	1
[c]Selkirk.................	1	0	0	0	0	0
Stanceu, p..............	1	0	0	0	0	0
Total	42	5	14	30	13	1

[a]Batted for Rowe in seventh.
[b]Batted for Crosetti in eighth.
[c]Batted for Donald in eighth.
[d]One out when winning run scored.

Detroit	0	1	0	0	0	0	2	1	0	0 —	4
New York	1	0	0	1	0	0	0	0	2	1 —	5

Runs batted in—DiMaggio, Tebbetts, Rolfe 2, Mullin 2, McNair, Henrich 2.
Two-base hits—Tebbetts, Donald, Sturm, Rolfe, Radcliff, Henrich. Three-base hit—Rolfe. Home run—Mullin. Double plays—Rolfe and Sturm; Keller, Rolfe, Sturm, and Gordon. Bases on balls—off Rowe 2, off Stanceu 2, off Donald 4, off Benton 3. Struck out—by Rowe 2, by Donald 7, by Benton 3, by Stanceu 2. Hits—off Rowe 9 in 6 innings, off Donald 7 in 7 innings. Hit by pitcher—by Donald 1. Winning pitcher—Stanceu. Losing pitcher—Benton. Umpires—Rue, Summers, and Stewart. Time of game—2:47. Attendance—10,596.

APPENDIX

GAME 8: MAY 22

DETROIT	ab	r	h	po	a	e
Mullin, cf	3	3	1	2	0	0
Gehr'ger, 2b	5	0	2	3	0	0
Radcliff, lf	4	1	2	1	0	0
York, 1b	5	0	1	3	1	0
Campbell, rf	5	1	2	3	0	1
McNair, 3b	4	0	1	3	2	0
aStainback	0	0	0	0	0	0
Sullivan, c	4	0	1	7	1	0
Croucher, ss	2	0	1	1	3	0
Newsom, p	3	0	0	1	0	0
McKain, p	0	0	0	0	1	0
bTebbetts	1	0	0	0	0	0
Total	36	5	11	24	8	1

NEW YORK	ab	r	h	po	a	e
Sturm, 1b	5	1	2	8	0	1
Rolfe, 3b	4	1	2	0	1	0
Henrich, rf	3	1	2	1	0	0
DiMaggio, cf	4	0	1	1	0	0
Keller, lf	4	0	0	1	0	0
Gordon, 2b	4	1	1	6	5	0
Dickey, c	4	2	2	6	1	0
Crosetti, ss	4	0	2	4	3	1
Peek, p	3	0	0	0	3	0
Branch, p	1	0	0	0	0	0
Total	36	6	12	27	13	2

aBatted for McNair in eighth.
bBatted for McKain in ninth.

Detroit	1	0	0	1	0	1	1	0	1	—	5
New York	2	0	1	0	0	2	0	1	X	—	6

Runs batted in—Radcliff 2, Henrich 2, DiMaggio, Campbell, Sullivan, Dickey 2, Crosetti, York. Two-base hits—Sullivan, Dickey. Three-base hit—Crosetti. Home runs—Henrich, Dickey. Double plays—Gordon, Crosetti, and Sturm; Crosetti, Gordon, and Sturm; Gordon and Sturm. Bases on balls—off Peek 4, off Branch 1, off Newsom 1. Struck out—by Peek 4, by Newsom 4, by McKain 3, by Branch 1. Hits—off Newsom 8 in 5⅓ innings, off Peek 9 in 7 innings (none out in eighth). Hit by pitcher—by Newsom 1. Winning pitcher—Peek. Losing pitcher—Newsom. Umpires—Summers, Stewart, and Rue. Time of game—2:25. Attendance—10,156.

GAME 9: MAY 23

BOSTON	ab	r	h	po	a	e		NEW YORK	ab	r	h	po	a	e
D. DiM'gio, cf	4	1	2	1	0	1		Sturm, 1b	5	2	1	7	0	0
Finney, 1b	6	2	2	10	0	0		Rolfe, 3b	5	2	1	1	1	0
Williams, lf	3	0	1	3	0	0		Henrich, rf	2	2	1	2	0	0
Foxx, 3b	4	0	0	2	0	1		J. DiMaggio, cf	5	0	1	3	0	0
Cronin, ss	4	2	2	0	1	0		Keller, lf	3	3	3	2	0	0
Fox, rf	4	1	2	4	0	0		Gordon, 2b	3	0	1	2	4	0
L. Newsome, 2b	4	0	1	1	7	0		Priddy, 2b	2	0	0	0	1	0
Peacock, c	4	1	1	6	1	0		Dickey, c	4	0	1	6	1	0
Dobson, p	0	0	0	0	0	0		Crosetti, ss	3	0	1	4	4	0
Harris, p	0	1	0	0	1	0		Chandler, p	3	0	0	0	0	0
[a]Spence	1	0	0	0	0	0		Stanceu, p	0	0	0	0	0	0
Dickman, p	0	0	0	0	0	0		Breuer, p	1	0	0	0	0	1
[b]Pytlak	1	1	1	0	0	0		Murphy, p	0	0	0	0	0	0
H. Newsome, p	0	0	0	0	0	0		[d]Selkirk	1	0	0	0	0	0
[c]Judd	1	0	1	0	0	0								
Ryba, p	0	0	0	0	1	0								
Total	36	9	13	27	11	2		Total	37	9	10	27	11	1

[a]Batted for Harris in sixth.
[b]Batted for Dickman in eighth.
[c]Batted for H. Newsome in ninth.
[d]Batted for Murphy in ninth.

Boston	2	0	0		0	2	1		0	2	2	—	9
New York	2	2	1		0	1	0		1	2	0	—	9

Stopped by darkness.

Runs batted in—Finney 3, Keller, J. DiMaggio 2, Henrich 2, Dickey, Williams 3, D. DiMaggio, Priddy, Judd 2.

Two-base hits—Keller 2. Three-base hit—Keller. Home runs—Henrich, Finney. Double plays—Gordon, Crosetti, and Sturm 2; Rolfe, Gordon, and Sturm. Bases on balls—off Chandler 3, off Harris 1, off Stanceu 3, off Dickman 2, off Breuer 2, off H. Newsome 2, off Dobson 4, off Murphy 1, off Ryba 1. Struck out—by Chandler 1, by Harris 2, by Breuer 2, by Dickman 2, by Ryba 1. Hits—off Dobson 3 in 1⅔ innings, off Harris 4 in 3⅓ innings, off Dickman 1 in 2 innings, off H. Newsome 2 in 1 inning, off Chandler 7 in 5 innings (none out in sixth), off Stanceu 2 in 1 inning (none out in seventh), off Breuer 3 in 2 innings (none out in ninth). Wild pitch—Chandler. Umpires—Hubbard, Ormsby, and Rommel. Time of game—3:05. Attendance—8,584. Ladies day.

GAME 10: MAY 24

BOSTON	ab	r	h	po	a	e	NEW YORK	ab	r	h	po	a	e
D. DiM'gio, cf	4	0	1	0	0	1	Sturm, 1b	5	1	1	8	0	0
Finney, 1b	4	0	0	10	1	0	Rolfe, 3b	4	1	0	1	0	0
Williams, lf	3	3	2	1	0	0	Henrich, rf	4	1	1	4	0	0
Foxx, 3b	4	1	1	2	2	1	J. DiMaggio, cf	4	2	1	1	0	0
Cronin, ss	4	1	2	1	3	0	Gordon, 2b	4	0	0	4	3	0
Fox, rf	4	0	2	2	0	1	Keller, lf	3	0	1	3	0	0
L. Newsome, 2b	3	0	0	2	2	0	Rosar, c	4	1	3	3	1	0
dJudd	1	0	0	0	0	0	Crosetti, ss	3	1	1	3	3	1
Pytlak, c	5	0	0	5	0	1	Gomez, p	2	0	0	0	0	0
Johnson, p	3	1	1	1	1	0	Branch, p	0	0	0	0	0	0
Fleming, p	0	0	0	0	0	0	aRuffing	1	0	1	0	0	0
cSpence	1	0	0	0	0	0	bBordagaray	0	0	0	0	0	0
Wilson, p	0	0	0	0	0	0	Murphy, p	1	0	0	0	1	0
Total	36	6	9	24	9	4	Total	35	7	9	27	8	1

aBatted for Branch in seventh.
bRan for Ruffing in seventh.
cBatted for Fleming in eighth.
dBatted for L. Newsome in ninth.

```
Boston ..............................................  0 0 2   1 1 0   2 0 0  —  6
New York ...........................................  0 0 0   2 0 1   4 0 X  —  7
```

Runs batted in—Foxx, Cronin 2, D. DiMaggio, Keller, Fox 2, Gordon, Sturm 2, J. DiMaggio. Two-base hit—Cronin. Three-base hits—Foxx, D. DiMaggio. Bases on balls—off Gomez 5, off Murphy 3, off Wilson 2. Struck out—by Gomez 2, by Johnson 3, by Fleming 1, by Wilson 1. Hits—off Gomez 9 in 6⅓ innings, off Branch 0 in ⅔ inning, off Johnson 9 in 6⅔ innings, off Fleming 0 in ⅓ inning. Passed ball—Pytlak. Winning pitcher—Branch. Losing pitcher—Johnson. Umpires—Ormsby, Rommel, and Hubbard. Time of game—2:23. Attendance—20,935.

GAME 11: MAY 25

BOSTON	ab	r	h	po	a	e
D. DiM'gio, cf............	4	3	1	3	0	0
Finney, 1b................	4	3	2	11	1	0
Williams, lf..............	5	2	4	1	0	0
Foxx, 3b..................	5	0	1	3	1	2
Cronin, ss................	3	2	3	2	1	1
Fox, rf...................	4	0	0	2	0	0
L. Newsome, 2b..........	5	0	1	3	3	0
Peacock, c................	5	0	2	2	0	1
Grove, p..................	5	0	0	0	3	0
Total	40	10	14	27	9	4

NEW YORK	ab	r	h	po	a	e
Sturm, 1b	3	0	1	4	1	0
Rolfe, 3b	4	0	0	0	0	0
Henrich, rf.............	4	0	0	0	0	0
J. DiMaggio, cf.........	4	0	1	2	0	1
Rosar, c	4	1	1	14	1	0
Gordon, 2b.............	4	1	0	2	0	0
Keller, lf................	4	1	1	1	0	0
Crosetti, ss	3	0	1	3	2	0
Russo, p................	2	0	1	1	2	0
Stanceu, p..............	0	0	0	0	0	0
[a]Bordagaray	1	0	1	0	0	0
Bonhan, p..............	0	0	0	0	0	0
[b]Rizzuto.................	1	0	0	0	0	0
Total	34	3	7	27	6	1

[a]Batted for Stanceu in seventh.
[b]Batted for Bonham in ninth.

Boston	0	1	3	0	0	0	4	2	0	—	10
New York...	0	0	0	3	0	0	0	0	0	—	3

Runs batted in—L. Newsome, Williams 2, Fox 2, Keller 3, Peacock 2, Foxx 2.

Two-base hits—Cronin, D. DiMaggio, Williams. Home run—Keller. Stolen bases—L. Newsome, Gordon. Double play—Foxx, Newsome, and Finney. Bases on balls—off Russo 2, off Stanceu 2, off Bonham 2, off Grove 2. Struck out—by Russo 8, by Stanceu 2, by Bonham 1, by Grove 1. Hits—off Russo 10 in 6 innings (none out in seventh), off Stanceu 1 in 1 inning. Losing pitcher—Russo. Umpires—Rommel, Hubbard, and Ormsby. Time of game—2:36. Attendance—36,461.

GAME 12: MAY 27

NEW YORK	ab	r	h	po	a	e	WASHINGTON	ab	r	h	po	a	e
Sturm, 1b	6	2	3	5	3	0	Case, lf	5	0	2	1	1	0
Rolfe, 3b	3	1	1	2	3	1	Lewis, rf	4	1	1	6	0	1
Henrich, rf	4	2	1	1	0	0	Cramer, cf	5	2	2	3	1	0
DiMaggio, cf	5	3	4	2	0	0	Travis, ss	4	2	1	0	2	0
Rosar, c	4	0	1	1	0	0	Vernon, 1b	5	1	2	4	1	0
Gordon, 2b	5	0	3	6	3	0	Bloodw'th, 3b	4	0	0	1	0	1
Keller, lf	5	0	0	5	0	0	Myer, 2b	3	2	2	6	1	1
Crosetti, ss	5	2	3	3	2	1	Early, c	4	0	1	4	1	0
Ruffing, p	3	0	2	0	0	0	Chase, p	0	0	0	1	1	0
Murphy, p	1	0	0	0	0	0	Anderson, p	1	0	1	0	0	0
Chandler, p	1	0	0	2	0	0	[a]Welaj	1	0	0	0	0	0
							Carrasquel, p	0	0	0	0	0	0
Total	42	10	18	27	11	2	[b]Archie	0	0	0	0	0	0
							Zuber, p	0	0	0	1	1	0
							[c]Kennedy	1	0	0	0	0	0
							Masterson, p	0	0	0	0	0	0
							Total	37	8	12	27	9	3

[a]Batted for Anderson in fifth.
[b]Batted for Carrasquel in sixth.
[c]Batted for Zuber in eighth.

New York	1	0	1	4	1	2	0	1	0	—	10
Washington	0	0	1	0	0	5	2	0	0	—	8

Runs batted in—Rosar, Gordon 4, Case, Sturm, DiMaggio 3, Ruffing, Vernon, Bloodworth 2, Myer 2, Early.

Two-base hits—Sturm, Gordon, Early, Myer, Henrich. Home run—DiMaggio. Stolen base—Gordon. Double plays—Chase and Vernon; Gordon and Sturm 2. Bases on balls—off Chase 1, off Anderson 2, off Ruffing 3, off Murphy 1. Struck out—by Anderson 1, by Chandler 1, by Zuber 1, by Masterson 1. Hits—off Ruffing 8 in 5⅓ innings, off Murphy 3 in ⅔ innings (none out in seventh), off Chase 6 in 1⅔ innings, off Anderson 6 in 3⅓ innings, off Carrasquel 3 in 1 inning, off Zuber 3 in 2 innings. Wild pitch—Chandler. Winning pitcher—Ruffing. Losing pitcher—Anderson. Umpires—Hubbard, Ormsby, and Rommel. Time of game—2:33. Attendance—6,000.

GAME 13: MAY 28

NEW YORK	ab	r	h	po	a	e
Sturm, 1b	5	0	2	7	0	0
Rolfe, 3b	4	0	0	1	4	0
Henrich, rf	5	1	1	2	0	0
DiMaggio, cf	4	1	1	3	0	0
Keller, lf	3	1	1	2	0	0
Gordon, 2b	4	1	0	4	2	0
Dickey, c	3	1	0	3	0	0
Crosetti, ss	3	0	1	5	2	0
[a]Selkirk	1	1	1	0	0	0
Rizzuto, ss	0	0	0	0	0	0
Peek, p	4	0	0	2	2	0
Breuer, p	0	0	0	0	0	0
Total	36	6	7	27	10	0

WASHINGTON	ab	r	h	po	a	e
Case, lf	4	2	1	2	0	0
Lewis, rf	5	1	2	1	0	0
Cramer, cf	4	1	1	2	0	0
Travis, ss	4	1	3	2	2	1
Vernon, 1b	4	0	1	7	0	0
Myer, 2b	4	0	1	2	2	0
Early, c	3	0	2	7	0	0
Bloodw'th, 3b	4	0	0	3	1	0
Hudson, p	3	0	0	1	1	1
Carrasquel, p	0	0	0	0	0	0
[b]Welaj	1	0	0	0	0	0
Total	36	5	11	27	6	2

[a]Batted for Crosetti in eighth.
[b]Batted for Carrasquel in ninth.

New York	0	0	0	0	1	0	5	0	0	— 6
Washington	2	0	1	0	0	0	0	1	1	— 5

Night game.

Runs batted in—Vernon, Myer, Travis, Henrich, Gordon, Selkirk 4, Early, Lewis.

Three-base hits—DiMaggio, Case, Early. Home runs—Henrich, Selkirk. Stolen base—Case. Double play—Crosetti unassisted. Bases on balls—off Hudson 4, off Peek 3. Struck out—by Peek 2, by Hudson 4, by Carrasquel 2, by Breuer 1. Hits—off Peek 10 in 8 innings, off Hudson 7 in 7⅓ innings. Winning pitcher—Peek. Losing pitcher—Hudson. Umpires—Ormsby, Rommel, Hubbard, and Pipgras. Time of game—2:30. Attendance—25,000.

GAME 14: MAY 29

NEW YORK	ab	r	h	po	a	e
Sturm, 1b	3	0	0	8	0	1
Rolfe, 3b	3	0	1	0	2	0
Henrich, rf	3	1	2	0	0	0
DiMaggio, cf	3	1	1	0	0	0
Keller, lf	2	0	0	0	0	0
Gordon, 2b	2	0	0	0	0	1
Dickey, c	2	0	2	5	0	0
Rosar, c	0	0	0	1	0	0
Crosetti, ss	2	0	1	1	3	0
Russo, p	2	0	0	0	4	0
Total	22	2	7	15	9	2

WASHINGTON	ab	r	h	po	a	e
Case, lf	3	0	0	3	0	0
Lewis, rf	3	1	1	5	0	0
Cramer, cf	3	0	2	1	0	0
Travis, ss	3	1	1	0	1	0
Archie, 1b	3	0	2	4	0	0
Myer, 2b	3	0	0	0	1	0
Evans, c	2	0	0	2	0	0
Bloodw'th, 3b	2	0	0	0	2	0
Sundra, p	1	0	0	0	0	0
Total	23	2	6	15	4	0

New York	0	0	0	1	1	— 2
Washington	0	0	1	0	1	— 2

Stopped by rain.

Runs batted in—Archie 2, Crosetti, Henrich.

Three-base hit—Archie. Home run—Henrich. Stolen base—Rolfe. Bases on balls—off Russo 1. Struck out—by Russo 6, by Sundra 2. Umpires—Rommel, Hubbard, Pipgras, and Ormsby. Time of game—1:26. Attendance—1,500.

APPENDIX

GAME 15: MAY 30 (first game)

NEW YORK	ab	r	h	po	a	e
Sturm, 1b	4	0	0	8	2	0
Rolfe, 3b	4	1	2	3	0	0
Henrich, rf	3	0	0	4	0	0
bRuffing	1	0	1	0	0	0
cRizzuto	0	1	0	0	0	0
Selkirk, rf	0	0	0	0	0	0
J. DiMaggio, cf	2	1	1	2	0	1
Rosar, c	4	0	0	3	2	0
Gordon, 2b	3	1	0	0	3	0
Keller, lf	3	0	0	2	0	1
Crosetti, ss	4	0	1	4	3	0
Donald, p	2	0	0	1	3	0
aBordagaray	1	0	0	0	0	0
Breuer, p	1	0	0	0	0	0
Total	32	4	5	27	13	2

BOSTON	ab	r	h	po	a	e
D. DiM'gio, cf	5	0	2	1	0	0
Finney, 1b	4	0	0	13	0	0
Williams, lf	2	2	1	3	0	0
Cronin, ss	4	0	2	1	1	0
Fox, rf	4	0	2	1	1	0
Tabor, 3b	4	0	1	0	5	1
L. Newsome, 2b	4	0	0	0	1	0
Peacock, c	4	0	0	8	0	0
Johnson, p	3	1	2	0	3	0
dSpence	1	0	0	0	0	0
Total	35	3	10	27	11	1

aBatted for Donald in eighth.
bBatted for Henrich in ninth.
cRan for Ruffing in ninth.
dBatted for Johnson in ninth.

New York .... 0 0 0   1 0 0   0 0 3 — 4
Boston .... 0 0 1   0 0 1   0 1 0 — 3

Runs batted in—Rolfe, Keller, Crosetti 2, Finney, Cronin, Tabor.
Two-base hits—D. DiMaggio, Williams. Home run—Rolfe. Double plays—Sturm, Crosetti, and Sturm; Rosar and Crosetti; Gordon, Crosetti, and Sturm. Bases on balls—off Donald 1, off Breuer 1, off Johnson 4. Struck out—by Donald 3, by Breuer 1, by Johnson 6. Hits—off Donald 9 in 7 innings. Winning pitcher—Breuer. Umpires—Summers, Rue, and Steward. Time of game—2:03. Attendance—34,500.

GAME 16: MAY 30 (second game)

NEW YORK	ab	r	h	po	a	e	BOSTON	ab	r	h	po	a	e
Sturm, 1b	4	0	0	9	0	1	D. DiM'gio, cf	4	0	1	5	0	1
Rolfe, 3b	2	0	0	0	4	0	Finney, 1b	6	1	2	5	0	0
Priddy, 3b	2	0	1	0	1	0	Williams, lf	3	2	2	1	0	0
Henrich, rf	4	0	0	0	0	1	Spence, lf	0	0	0	1	0	0
J. DiM'gio, cf	3	0	1	4	0	3	Cronin, ss	4	2	2	1	1	0
Rosar, c	3	0	0	6	1	0	Carey, ss	1	0	0	0	2	0
Gordon, 2b	3	0	0	1	3	1	Fox, rf	5	1	2	3	0	0
Keller, lf	2	0	0	1	0	0	Tabor, 3b	5	3	3	1	0	0
Bordagaray	1	0	0	1	0	0	L. Newsome, 2b	3	1	1	2	0	0
Crosetti, ss	3	0	0	2	1	0	Pytlak, c	5	1	2	8	0	0
Stanceu, p	1	0	0	0	0	0	Harris, p	3	2	1	0	0	0
Chandler, p	0	0	0	0	0	0							
Branch, p	1	0	0	0	0	0	Total	39	13	16	27	3	1
aRizzuto	1	0	0	0	0	0							
Total	30	0	2	24	10	6							

aBatted for Branch in ninth.

New York	0 0 0	0 0 0	0 0 0	—	0
Boston	3 0 2	5 2 0	1 0 X	—	13

Runs batted in—Williams, Fox 2, Pytlak 2, D. DiMaggio, Finney 2, Tabor 2.
Two-base hits—J. DiMaggio, Cronin, Harris, Tabor 2. Home run—Tabor. Stolen bases—L. Newsome 2, Pytlak, Harris. Bases on balls—off Stanceu 1, off Chandler 3, off Branch 5. Struck out—by Stanceu 2, by Branch 3, by Harris 6. Hits—off Stanceu 9 in 2⅔ innings, off Chandler 4 in 1 inning. Wild pitch—Chandler. Losing pitcher—Stanceu. Umpires—Summers, Rue, and Stewart. Time of game—2:30. Attendance—34,500.

GAME 17: JUNE 1 (first game)

NEW YORK	ab	r	h	po	a	e	CLEVELAND	ab	r	h	po	a	e
Sturm, 1b	4	0	2	9	2	0	Boudreau, ss	4	0	1	1	6	0
Rolfe, 3b	4	0	0	2	1	0	W'therley, cf	4	0	2	1	0	0
Henrich, rf	3	0	1	1	0	0	Walker, lf	4	0	2	2	1	0
DiMaggio, cf	4	1	1	3	0	0	Trosky, 1b	4	0	0	12	0	0
Rosar, c	3	0	1	1	1	0	Heath, rf	3	0	1	2	0	0
Gordon, 2b	3	0	0	2	4	0	Keltner, 3b	3	0	0	2	3	0
Keller, lf	3	1	1	1	0	0	Mack, 2b	3	0	1	3	5	0
Selkirk, lf	0	0	0	1	0	0	Hemsley, c	2	0	1	3	1	0
Crosetti, ss	3	0	1	7	2	0	aRosenthal	1	0	0	0	0	0
Ruffing, p	4	0	0	0	3	0	Susce, c	0	0	0	1	0	0
							Milnar, p	2	0	0	0	0	0
Total	31	2	7	27	13	0	bCampbell	1	0	0	0	0	0
							Heving, p	0	0	0	0	0	0
							Total	31	0	8	27	16	0

aBatted for Hemsley in eighth.
bBatted for Milnar in eighth.

New York	0 1 1	0 0 0	0 0 0	—	2
Cleveland	0 0 0	0 0 0	0 0 0	—	0

Runs batted in—Crosetti, Rosar.
Two-base hit—Rosar. Stolen base—Keller. Double plays—Boudreau, Mack, and Trosky; Gordon and Sturm; Ruffing, Crosetti, and Sturm; Crosetti, Gordon, and Sturm. Bases on balls—off Milnar 5. Struck out—by Ruffing 1, by Milnar 3, by Heving 1. Hits—off Milnar 7 in 8 innings. Wild pitch—Milnar. Umpires—Rummel, Hubbard, and Ormsby. Time of game—1 57. Attendance—52,081.

APPENDIX

GAME 18: JUNE 1 (second game)

NEW YORK	ab	r	h	po	a	e	CLEVELAND	ab	r	h	po	a	e
Sturm, 1b	4	1	1	2	2	0	Boudreau, ss	4	0	0	0	3	0
Rolfe, 3b	4	1	1	3	1	0	W'therley, cf	4	0	1	3	0	0
Selkirk, lf	4	1	1	2	0	0	Keltner, 3b	4	2	3	2	2	0
DiMaggio, cf	4	0	1	4	0	0	Heath, rf	4	1	1	2	0	0
Henrich, rf	3	1	0	2	0	0	Walker, lf	4	0	0	3	0	0
Rosar, c	4	0	0	7	0	0	Trosky, 1b	3	0	0	11	3	0
Gordon, 2b	4	0	2	3	1	1	Mack, 2b	4	0	0	2	0	0
Crosetti, ss	4	1	1	3	0	0	Hemsley, c	3	0	1	3	0	0
Gomez, p	2	0	0	1	1	0	Harder, p	2	0	0	3	2	0
Breuer, p	0	0	0	0	0	0	[a]Bell	1	0	0	0	0	0
							Brown, p	0	0	0	0	1	0
Total	33	5	7	27	5	1	Total	33	3	6	27	13	0

[a]Batted for Harder in eighth.

New York	0	0	0		0	1	0		0	4	0	— 5
Cleveland	1	0	0		0	0	0		0	0	2	— 3

Runs batted in—Keltner, Gordon, Sturm 2, Selkirk 2, Heath, Walker.

Two-base hits—Gordon 2, Keltner. Three-base hit—Heath. Home runs—Keltner, Sturm, Selkirk. Double play—Rolfe, Gordon, and Sturm. Bases on balls—off Harder 1, off Breuer 1. Struck out—by Gomez 5, by Harder 2. Hits—off Harder 7 in 8 innings, off Gomez 6 in 8 innings (none out in ninth). Wild pitch—Gomez. Winning pitcher—Gomez. Losing pitcher—Harder. Umpires—Rommel, Hubbard, and Ormsby. Time of game—1:53. Attendance—52,081.

GAME 19: JUNE 2

NEW YORK	ab	r	h	po	a	e	CLEVELAND	ab	r	h	po	a	e
Sturm, 1b	5	0	1	10	2	0	Boudreau, ss	3	0	1	3	1	0
Rolfe, 3b	4	0	1	0	1	0	W'therley, cf	5	1	1	3	0	0
Selkirk, lf	4	0	0	2	0	0	Keltner, 3b	4	2	1	1	2	0
DiMaggio, cf	4	2	2	3	0	0	Heath, rf	5	2	2	2	0	0
Henrich, rf	3	3	2	3	0	0	Walker, lf	4	0	2	5	0	0
Rosar, c	2	0	1	2	0	0	Trosky, 1b	4	0	0	4	1	0
Gordon, 2b	4	0	0	2	2	1	Mack, 2b	3	1	1	1	1	0
Crosetti, ss	4	0	0	1	3	0	Hemsley, c	3	1	1	7	0	0
Russo, p	2	0	0	0	2	0	Feller, p	3	0	1	1	1	0
Stanceu, p	0	0	0	0	0	0							
[a]Keller	1	0	0	0	0	0							
Chandler, p	0	0	0	1	0	0	Total	34	7	10	27	6	0
[b]Dickey	1	0	0	0	0	0							
Total	34	5	7	24	10	1							

[a]Batted for Stanceu in seventh.

[b]Batted for Chandler in ninth.

New York	0	2	0		1	0	0		0	2	0	— 5
Cleveland	2	1	0		0	2	2		0	0	X	— 7

Runs batted in—Rosar, Crosetti, Henrich 3, Walker 2, Boudreau 2, Heath 2, Feller.

Two-base hits—Boudreau, DiMaggio, Sturm. Three-base hits—Mack, Keltner. Home runs—Henrich 2, Heath. Double play—Sturm and Crosetti. Bases on balls—off Russo 6, off Feller 4. Struck out—by Chandler 2, by Feller 6. Hits—off Russo 10 in 5 innings (none out in sixth), off Stanceu 0 in 1 inning. Wild pitch—Feller. Losing pitcher—Russo. Umpires—Hubbard, Ormsby, and Rommel. Time of game—2:23. Attendance—6,000.

241

GAME 20: JUNE 3

NEW YORK	ab	r	h	po	a	e	DETROIT	ab	r	h	po	a	e
Sturm, 1b	4	1	0	6	0	0	Mullin, cf	4	0	1	5	0	0
Rolfe, 3b	4	0	3	2	1	0	Gehr'ger, 2b	3	0	0	3	5	0
Selkirk, lf	3	0	0	3	0	0	Radcliff, lf	4	1	0	2	0	0
DiMaggio, cf	4	1	1	4	0	0	York, 1b	3	1	2	7	0	0
Henrich, rf	3	0	1	3	0	0	Campbell, rf	4	1	1	1	0	0
Rosar, c	4	0	1	3	0	0	Higgins, 3b	4	1	2	0	1	0
Gordon, 2b	4	0	1	1	4	1	Tebbetts, c	4	0	1	3	1	0
Crosetti, ss	3	0	0	2	0	0	Croucher, ss	3	0	0	6	3	0
ªDickey	1	0	0	0	0	0	Trout, p	3	0	0	0	1	0
Peek, p	3	0	1	0	1	0							
ᵇKeller	1	0	0	0	0	0	Total	32	4	7	27	11	0
Total	34	2	8	24	6	1							

ªBatted for Crosetti in seventh.
ᵇBatted for Peek in ninth.

New York	0	0	0	1	0	0	1	0	0	—	2
Detroit	4	0	0	0	0	0	0	0	X	—	4

Runs batted in—Campbell, Higgins 2, Tebbetts, DiMaggio, Selkirk.
Two-base hits—Higgins, Tebbetts, Rolfe. Home run—DiMaggio. Double play—Gehringer, Croucher, and York. Bases on balls—off Peek 2, off Trout 3. Struck out—by Peek 2, by Trout 3. Umpires—Rue, Stewart, and Summers. Time of game—1:39. Attendance—3,523.

GAME 21: JUNE 5

NEW YORK	ab	r	h	po	a	e	DETROIT	ab	r	h	po	a	e
Bordagaray, 1f	4	0	0	0	0	0	Mullin, cf	4	1	3	3	0	0
Rolfe, 3b	4	1	1	0	3	0	Gehr'ger, 2b	4	1	1	2	2	0
Henrich, rf	4	2	1	1	1	0	Radcliff, 1f	4	1	1	1	0	0
DiMaggio, cf	5	1	1	5	0	0	York, 1b	3	2	1	8	1	0
Rosar, c	3	0	3	4	2	0	Campbell, rf	5	0	1	0	0	0
Gordon, 2b-1b	5	0	1	3	3	0	Higgins, 3b	3	0	1	2	1	0
Crosetti, ss	4	0	0	6	2	0	Tebbetts, c	4	0	1	10	0	1
Sturm, 1b	2	0	1	9	0	0	Croucher, ss	4	0	1	4	1	1
ªRuffing	1	0	0	0	0	0	Newhouser, p	3	0	0	0	2	0
Priddy, 2b	1	0	0	0	0	0	Newsom, p	1	0	0	0	1	0
Donald, p	3	0	0	0	1	1							
ᵇRizzuto	1	0	0	0	0	0	Total	35	5	10	30	8	2
Breuer, p	1	0	0	0	2	0							
Murphy, p	0	0	0	0	0	0							
Total	38	4	8	ᶜ28	14	1							

ªBatted for Sturm in eighth.
ᵇBatted for Donald in eighth.
ᶜOne out when winning run scored.

New York	0	0	0	0	0	2	0	0	2	0	—	4
Detroit	0	0	0	0	0	3	0	1	0	1	—	5

Runs batted in—DiMaggio, Rosar, Henrich 2, Higgins, Campbell.
Two-base hit—Mullin. Three-base hit—DiMaggio. Home run—Henrich. Stolen bases—Bordagaray, York. Double play—Gordon, Crosetti, and Sturm. Bases on balls—off Donald 3, off Breuer 1, off Murphy 2, off Newhouser 7. Struck out—by Donald 1, by Breuer 1, by Newhouser 8, by Newsom 1. Hits—off Donald 7 in 7 innings, off Breuer 2 in 2 innings (none out in tenth), off Newhouser 8 in 8⅔ innings. Wild pitches—Donald 2, Newhouser. Winning pitcher—Newsom. Losing pitcher—Breuer. Umpires—Stewart, Summers, and Rue. Time of game—2:43. Attendance—8,230.

GAME 22: JUNE 7

NEW YORK	ab	r	h	po	a	e
Sturm, 1b	6	1	2	6	0	0
Rolfe, 3b	5	2	2	3	1	0
Henrich, rf	3	2	1	1	0	0
DiMaggio, cf	5	2	3	6	1	0
Keller, lf	4	2	3	1	0	0
Dickey, c	5	0	1	7	0	0
Gordon, 2b	4	1	0	2	1	0
Crosetti, ss	4	1	2	1	2	1
Gomez, p	2	0	0	0	0	1
Chandler, p	2	0	1	0	0	0
Stanceu, p	1	0	0	0	0	0
Total	41	11	15	27	5	2

ST. LOUIS	ab	r	h	po	a	e
Lucadello, 2b	3	2	1	2	1	0
McQuinn, 1b	4	0	1	10	0	0
Laabs, rf	3	1	1	2	0	0
Allen, p	0	0	0	0	0	0
Trotter, p	0	0	0	0	1	0
Cullenbine, lf	4	0	0	3	0	0
Clift, 3b	3	2	0	4	3	0
Grace, rf	4	0	3	0	1	1
Berardino, ss	5	0	0	2	4	0
Ferrell, c	5	1	1	4	0	0
Muncrief, p	1	0	0	0	0	0
Kramer, p	1	0	0	0	0	0
ªEstalella	1	0	0	0	0	0
Caster, p	0	0	0	0	1	0
ᵇJudnich, cf	1	1	1	0	0	0
Total	35	7	8	27	11	1

ªBatted for Kramer in fifth.
ᵇBatted for Caster in eighth.

New York	0	1	5	0	0	0	0	0	5	—	11
St. Louis	1	0	2	0	1	0	0	3	0	—	7

Runs batted in—Crosetti, DiMaggio, Keller 4, Grace 2, Judnich 2, Cullenbine, Henrich, Dickey 2, Sturm 2.

Two-base hits—Rolfe, Laabs, Keller, Ferrell, Henrich. Home runs—Keller, Judnich. Double plays—Crosetti, Gordon, and Sturm; DiMaggio and Rolfe. Bases on balls—off Gomez 7, off Chandler 1, off Muncrief 2, off Kramer 2, off Allen 1. Struck out—by Gomez 1, by Chandler 3, by Stanceu 2, by Muncrief 1, by Caster 1. Hits—off Gomez 4 in 4⅓ innings, off Chandler 4 in 2⅔ innings (none out in eighth), off Muncrief 6 in 2 innings (none out in third), off Kramer 1 in 3 innings, off Caster 2 in 3 innings, off Allen 4 in 0 innings. Winning pitcher—Stanceu. Losing pitcher—Allen. Umpires—Grieve, McGowan, and Quinn. Time of game—2:41. Attendance—2,394.

STREAK

GAME 23: JUNE 8 (first game)

NEW YORK	ab	r	h	po	a	e
Sturm, 1b	5	0	0	3	0	0
Rolfe, 3b	4	2	2	4	1	0
Henrich, rf	4	2	2	4	0	0
DiMaggio, cf	4	3	2	2	0	0
Keller, lf	4	1	1	2	0	0
Dickey, c	4	0	1	9	0	0
Gordon, 2b	4	0	2	0	0	0
Crosetti, ss	4	0	0	3	1	0
Ruffing, p	4	1	1	0	0	0
Total	37	9	11	27	2	0

ST. LOUIS	ab	r	h	po	a	e
Lucadello, 2b	5	0	0	2	5	0
McQuinn, 1b	4	1	1	12	1	0
Judnich, cf	3	0	1	2	0	0
Cullenbine, lf	3	0	2	2	0	0
Clift, 3b	3	1	1	1	1	0
Grace, rf	4	0	0	0	0	0
Berardino, ss	3	0	1	2	2	0
Swift, c	3	0	0	5	0	0
[a]Ferrell	1	0	0	0	0	0
Auker, p	3	1	1	1	1	0
Osterm'ler, p	0	0	0	0	0	0
[b]Laabs	1	0	0	0	0	0
Total	33	3	7	27	10	0

[a]Batted for Swift in ninth.
[b]Batted for Ostermueller in ninth.

New York	0	0	3	0	0	1	0	3	2	— 9
St. Louis	1	0	0	1	1	0	0	0	0	— 3

Runs batted in—Cullenbine, DiMaggio 4, Clift, McQuinn, Henrich, Gordon 2, Rolfe 2.
Two-base hits—McQuinn, Cullenbine, Berardino, Judnich, Gordon. Three-base hit—Auker. Home runs—DiMaggio 2, Henrich, Rolfe, Clift. Double plays—Dickey unassisted; Lucadello, Berardino, and McQuinn. Struck out—by Ruffing 5, by Auker 4. Hits—off Auker 10 in 8⅓ innings. Losing pitcher—Auker. Umpires—Quinn, Grieve, and McGowan. Time of game—2:05. Attendance—10,546.

GAME 24: JUNE 8 (second game)

NEW YORK	ab	r	h	po	a	e	ST. LOUIS	ab	r	h	po	a	e
Sturm, 1b	3	2	2	9	1	0	Lucadello, 2b	4	0	0	2	1	1
Rolfe, 3b	4	1	1	0	2	0	McQuinn, 1b	4	1	2	7	0	0
Henrich, rf	3	1	0	1	0	0	Laabs, cf	4	2	2	4	0	0
DiMaggio, cf	4	1	2	0	0	0	Cullenbine, lf	2	0	0	0	0	0
Keller, lf	1	1	1	0	0	1	Clift, 3b	3	0	2	1	3	0
Rosar, c	4	1	2	6	0	0	Grace, rf	3	0	1	2	0	0
Gordon, 2b	4	1	1	2	2	1	Berardino, ss	2	0	0	1	1	0
Crosetti, ss	3	0	0	2	8	0	Ferrell, c	4	0	1	4	1	0
Russo, p	2	0	0	0	0	0	Harris, p	0	0	0	0	0	0
Breuer, p	1	0	0	1	0	0	Caster, p	0	0	0	0	0	0
							[a]Heffner	1	0	0	0	0	0
Total	29	8	9	21	13	2	Muncrief, p	1	0	0	0	0	0
							[b]Judnich	0	0	0	0	0	0
							Kramer, p	0	0	0	0	0	0
							Total	28	3	8	21	6	1

[a]Batted for Caster in second.
[b]Batted for Muncrief in sixth.

New York	5	2	0	0	0	0	1		—	8
St. Louis	2	0	1	0	0	0	0		—	3

Runs batted in—Henrich, Keller 2, Gordon 2, Clift 2, DiMaggio 3, Laabs.
Two-base hits—Rosar, Laabs, DiMaggio, McQuinn. Double plays—Gordon, Crosetti, and Sturm; Berardino, Lucadello, and McQuinn. Bases on balls—off Russo 2, off Breuer 4, off Caster 2, off Muncrief 2, off Kramer 1. Struck out—by Russo 2, by Breuer 3, by Muncrief 2, by Caster, by Kramer. Hits—off Russo 6 in 2⅔ innings, off Harris 5 in ⅔ innings, off Caster 2 in 1⅓ innings, off Muncrief 1 in 4 innings. Hit by pitcher—by Breuer 1. Winning pitcher—Breuer. Losing pitcher—Harris. Umpires—Quinn, Grieve, and McGowan. Time of game—2:01. Attendance—10,546.

GAME 25: JUNE 10

NEW YORK	ab	r	h	po	a	e	CHICAGO	ab	r	h	po	a	e
Sturm, 1b	4	0	2	10	0	0	Webb, 2b	4	0	1	3	2	0
Rolfe, 3b	5	0	3	0	1	0	Appling, ss	4	1	0	0	3	0
Henrich, rf	4	1	1	3	1	0	Kuhel, 1b	4	1	1	8	0	0
DiMaggio, cf	5	1	1	8	0	0	Chapman, rf	4	1	1	3	0	0
Keller, lf	4	2	2	1	0	0	Lodig'ni, 3b	4	0	1	3	5	0
W. Dickey, c	4	2	2	1	0	0	Kreevich, cf	4	0	1	2	0	0
Gordon, 2b	5	1	2	3	4	0	Hoag, lf	4	0	1	3	0	0
Crosetti, ss	4	1	1	1	3	1	Tresh, c	1	0	0	4	0	0
Peek, p	5	0	0	0	1	0	G. Dickey, c	1	0	0	1	0	0
							Rigney, p	2	0	0	0	1	0
Total	40	8	14	27	10	1	Haynes, p	1	0	0	0	0	0
							Total	33	3	6	27	11	0

New York	0	0	0	0	0	5	3	0	0	—	8
Chicago	0	0	0	0	0	0	0	0	3	—	3

Runs batted in—Gordon 2, Crosetti 4, Keller 2, Chapman, Lodigiani, Kreevich.
Two-base hit—W. Dickey. Home runs—Crosetti, Keller. Double play—Appling, Webb, and Kuhel. Bases on balls—off Peek 1, off Rigney 4, off Haynes 1. Struck out—by Peek 1, by Rigney 3, by Haynes 1. Hits—off Rigney 11 in 7 innings. Wild pitches—Rigney 2. Passed ball—Tresh. Losing pitcher—Rigney. Umpires—Passarella, Basil, Pipgras, and Geisel. Time of game—1:57. Attendance—2,832.

GAME 26: JUNE 12

NEW YORK	ab	r	h	po	a	e
Sturm, 1b	3	0	0	15	0	0
ᶜBordagaray..............	1	0	0	0	0	0
Murphy, p	0	0	0	0	0	0
Rolfe, 3b	5	0	0	1	6	0
Henrich, rf..............	5	0	1	0	0	0
DiMaggio, cf	4	1	2	2	1	0
Rosar, c	3	0	0	4	0	1
Gordon, 2b-1b	3	2	2	3	3	0
Keller, lf	4	0	0	1	0	0
Crosetti, ss	4	0	0	3	5	0
Chandler, p	3	0	2	0	3	0
ᵃRuffing.................	1	0	1	0	0	0
ᵇPriddy, 2b..............	0	0	0	1	0	0
Total	36	3	8	30	18	1

CHICAGO	ab	r	h	po	a	e
Chapman, rf	4	0	0	2	0	0
Kreevich, cf	5	1	2	3	1	0
Lodig'ni, 3b	5	0	2	1	3	0
Kuhel, 1b	3	0	1	10	0	0
Appling, ss	4	0	2	2	1	0
Hoag, lf	4	1	1	1	1	0
Tresh, c	3	0	0	8	0	0
Webb, 2b................	4	0	0	3	4	0
Lee, p	4	0	1	0	1	0
Total	36	2	9	30	11	0

ᵃBatted for Chandler in ninth.
ᵇRan for Ruffing in ninth.
ᶜBatted for Sturm in ninth.

New York...	0 0 0	0 0 1	0 0 1	1 — 3
Chicago	0 1 0	0 1 0	0 0 0	0 — 2

Night game.
Runs batted in—Gordon, Ruffing, DiMaggio, Lee, Lodigiani.
   Two-base hits—Lodigiani, Ruffing. Three-base hit—Kreevich. Home runs—Gordon, DiMaggio. Stolen base—Appling. Double play—Lodigiani, Webb, and Kuhel. Bases on balls—off Chandler 3, off Lee 4. Struck out—by Chandler 1, by Lee 7. Hits—off Chandler 8 in 8 innings. Winning pitcher—Murphy. Umpires—Basil, Geisel, Pipgras, and Passarella. Time of game—2:35. Attendance—27,102.

GAME 27: JUNE 14

CLEVELAND	ab	r	h	po	a	e
Boudreau, ss	2	0	0	5	3	0
Keltner, 3b..............	3	0	0	0	1	0
Walker, lf	4	0	1	2	0	0
Heath, rf................	4	0	1	1	0	0
Campbell, cf	4	0	0	2	0	0
Trosky, 1b	3	0	0	9	0	0
Mack, 2b	3	0	0	6	0	0
Hemsley, c	3	1	1	5	0	0
Feller, p.................	2	0	0	0	2	0
ᵃRosenthal	1	0	0	0	0	0
Eisenstat, p..............	0	0	0	0	0	0
Total	29	1	3	24	12	0

NEW YORK	ab	r	h	po	a	e
Sturm, 1b	4	0	0	8	3	0
Rolfe, 3b	4	2	2	1	2	0
Henrich, rf	3	2	2	2	0	0
DiMaggio, cf	2	0	1	1	0	0
Keller, lf	4	0	1	0	0	0
Dickey, c	4	0	0	6	0	0
Gordon, 2b..............	3	0	0	5	2	0
Crosetti, ss	2	0	0	2	5	0
Donald, p	3	0	0	2	1	0
Total	29	4	6	27	13	0

ᵃBatted for Feller in eighth.

Cleveland	0 0 0	0 1 0	0 0 0	— 1
New York...	1 0 1	0 2 0	0 0 0	— 4

   Runs batted in—Henrich, DiMaggio, Hemsley, Keller 2.
   Two-base hit—DiMaggio. Home runs—Henrich, Hemsley. Double plays—Gordon, Crosetti, and Sturm; Mack, Boudreau, and Trosky. Bases on balls—off Feller 3, off Donald 3, off Eisenstat 1. Struck out—by Feller 5, by Donald 4. Hits—off Feller 6 in 7 innings. Hit by pitcher—by Donald 1. Wild pitch—Feller. Losing pitcher—Feller. Umpires—Quinn, Grieve, and McGowan. Time of game—2:10. Attendance—44,161.

APPENDIX

GAME 28: JUNE 15

CLEVELAND	ab	r	h	po	a	e
Boudreau, ss	4	0	1	2	3	0
Keltner, 3b	4	0	0	0	1	0
Walker, lf	4	1	0	3	0	0
Heath, rf	4	1	1	1	0	0
Campbell, cf	3	0	2	3	0	0
Trosky, 1b	4	0	1	8	2	0
Mack, 2b	3	0	0	3	4	0
Hemsley, c	3	0	0	3	2	0
aRosenthal	1	0	0	0	0	0
Bagby, p	1	0	0	1	0	0
Smith, p	3	0	1	0	0	0
Total	**34**	**2**	**6**	**24**	**12**	**0**

NEW YORK	ab	r	h	po	a	e
Sturm, 1b	3	1	2	10	0	0
Rolfe, 3b	4	0	2	0	2	0
Henrich, rf	4	0	0	2	0	0
DiMaggio, cf	3	1	1	5	0	0
Keller, lf	4	0	0	2	0	0
Dickey, c	3	0	0	4	0	0
Gordon, 2b	3	0	0	3	7	1
Crosetti, ss	1	0	0	1	3	0
Ruffing, p	2	1	0	0	0	0
Total	**27**	**3**	**5**	**27**	**12**	**1**

aBatted for Hemsley in ninth.

Cleveland	0	0	0	0	0	0	0	2	0	—	2
New York	1	1	1	0	0	0	0	0	0	—	3

Runs batted in—Henrich, Rolfe, DiMaggio, Heath, Trosky.

Two-base hit—Rolfe. Home run—DiMaggio. Double play—Mack and Boudreau. Bases on balls—off Bagby 2, off Ruffing 3. Struck out—by Ruffing 3, by Smith 2, by Bagby 1. Hits—off Bagby 4 in 3⅓ innings. Hit by pitcher—by Bagby 2. Losing pitcher—Bagby. Umpires—Grieve, McGowan, and Quinn. Time of game—1:45. Attendance—43,962.

STREAK

GAME 29: JUNE 16

CLEVELAND	ab	r	h	po	a	e
Boudreau, ss	4	2	1	2	1	1
Keltner, 3b	5	0	1	2	0	0
Walker, lf	5	1	1	0	0	0
Heath, rf	3	0	1	2	0	0
Campbell, cf	4	0	3	4	0	0
Trosky, 1b	4	0	1	6	1	0
Mack, 2b	3	0	1	5	5	1
Hemsley, c	4	1	2	3	0	0
Milnar, p	4	0	1	0	1	0
Brown, p	0	0	0	0	0	0
Total	36	4	12	24	8	2

NEW YORK	ab	r	h	po	a	e
Sturm, 1b	4	0	1	8	1	0
dDickey, c	1	0	1	1	0	0
Rolfe, 3b	4	0	1	3	2	0
Henrich, rf	4	0	1	2	1	0
DiMaggio, cf	5	0	1	1	0	0
Rosar, c	3	1	0	3	0	0
Gordon, 2b-1b	3	1	2	6	6	0
Keller, lf	4	1	1	0	0	0
Crosetti, ss	0	0	0	2	0	1
Rizzuto, ss	3	2	2	0	4	0
Gomez, p	1	0	0	0	0	0
aBordagaray	1	0	0	0	0	0
Murphy, p	0	0	0	0	0	0
bRuffing	1	0	0	0	0	0
cPriddy	0	1	0	1	0	0
Total	34	6	10	27	14	1

aBatted for Gomez in seventh.
bBatted for Murphy in eighth.
cBatted for Sturm in eighth.
dRan for Ruffing in eighth.

Cleveland	1	0	0	2	0	0	1	0	0	—	4
New York	0	0	1	2	0	0	0	3	X	—	6

Runs batted in—Sturm, Boudreau 2, Gordon 2, Campbell, Dickey 2.
Two-base hits—Hemsley, DiMaggio. Home runs—Boudreau, Gordon. Stolen base—Heath. Double plays—Henrich and Rolfe; Rizzuto, Gordon, and Sturm 2; Mack, Boudreau, and Trosky. Bases on balls—off Gomez 4, off Milnar 5. Struck out—by Gomez 2, by Milnar 2, by Russo 1. Hits—off Gomez 10 in 7 innings, off Murphy 2 in 1 inning, off Milnar 10 in 7⅔ innings. Winning pitcher—Murphy. Losing pitcher—Milnar. Umpires—McGowan, Quinn, and Grieve. Time of game—2:10. Attendance—12,052.

GAME 30: JUNE 17

CHICAGO	ab	r	h	po	a	e		NEW YORK	ab	r	h	po	a	e
Knick'ker, 2b	5	1	2	1	2	0		Sturm, 1b	4	0	2	10	1	0
Kreevich, cf	2	0	0	5	0	0		Rolfe, 3b	5	0	0	2	1	0
Chapman, cf	1	1	0	2	0	0		Henrich, rf	4	1	1	2	0	0
Lodig'ni, 3b	2	0	1	1	1	0		dRuffing	1	0	0	0	0	0
Kuhel, 1b	5	2	1	7	1	0		DiMaggio, cf	4	1	1	3	0	0
Appling, ss	4	1	1	0	2	0		Keller, lf	4	2	2	2	0	0
Hoag, lf	5	0	2	1	0	0		Dickey, c	3	0	0	2	1	0
Wright, rf	5	1	1	3	1	0		Gordon, 2b	3	2	1	3	4	0
Tresh, c	4	0	0	7	0	0		Rizzuto, ss	4	1	2	2	4	1
Rigney, p	4	2	3	0	1	0		Peek, p	2	0	0	1	2	1
Hallett, p	0	0	0	0	1	0		Stanceu, p	0	0	0	0	1	0
Smith, p	0	0	0	0	0	0		aSelkirk	1	0	0	0	0	0
								Murphy, p	0	0	0	0	1	0
Total	37	8	11	27	9	0		bRosar	0	0	0	0	0	0
								cBordagaray	0	0	0	0	0	0
								Total	35	7	9	27	15	2

aBatted for Stanceu in seventh.
bBatted for Murphy in ninth.
cRan for Rosar in ninth.
dBatted for Henrich in ninth.

Chicago .... 0 2 0   0 1 0   4 0 1   — 8
New York .... 0 0 2   0 0 0   3 2 0   — 7

Runs batted in—Tresh, Rigney, Peek, Sturm 2, Lodigiani 2, Kuhel, Rizzuto 2, Keller 2, Hoag.
Home run—Keller. Stolen bases—Kuhel, Hoag. Double play—Gordon, Rizzuto, and Sturm. Bases on balls—off Rigney 2, off Hallett 2, off Peek 5. Struck out—by Rigney 5, by Hallett 1, by Peek 1, by Murphy 1. Hits—off Peek 8 in 6⅓ innings, off Stanceu 0 in ⅔ inning, off Rigney 9 in 7⅔ innings, off Hallett 0 in ⅔ inning. Wild pitch—Peek. Winning pitcher—Hallett. Losing pitcher—Murphy. Umpires—Quinn, Grieve, and McGowan. Time of game—2:03. Attendance—10,442.

GAME 31: JUNE 18

CHICAGO	ab	r	h	po	a	e
Knick'ker, 2b.............	4	0	0	5	3	1
Kreevich, cf	3	0	0	2	0	0
Lodig'ni, 3b	4	0	0	1	4	0
Kuhel, 1b	5	1	1	7	1	0
Appling, ss	4	1	1	1	3	0
Hoag, lf	3	1	0	2	0	0
Wright, rf	4	0	1	4	0	0
G. Dickey, c	3	0	1	5	1	0
Lee, p	4	0	1	0	0	0
Total	34	3	5	27	12	1

NEW YORK	ab	r	h	po	a	e
Sturm, 1b	3	0	1	10	0	1
Rolfe, 3b	4	0	1	3	4	0
Henrich, rf.............	4	0	1	2	0	0
DiMaggio, cf	3	0	1	1	0	0
Rosar, c	4	0	2	5	1	0
Gordon, 2b.............	3	1	0	4	3	1
Keller, lf	3	1	2	2	0	0
Rizzuto, ss	4	0	1	0	4	0
Chandler, p	2	0	0	0	0	0
aRuffing................	1	0	1	0	0	0
bSelkirk	0	0	0	0	0	0
Total	31	2	10	27	12	2

aBatted for Chandler in ninth.
bRan for Ruffing in ninth.

Chicago	0	1	0		0	0	0		0	2	0	— 3
New York...	0	2	0		0	0	0		0	0	0	— 2

Runs batted in—G. Dickey 2, Keller 2, Wright.
Two-base hit—Appling. Home run—Keller. Stolen base—Kuhel. Double plays—Lodigiani and Knickerbocker; Appling, Knickerbocker, and Kuhel. Bases on balls—off Chandler 7, off Lee 4. Struck out—by Chandler 4, by Lee 3. Hit by pitcher—by Lee 1. Umpires—Grieve, McGowan, and Quinn. Time of game—2:07. Attendance—11,918.

GAME 32: JUNE 19

CHICAGO	ab	r	h	po	a	e
Knick'ker, 2b.............	3	0	0	1	4	0
Kreevich, cf	4	0	0	1	0	0
Lodig'ni, 3b	3	1	0	0	1	1
Kuhel, 1b	3	0	2	12	0	0
Appling, ss	4	0	0	2	5	0
Hoag, lf	4	0	0	1	0	0
Wright, rf	4	0	1	2	0	0
G. Dickey, c	4	1	1	5	0	0
Smith, p..................	2	0	1	0	0	0
Ross, p	1	0	0	0	0	0
Total	32	2	5	24	10	1

NEW YORK	ab	r	h	po	a	e
Sturm, 1b	4	0	0	7	0	0
Rolfe, 3b	4	1	1	5	3	0
Henrich, rf.............	4	1	1	3	0	0
DiMaggio, cf	3	2	3	3	0	0
Rosar, c	4	1	1	5	0	0
Gordon, 2b.............	3	1	0	2	4	1
Keller, lf	3	1	1	1	0	0
Rizzuto, ss	4	0	2	1	1	0
Breuer, p	4	0	0	0	1	0
Total	33	7	9	27	9	1

Chicago	0	0	0		1	0	0		1	0	0	— 2
New York...	0	0	0		5	1	0		0	1	X	— 7

Runs batted in—Rosar, Keller 4, DiMaggio 2, G. Dickey.
Three-base hit—Henrich. Home runs—Keller, G. Dickey, DiMaggio. Double plays—Appling, Knickerbocker, and Kuhel; Rolfe, Gordon, and Sturm. Bases on balls—off Breuer 3, off Smith 2, off Ross 1. Struck out—by Breuer 4, by Smith 2, by Ross 3. Hits—off Smith 5 in 4 innings. Losing pitcher—Smith. Umpires—McGowan, Quinn, and Grieve. Time of game—1:45. Attendance—9,609.

GAME 33: JUNE 20

DETROIT	ab	r	h	po	a	e	NEW YORK	ab	r	h	po	a	e
Croucher, ss	4	1	1	2	3	1	Sturm, 1b	5	2	3	5	0	0
McCosky, lf	4	1	1	2	0	0	Rolfe, 3b	4	2	1	0	2	0
Mullin, cf	4	1	1	3	0	0	Henrich, rf	5	1	1	1	0	0
York, 1b	5	0	0	10	0	0	DiMaggio, cf	5	3	4	5	0	1
Campbell, rf	3	0	2	5	0	0	Keller, lf	5	2	2	2	0	0
Higgins, 3b	4	0	2	0	2	0	Dickey, c	5	1	2	8	1	0
Gehr'ger, 2b	0	0	0	0	2	0	Gordon, 2b	4	1	2	4	1	0
Perry, 2b	2	0	0	1	3	1	Rizzuto, ss	5	1	1	2	3	0
Tebbetts, c	4	0	0	1	0	0	Russo, p	4	1	1	0	1	0
Newsom, p	1	0	0	0	0	0							
McKain, p	2	0	0	0	2	0	Total	42	14	17	27	8	1
ªRadcliff	0	1	0	0	0	0							
Total	33	4	7	24	12	2							

ªBatted for McKain in ninth.

Detroit	1	0	0	0	0	0	0	1	2	—	4
New York	4	0	3	0	7	0	0	0	X	—	14

Runs batted in—York, Henrich 3, Keller 3, Dickey 2, Gordon, Rizzuto, Russo, Rolfe, DiMaggio, Higgins, Croucher, McCosky.

Two-base hits—Gordon, Keller, Rolfe, DiMaggio. Three-base hits—Rizzuto, Croucher. Home runs—Henrich, Keller. Double plays—Rizzuto, Gordon, and Sturm; Perry, Croucher, and York. Bases on balls—off Russo 7, off Newsom 1, off McKain 1. Struck out—by Russo 8, by Newsom 1. Hits—off Newsom 7 in 2⅔ innings. Wild pitch—McKain. Losing pitcher—Newsom. Umpires—Geisel, Passarella, Rommel, and Basil. Time of game—2:07. Attendance—10,129.

GAME 34: JUNE 21

DETROIT	ab	r	h	po	a	e
Croucher, ss..............	5	1	2	2	5	0
McCosky, lf	4	1	1	1	0	0
Mullin, cf	5	1	2	3	0	0
York, 1b..................	4	0	1	9	2	0
Campbell, rf	5	2	2	4	0	0
Higgins, 3b...............	4	1	1	0	1	0
Gehr'ger, 2b	4	0	0	3	3	0
Tebbetts, c	4	0	1	4	0	0
Trout, p.................	3	1	2	0	0	0
Benton, p	1	0	0	1	0	0
Total	39	7	12	27	11	0

NEW YORK	ab	r	h	po	a	e
Sturm, 1b	3	1	2	7	0	1
Rolfe, 3b	3	0	2	0	0	0
Henrich, rf.............	4	0	0	6	0	0
DiMaggio, cf	4	0	1	3	0	0
Keller, lf	3	0	0	0	0	0
Dickey, c	4	0	1	7	1	0
Gordon, 2b..............	4	0	0	3	1	0
Rizzuto, ss...............	4	1	2	1	3	0
Donald, p	2	0	0	0	1	0
Bonham, p...............	0	0	0	0	0	0
aBordagaray	1	0	0	0	0	0
Branch, p	0	0	0	0	0	0
bSelkirk	1	0	0	0	0	0
Total	33	2	8	27	6	1

aBatted for Bonham in seventh.
bBatted for Branch in ninth.

Detroit..	0	2	2	0	0	0	3	0	0	— 7
New York..	1	0	0	0	0	0	1	0	0	— 2

Runs batted in—DiMaggio, Trout 2, Campbell 2, York 2, Rizzuto.
Two-base hits—Dickey, York. Home runs—Campbell, Rizzuto. Stolen bases—Rizzuto, McCosky. Double plays—Gehringer, Croucher, and York; York, Croucher, and York. Bases on balls—off Trout 3, off Branch 2. Struck out—by Donald 2, by Trout 3, by Branch 1, by Benton 1. Hits—off Donald 10 in 6⅔ innings, off Bonham 0 in ⅓ inning, off Trout 8 in 6⅓ innings. Wild pitch—Donald. Winning pitcher—Trout. Losing pitcher—Donald. Umpires—Passarella, Rommel, Basil, and Geisel. Time of game—2:14. Attendance—20,067.

GAME 35: JUNE 22

DETROIT	ab	r	h	po	a	e
Croucher, ss............	5	0	1	3	2	0
McCosky, lf	5	0	0	3	0	0
Mullin, cf	3	1	1	2	0	0
York, 1b.................	3	1	0	5	0	0
Campbell, rf	3	1	1	1	0	0
Higgins, 3b.............	3	1	2	1	2	0
Gehr'ger, 2b	3	0	0	5	2	0
Sullivan, c..............	2	0	1	6	0	0
Newhouser, p..........	2	0	0	0	1	0
[a]McNair.................	1	0	0	0	0	0
Newsom, p.............	1	0	0	0	0	0
Total	**31**	**4**	**6**	**[c]26**	**7**	**0**

NEW YORK	ab	r	h	po	a	e
Sturm, 1b	5	1	1	9	1	0
Rolfe, 3b	4	2	2	2	3	0
Henrich, rf.............	3	1	1	2	0	0
DiMaggio, cf	5	1	2	5	0	0
Rosar, c	2	0	0	1	0	0
Dickey, c	0	0	0	1	0	0
Gordon, 2b.............	4	0	2	0	4	1
Keller, lf	2	0	0	2	0	0
Rizzuto, ss.............	4	0	0	4	2	0
Ruffing, p..............	3	0	0	1	1	0
Murphy, p	0	0	0	0	1	0
[b]Selkirk	1	0	0	0	0	0
Total	**33**	**5**	**8**	**27**	**12**	**1**

[a]Batted for Newhouser in seventh.
[b]Batted for Murphy in ninth.
[c]Two out when winning run scored.

Detroit...................................	0	1	0	1	0	0	0	2	0	—	4
New York................................	0	0	2	0	0	1	0	0	2	—	5

Runs batted in—Henrich, DiMaggio 2, Sullivan, Higgins 2, Rolfe, Gordon.
Two-base hit—DiMaggio. Home runs—DiMaggio, Higgins, Rolfe. Double plays—Gordon, Rizzuto, and Sturm; Higgins, Gehringer, and York. Bases on balls—off Ruffing 5, off Newhouser 4, off Newsom 4, off Murphy 1. Struck out—by Ruffing 1, by Newhouser 1, by Newsom 2, by Murphy 1. Hits—off Newhouser 5 in 6 innings, off Ruffing 6 in 8 innings. Hit by pitcher—by Newsom 1. Winning pitcher—Murphy. Losing pitcher—Newsom. Umpires—Rommel, Basil, Geisel, and Passarella. Time of game—2:32. Attendance—27,072.

GAME 36: JUNE 24

ST. LOUIS	ab	r	h	po	a	e
Lucadello, 2b	5	0	0	1	3	0
McQuinn, 1b...........	4	0	0	12	1	0
Judnich, cf.............	4	0	0	1	0	0
Cullenbine, 1f..........	3	0	2	4	1	0
Clift, 3b	3	1	0	1	2	0
Laabs, rf	2	0	1	0	1	0
Berardino, ss...........	4	0	1	1	4	0
Ferrell, c	4	0	1	4	0	0
Muncrief, p	2	0	0	0	0	0
Kramer, p..............	0	0	0	0	0	0
[a]Estalella	0	0	0	0	0	0
Total	**31**	**1**	**5**	**24**	**12**	**0**

NEW YORK	ab	r	h	po	a	e
Sturm, 1b	3	2	1	5	1	0
Rolfe, 3b	3	2	1	0	4	0
Henrich, rf.............	3	1	2	2	0	0
DiMaggio, cf	4	1	1	1	0	0
Keller, lf	3	1	1	5	0	0
Dickey, c	4	1	1	4	0	0
Gordon, 2b.............	4	1	2	5	2	0
Rizzuto, ss.............	4	0	0	4	3	1
Gomez, p................	4	0	1	1	0	0
Total	**32**	**9**	**10**	**27**	**10**	**1**

[a]Batted for Kramer in ninth.

St. Louis...................................	0	0	0	0	0	0	0	0	1	—	1
New York................................	2	0	1	1	0	0	0	5	X	—	9

Runs batted in—Rolfe 2, Henrich 3, Gomez, Dickey, Gordon 2, Berardino.
Home runs—Rolfe, Henrich, Gordon. Double plays—Cullenbine, Berardino, and McQuinn; Rolfe, Gordon, and Sturm. Bases on balls—off Gomez 6, off Muncrief 4. Struck out—by Muncrief 3, by Gomez 4. Hits—off Muncrief 10 in 7⅓ innings. Losing pitcher—Muncrief. Umpires—Basil, Geisel, Passarella, and Rommel. Time of game—2:05. Attendance—9,081.

GAME 37: JUNE 25

ST. LOUIS	ab	r	h	po	a	e	NEW YORK	ab	r	h	po	a	e
Heffner, 2b	4	0	0	3	5	1	Sturm, 1b	4	1	1	12	0	0
ªLucadello	1	0	0	0	0	0	Rolfe, 3b	4	0	0	3	0	0
McQuinn, 1b	4	1	2	7	3	0	Henrich, rf	3	1	1	0	0	0
Judnich, cf	5	0	0	3	0	0	DiMaggio, cf	4	1	1	3	0	0
Cullenbine, lf	5	2	4	3	1	0	Keller, lf	3	1	1	3	0	0
Clift, 3b	2	2	1	0	0	0	Dickey, c	4	0	1	4	2	0
Laabs, rf	4	0	0	0	0	0	Gordon, 2b	2	1	1	1	5	0
Berardino, ss	4	0	3	5	1	0	Rizzuto, ss	4	1	1	1	3	1
Ferrell, c	4	0	1	1	1	0	Chandler, p	1	1	0	0	2	0
Galehouse, p	1	0	0	2	1	0	Murphy, p	1	0	1	0	1	0
Allen, p	2	0	0	0	0	0							
Total	36	5	11	24	12	1	Total	30	7	8	27	13	1

ªBatted for Heffner in ninth.

St. Louis	0	1	0	0	0	2	0	2	0	—	5
New York	0	0	0	2	2	0	0	3	X	—	7

Runs batted in—Berardino 2, DiMaggio 3, Cullenbine, Clift 2, Gordon, Rizzuto, Sturm.
Two-base hits—McQuinn, Keller. Home runs—DiMaggio, Clift. Stolen bases—Berardino, Gordon. Double play—Dickey and Rolfe. Bases on balls—off Chandler 3, off Galehouse 6, off Murphy 1, off Allen 1. Struck out—by Chandler 2, by Galehouse 1, by Murphy 2. Hits—off Galehouse 3 in 4⅓ innings, off Chandler 7 in 5⅔ innings. Wild pitches—Galehouse, Allen. Winning pitcher—Murphy. Losing pitcher—Allen. Umpires—Geisel, Passarella, Rommel, and Basil. Time of game—2:25. Attendance—9,249.

GAME 38: JUNE 26

ST. LOUIS	ab	r	h	po	a	e	NEW YORK	ab	r	h	po	a	e
Heffner, 2b	4	0	0	5	2	0	Sturm, 1b	4	0	0	13	0	0
McQuinn, 1b	3	1	1	6	1	0	Rolfe, 3b	3	1	0	1	2	0
Judnich, cf	3	0	0	6	0	0	Henrich, rf	3	1	1	2	0	0
Cullenbine, lf	3	0	0	1	0	0	DiMaggio, cf	4	0	1	4	0	0
Clift, 3b	2	0	0	2	1	0	Keller, lf	3	1	0	1	0	0
Laabs, rf	3	0	0	2	0	0	Dickey, c	3	0	1	3	2	0
Berardino, ss	3	0	0	0	2	1	Gordon, 2b	2	1	2	2	6	0
Ferrell, c	2	0	0	2	1	0	Rizzuto, ss	3	0	1	0	2	0
Auker, p	2	0	0	0	0	0	Russo, p	2	0	0	1	1	0
ªLucadello	1	0	0	0	0	0							
Total	26	1	1	24	7	1	Total	27	4	6	27	13	0

ªBatted for Auker in ninth.

St. Louis	0	0	0	0	0	0	1	0	3	—	1
New York	0	1	0	0	1	1	0	1	X	—	4

Runs batted in—Gordon, Rizzuto, Henrich, McQuinn, DiMaggio.
Two-base hit—DiMaggio. Three-base hit—Gordon. Home runs—Henrich, McQuinn. Double plays—Rizzuto, Gordon, and Sturm; Berardino, Heffner, and McQuinn 2; Dickey and Gordon. Bases on balls—off Russo 2, off Auker 3. Struck out—by Russo 3, by Auker 1. Umpires—Passarella, Rommel, Basil, and Geisel. Time of game—1:35. Attendance—8,692.

GAME 39: JUNE 27

NEW YORK	ab	r	h	po	a	e
Sturm, 1b	3	1	1	6	0	0
Priddy, 2b	0	0	0	0	0	0
Rolfe, 3b	4	0	0	2	2	0
Crosetti, 3b	1	0	1	0	0	0
Henrich, rf	4	0	0	0	0	0
DiMaggio, cf	3	1	2	4	1	0
Rosar, c	4	0	0	3	1	0
Dickey, c	1	0	0	1	0	0
Gordon, 2b-1b	3	1	1	1	5	0
Keller, lf	4	1	2	5	0	0
Rizzuto, ss	4	0	1	3	2	1
Breuer, p	3	0	0	0	0	0
Stanceu, p	0	0	0	0	0	0
Branch, p	0	0	0	0	0	0
[a]Bordagaray	1	1	1	0	0	0
[b]Ruffing	1	0	1	0	0	0
[c]Silvestri	0	1	0	0	0	0
Total	36	6	10	[d]25	11	1

PHILADELPHIA	ab	r	h	po	a	e
Brancato, ss	5	0	0	4	3	0
Collins, rf	4	1	1	2	0	0
McCoy, 2b	5	0	1	3	5	1
Johnson, cf	4	1	1	0	0	0
Siebert, 1b	5	2	3	11	2	0
Simmons, lf	4	1	1	2	0	0
Hayes, c	3	2	2	2	2	0
Suder, 3b	4	0	3	2	4	1
Dean, p	3	0	1	1	1	0
Ferrick, p	0	0	0	0	0	0
Total	37	7	13	27	17	2

[a]Batted for Stanceu in ninth.
[b]Batted for Sturm in ninth.
[c]Ran for Ruffing in ninth.
[d]One out when the winning run scored.

New York	1	1	0	0	0	1	1	0	2	—	6
Philadelphia	1	1	0	1	0	2	0	1	1	—	7

Runs batted in—DiMaggio 2, McCoy, Keller, Suder, Dean 2, Rizzuto, Hayes, Ruffing, Siebert.
Two-base hits—Collins, Gordon, Suder 2, Siebert 2, Sturm, Rizzuto, Ruffing. Home runs—DiMaggio, Hayes. Double plays—Brancato, McCoy, and Siebert; Suder and Siebert; Rizzuto, Gordon, and Sturm. Bases on balls—off Dean 5, off Breuer 3, off Stanceu 1, off Ferrick 1. Struck out—by Dean 2, by Stanceu 1, by Branch 1. Hits—off Breuer 9 in 6 innings, off Stanceu 2 in 2 innings, off Dean 9 in 8 innings (none out in ninth). Winning pitcher—Ferrick. Losing pitcher—Branch. Umpires—Stewart, Summers, and Rue. Time of game—2:14. Attendance—8,107.

GAME 40: JUNE 28

NEW YORK	ab	r	h	po	a	e
Sturm, 1b	5	0	1	8	1	0
Rolfe, 3b	5	1	2	0	1	0
Henrich, rf	5	1	2	3	0	1
DiMaggio, cf	5	1	2	1	0	0
Keller, lf	5	1	2	3	0	0
Dickey, c	5	1	1	4	1	0
Gordon, 2b	4	0	2	5	2	0
Rizzuto, ss	3	1	2	2	4	0
Donald, p	3	1	0	1	3	0
Murphy, p	0	0	0	0	0	0
Total	40	7	14	27	12	1

PHILADELPHIA	ab	r	h	po	a	e
Brancato, ss	5	1	1	5	0	0
Collins, rf	3	1	0	2	0	0
McCoy, 2b	4	1	1	1	4	0
Johnson, cf	4	0	1	1	0	0
Siebert, 1b	4	1	1	6	3	0
Simmons, lf	3	0	1	2	0	0
Hayes, c	4	0	1	3	1	0
Suder, 3b	4	0	1	5	0	0
Babich, p	2	0	1	2	0	0
^aMiles	1	0	0	0	0	0
Harris, p	0	0	0	0	0	0
^bDean	0	0	0	0	0	0
^cF. Chapman	0	0	0	0	0	0
Total	34	4	8	27	8	0

[a]Batted for Babich in sixth.
[b]Batted for Harris in ninth.
[c]Ran for Dean in ninth.

New York	1	2	1	0	0	1	2	0	0	—	7
Philadelphia	0	0	0	1	3	0	0	0	0	—	4

Runs batted in—Keller 4, Rolfe 2, Hayes, McCoy 3, Rizzuto.
Two-base hits—Rizzuto, DiMaggio, Babich, Sturm. Three-base hits—Rolfe, Dickey. Home runs—McCoy, Keller. Stolen base—Gordon. Double plays—Donald, Rizzuto, and Sturm; Gordon, Rizzuto, and Sturm. Bases on balls—off Babich 1, off Harris 1, off Donald 4. Struck out—by Babich 1, by Harris 1, by Donald 3. Hits—off Babich 10 in 6 innings, off Donald 8 in 8⅓ innings. Passed ball—Hayes. Winning pitcher—Donald. Losing pitcher—Babich. Umpires—Summers, Rue, and Stewart. Time of game—2:30. Attendance—13,604.

APPENDIX

GAME 41: JUNE 29 (first game)

NEW YORK	ab	r	h	po	a	e	WASHINGTON	ab	r	h	po	a	e
Sturm, 1b	5	1	1	9	1	0	Archie, 1b	4	1	1	2	1	0
Rolfe, 3b	5	0	0	1	4	0	Cramer, cf	3	0	0	4	0	0
Henrich, rf	5	1	2	1	0	0	Lewis, rf	4	1	1	0	0	0
DiMaggio, cf	4	1	1	1	0	0	Travis, ss	4	1	2	1	2	0
Keller, lf	3	2	2	6	0	0	Vernon, 1b	4	1	1	12	1	0
Dickey, c	2	0	1	4	0	0	Early, c	4	0	1	3	1	1
Gordon, 2b	4	2	1	1	3	0	Case, lf	3	0	0	1	1	0
Rizzuto, ss	4	1	3	3	1	0	Bloodw'th, 2b	3	0	0	3	6	0
Ruffing, p	3	1	1	0	1	0	Leonard, p	1	0	0	1	2	0
Murphy, p	1	0	0	1	0	0	ªBolton	1	0	0	0	0	0
							Carrasquel, p	1	0	0	0	1	0
Total	36	9	12	27	10	0	Total	32	4	6	27	15	1

ªBatted for Leonard in sixth.

New York	0	0	0	0	3	3	0	1	2	—	9
Washington	0	0	0	0	0	4	0	0	0	—	4

Runs batted in—Ruffing 2, Rolfe, Travis, Vernon, Early 2, Rizzuto, Henrich 2. Two-base hits—Rizzuto, Ruffing, DiMaggio, Vernon. Three-base hit—Early. Home run—Henrich. Double plays—Leonard, Bloodworth, and Vernon; Rolfe, Gordon, and Sturm; Early and Travis. Bases on balls—off Leonard 2, off Ruffing 2, off Carrasquel 1. Struck out—by Leonard 2, by Ruffing 1, by Carrasquel 2, by Murphy 2. Hits—off Ruffing 6 in 5⅔ innings, off Leonard 8 in 6 innings. Hit by pitcher—by Carrasquel 1. Passed ball—Early. Winning pitcher—Ruffing. Losing pitcher—Leonard. Umpires—Grieve, McGowan, and Quinn. Time of game—2:08. Attendance—31,000.

GAME 42: JUNE 29 (second game)

NEW YORK	ab	r	h	po	a	e	WASHINGTON	ab	r	h	po	a	e
Sturm, 1b	5	1	3	11	1	0	Archie, 1b	5	1	2	1	2	0
Rolfe, 3b	4	1	1	0	2	0	Cramer, cf	4	2	2	3	0	0
Henrich, rf	4	0	0	1	0	0	Lewis, rf	5	1	3	3	1	0
DiMaggio, cf	5	1	1	2	0	0	Travis, ss	5	0	2	3	2	1
Keller, lf	5	1	2	1	0	0	Vernon, 1b	5	0	1	9	2	0
Gordon, 2b	3	2	2	5	5	3	Early, c	3	0	0	3	0	0
Rizzuto, ss	3	1	1	3	4	1	Case, lf	4	0	1	2	0	0
Silvestri, c	3	0	0	3	1	0	Bloodw'th, 2b	3	0	0	1	4	0
Stanceu, p	2	0	0	0	1	0	Hudson, p	1	0	0	0	0	0
bSelkirk	1	0	1	0	0	0	aMyer	1	1	1	0	0	0
Peek, p	1	0	0	1	0	0	Anderson, p	1	0	0	0	0	0
Bonham, p	0	0	0	0	0	0	Masterson, p	0	0	0	2	0	0
							cWelaj	1	0	0	0	0	0
Total	36	7	11	27	14	4	Kennedy, p	0	0	0	0	0	0
							Total	38	5	12	27	11	1

aBatted for Hudson in fourth.
bBatted for Stanceu in sixth.
cBatted for Masterson in eighth.

New York	2	1	0	1	0	2	1	0	0	—	7
Washington	1	0	2	1	0	0	0	0	1	—	5

Runs batted in—DiMaggio, Lewis 2, Gordon, Travis 2, Keller 2, Selkirk 2.

Two-base hits—Sturm, Lewis. Three-base hits—Sturm, Keller. Home runs—Gordon, Keller. Double plays—Bloodworth, Travis, and Vernon; Gordon, Rizzuto, and Sturm 3. Bases on balls—off Stanceu 1, off Anderson 3, off Peek 1, off Kennedy 3. Struck out—by Stanceu 3, by Hudson 2, by Kennedy 1, by Peek 1. Hits—off Stanceu 7 in 5 innings, off Peek 5 in 3⅔ innings, off Hudson 6 in 4 innings, off Anderson 5 in 2⅔ innings, off Masterson 0 in 1⅓ inning. Passed ball—Early. Winning pitcher—Stanceu. Losing pitcher—Anderson. Umpires—Grieve, McGowan, and Quinn. Time of game—2:15. Attendance—31,000.

APPENDIX

GAME 43: JULY 1 (first game)

BOSTON	ab	r	h	po	a	e
D. DiM'gio, cf	4	1	1	3	0	0
Finney, 1b	3	1	0	5	2	0
Williams, lf	4	0	1	1	0	0
Cronin, ss	4	0	1	1	1	0
Spence, rf	4	0	1	4	1	0
Tabor, 3b	4	0	1	2	2	1
Doerr, 2b	4	0	1	0	0	0
Pytlak, c	3	0	1	7	1	0
Harris, p	1	0	0	0	0	0
Ryba, p	1	0	0	0	1	0
bPeacock	1	0	0	0	0	0
Potter, p	0	0	0	1	0	0
Total	33	2	7	24	8	1

NEW YORK	ab	r	h	po	a	e
Sturm, 1b	4	0	2	12	0	0
Rolfe, 3b	5	2	2	2	2	0
Henrich, rf	5	0	2	3	1	0
J. DiM'gio, cf	4	0	2	2	0	0
Gordon, 2b	4	0	0	1	3	1
Keller, lf	5	1	1	0	0	0
Rizzuto, ss	4	1	3	2	7	0
Silvestri,c	2	2	2	5	1	0
Russo, p	2	1	1	0	1	0
aSelkirk	1	0	0	0	0	0
Chandler, p	1	0	0	0	0	0
Total	37	7	15	27	15	1

aBatted for Russo in sixth.
bBatted for Ryba in eighth.

Boston .... 0 0 0   0 0 2   0 0 0   — 2
New York.. 0 0 0   4 0 2   0 1 X   — 7

Runs batted in—Silvestri 2, Russo, Sturm, D. DiMaggio, Spence, Rolfe, J. DiMaggio, Gordon.
Two-base hits—Silvestri 2, Russo. Three-base hit—Rizzuto. Home run—D. DiMaggio. Double play—Spence and Pytlak. Bases on balls—off Harris 1, off Russo 1, off Ryba 1, off Potter 2. Struck out—by Russo 4, by Ryba 5, by Chandler 1. Hits—off Harris 8 in 3⅓ innings, off Ryba 6 in 3⅔ innings, off Russo 6 in 6 innings. Wild pitch—Potter. Winning pitcher—Russo. Losing pitcher—Harris. Umpires—Rue, Rommel, Stewart, and Summers. Time of game—2:32. Attendance—52,832.

GAME 44: JULY 1 (second game)

BOSTON	ab	r	h	po	a	e
D. DiM'gio, cf	2	0	0	1	0	0
Finney, 1b	2	0	1	7	1	1
Williams, lf	2	1	1	1	0	2
Cronin, ss	2	1	2	0	4	0
Spence, rf	2	0	0	0	0	0
Tabor, 3b	2	0	0	0	1	0
Doerr, 2b	2	0	0	1	0	0
Peacock, c	2	0	0	4	0	0
J. Wilson, p	1	0	0	1	1	0
Dobson, p	1	0	0	0	0	0
Total	18	2	4	15	7	3

NEW YORK	ab	r	h	po	a	e
Sturm, 1b	3	1	0	5	1	0
Rolfe, 3b	3	3	2	0	2	0
Henrich, rf	3	0	0	0	0	0
J. DiM'gio, cf	3	1	1	2	0	0
Keller, lf	3	2	3	1	0	0
Dickey, c	2	1	2	4	0	0
Gordon, 2b	3	1	1	2	1	0
Rizzuto, ss	3	0	1	1	1	0
Bonham, p	3	0	0	0	1	0
Total	26	9	10	15	6	0

Boston .... 0 0 0   2 0   — 2
New York.. 3 0 4   2 0   — 9

Stopped by darkness.
Runs batted in—Keller 2, Dickey 3, Rizzuto, Cronin 2, Henrich, J. DiMaggio.
Two-base hits—Keller, Dickey, Rolfe. Home runs—Dickey, Cronin. Double play—Sturm and Rizzuto. Bases on balls—off Dobson 2. Struck out—by Bonham 2, by Wilson 2, by Dobson 1. Hits—off Wilson 7 in 2⅔ innings. Wild pitch—Dobson. Losing pitcher—Wilson. Umpires—Rue, Rommel, Stewart, and Summers. Time of game—1:05. Attendance—52,832.

STREAK

GAME 45: JULY 2

BOSTON	ab	r	h	po	a	e
D. DiM'gio, cf	5	1	0	1	0	0
Finney, 1b	5	1	2	10	1	0
Williams, lf	3	1	1	1	0	0
Cronin, ss	2	1	1	0	1	1
L. Newsome, ss	0	0	0	1	1	0
Spence, rf	4	0	1	4	0	0
Tabor, 3b	4	0	2	1	2	0
Doerr, 2b	4	0	0	1	4	0
Pytlak, c	4	0	0	5	1	0
H. Newsome, p	2	0	1	0	0	0
Wilson, p	0	0	0	0	0	0
Potter, p	1	0	0	0	0	0
[a]Foxx	1	0	1	0	0	0
Total	35	4	9	24	10	1

[a]Batted for Potter in ninth.

NEW YORK	ab	r	h	po	a	e
Sturm, 1b	4	1	0	9	0	0
Rolfe, 3b	3	2	2	0	4	0
Henrich, rf	5	0	3	3	0	0
J. DiM'gio, cf	5	1	1	3	0	0
Keller, lf	4	2	2	4	0	0
Dickey, c	3	1	0	3	0	0
Gordon, 2b	5	1	0	2	3	0
Rizzuto, ss	4	0	2	3	4	1
Gomez, p	3	0	1	0	1	0
Murphy, p	1	0	0	0	0	0
Total	37	8	11	27	12	1

Boston	0	0	0	0	0	3	1	0	0	—	4
New York	0	1	1	0	6	0	0	0	X	—	8

Runs batted in—Keller, J. DiMaggio 3, Rolfe, Gomez 2, Spence 2, Tabor, Cronin. Two-base hits—Rizzuto, Rolfe. Home runs—Keller, J. DiMaggio. Stolen base—Sturm. Double plays—Gomez, Rizzuto, and Sturm; Rolfe, Gordon, and Sturm. Bases on balls—off Gomez 2, off H. Newsome 3, off Wilson 1, off Murphy 1, off Potter 2. Struck out—by Gomez 2, by H. Newsome 2, by Wilson 1, by Murphy 1, by Potter 1. Hits—off H. Newsome 6 in 4⅓ innings, off Wilson 1 in ⅔ innings, off Gomez 5 in 5⅓ innings. Wild pitch—Gomez. Passed balls—Pytlak 2. Winning pitcher—Gomez. Losing pitcher—H. Newsome. Umpires—Rommel, Stewart, Summers, and Rue. Time of game—2:23. Attendance—8,682.

GAME 46: JULY 5

PHILADELPHIA	ab	r	h	po	a	e
Brancato, ss	4	0	1	1	2	1
Collins, rf	4	0	0	3	1	0
McCoy, 2b	4	0	0	1	3	0
Johnson, lf	4	0	0	0	0	0
Siebert, 1b	4	2	3	6	0	0
S. Chapman, cf	4	1	1	5	0	0
Hayes, c	4	1	3	4	0	0
Suder, 3b	4	1	1	4	0	0
Marchildon, p	2	0	0	0	0	0
[a]Moses	1	0	0	0	0	0
Total	35	5	9	24	6	1

[a]Batted for Marchildon in ninth.

NEW YORK	ab	r	h	po	a	e
Sturm, 1b	4	1	1	5	0	0
Rolfe, 3b	5	2	2	1	1	0
Henrich, rf	3	0	0	2	0	0
DiMaggio, cf	4	2	1	5	0	0
Keller, lf	4	2	2	3	0	0
Dickey, c	4	0	0	3	0	0
Gordon, 2b	4	2	0	6	0	0
Rizzuto, ss	3	1	2	2	2	0
Ruffing, p	4	0	3	0	2	0
Total	35	10	11	27	5	0

Philadelphia	0	0	2	2	0	1	0	0	0	—	5
New York	2	1	0	0	2	2	1	2	X	—	10

Runs batted in—DiMaggio 2, Ruffing 2, Brancato 2, Siebert 2, Suder, Keller 3, Henrich, Sturm, Rolfe. Two-base hit—Ruffing. Home runs—DiMaggio, Siebert 2, Keller 2, Sturm, Rolfe. Stolen base—Henrich. Bases on balls—off Marchildon 7. Struck out—by Ruffing 2, by Marchildon 1. Hit by pitcher—by Marchildon 1. Wild pitch—Marchildon. Umpires—Rommel, McGowan, Quinn, and Grieve. Time of game—2:10. Attendance—19,977.

GAME 47: JULY 6 (first game)

PHILADELPHIA	ab	r	h	po	a	e	NEW YORK	ab	r	h	po	a	e
Brancato, ss	5	1	3	2	1	0	Sturm, 1b	5	0	0	6	3	0
Collins, rf	5	0	0	1	0	0	Rolfe, 3b	5	2	4	1	1	0
McCoy, 2b	3	0	1	0	4	0	Henrich, rf	4	1	2	3	0	0
Johnson, lf	4	0	0	1	0	0	DiMaggio, cf	5	2	4	6	0	0
Siebert, 1b	2	0	1	1	0	0	Keller, lf	5	0	0	3	0	0
Davis, 1b	2	0	1	7	0	0	Dickey, c	4	1	2	3	1	0
S. Chapman, cf	4	1	1	3	0	0	Gordon, 2b	4	0	1	2	2	0
Wagner, c	3	1	0	8	0	0	Rizzuto, ss	4	1	2	1	1	1
Suder, 3b	3	1	0	1	2	0	Donald, p	1	1	1	1	2	0
Babich, p	0	0	0	0	0	0	Bonham, p	3	0	1	1	1	0
Hadley, p	1	0	0	0	1	0							
aMoses	1	0	0	0	0	0	Total	40	8	17	27	11	1
Total	33	4	7	24	8	0							

aBatted for Hadley in ninth.

Philadelphia...... 0 1 0   3 0 0   0 0 0   — 4
New York...... 4 2 0   0 1 0   0 1 X   — 8

Runs batted in—DiMaggio 2, Dickey 4, S. Chapman, Rolfe 2, Brancato 2, Collins.
Two-base hits—Brancato, DiMaggio. Three-base hit—Brancato. Home runs—S. Chapman, Dickey, Rolfe. Double plays—Dickey and Rolfe; McCoy, Brancato, and Davis. Bases on balls—off Donald 4, off Hadley 1. Struck out—by Hadley 6, by Donald 2, by Bonham 1. Hits—off Babich 6 in 1 inning (none out in second), off Donald 6 in 3⅓ innings. Winning pitcher—Bonham. Losing pitcher—Babich. Umpires—Quinn, Grieve, Rommel, and McGowan. Time of game—2:15. Attendance—60,948.

GAME 48: JULY 6 (second game)

PHILADELPHIA	ab	r	h	po	a	e	NEW YORK	ab	r	h	po	a	e
Brancato, ss	4	0	0	0	2	0	Sturm, 1b	4	0	1	7	0	0
Collins, rf	4	1	2	2	0	0	Rolfe, 3b	3	1	0	1	1	0
McCoy, 2b	3	0	0	2	7	1	Henrich, rf	3	1	1	4	0	0
Johnson, lf	4	0	1	2	0	0	DiMaggio, cf	4	0	2	4	0	0
Siebert, 1b	4	0	1	9	0	0	Keller, lf	4	0	1	2	0	0
S. Chapman, cf	3	0	0	2	0	0	Gordon, 2b	4	0	0	1	5	0
Hayes, c	3	0	0	7	1	0	Rosar, c	4	0	1	7	0	0
Suder, 3b	3	0	1	0	1	0	Rizzuto, ss	3	1	3	1	1	0
Knott, p	1	0	0	0	0	0	Breuer, p	2	0	0	0	0	0
aMoses	1	0	0	0	0	0							
Ferrick, p	1	0	0	0	1	0	Total	31	3	9	27	7	0
Total	31	1	5	24	12	1							

aBatted for Knott in seventh.

Philadelphia...... 0 0 0   0 0 0   0 0 1   — 1
New York...... 1 0 1   0 0 0   1 0 X   — 3

Runs batted in—DiMaggio 2, Sturm, McCoy.
Two-base hits—Brancato, DiMaggio. Three-base hits—DiMaggio, Rizzuto, Collins. Double plays—Gordon, Rizzuto, and Sturm; McCoy and Siebert; Ferrick, McCoy, and Siebert. Bases on balls—off Knott 2, off Breuer 1, off Ferrick 1. Struck out—by Breuer 7, by Knott 4, by Ferrick 2. Hits—off Knott 6 in 4 innings. Losing pitcher—Knott. Umpires—Quinn, Grieve, Rommel, and McGowan. Time of game—1:53. Attendance—60,948.

GAME 49: JULY 10

NEW YORK	ab	r	h	po	a	e
Sturm, 1b	2	0	0	3	1	0
Rolfe, 3b	1	0	0	1	1	0
Henrich, rf	2	0	0	2	0	0
DiMaggio, cf	2	0	1	2	0	0
Keller, lf	2	0	0	0	0	1
Dickey, c	2	0	0	1	0	0
Gordon, 2b	2	1	1	3	0	0
Rizzuto, ss	2	0	1	3	2	0
Gomez, p	2	0	0	0	2	0
Total	17	1	3	15	6	1

ST. LOUIS	ab	r	h	po	a	e
Heffner, 2b	3	0	2	1	1	0
Laabs, rf	3	0	0	1	0	0
Judnich, cf	2	0	1	1	0	0
Cull'bine, 1b	2	0	1	8	0	1
Clift, 3b	2	0	0	0	0	0
Estalella, lf	1	0	1	1	0	0
Ferrell, c	2	0	0	2	1	0
Strange, ss	1	0	0	1	0	0
Niggeling, p	2	0	0	0	1	0
Total	18	0	5	15	3	1

New York	0 1 0	0 0	—	1
St. Louis	0 0 0	0 0	—	0

Night game. Stopped by rain.

Run batted in—Gordon. Home run—Gordon. Double play—Sturm, Rizzuto, and Sturm. Bases on balls—off Gomez 2, off Niggeling 1. Struck out—by Gomez 1, by Niggeling 1. Umpires—Grieve, McGowan, and Quinn. Time of game—1:07. Attendance—12,682.

GAME 50: JULY 11

NEW YORK	ab	r	h	po	a	e
Sturm, 1b	5	0	0	10	0	0
Rolfe, 3b	3	2	3	1	2	1
Henrich, rf	5	1	2	4	0	0
DiMaggio, cf	5	1	4	2	0	0
Keller, lf	4	1	2	3	0	0
Dickey, c	5	0	1	1	0	0
Gordon, 2b	4	1	1	4	1	0
Rizzuto, ss	4	0	1	2	5	0
Russo, p	4	0	0	0	3	0
Total	39	6	14	27	11	1

ST. LOUIS	ab	r	h	po	a	e
Heffner, 2b	5	0	0	1	2	0
McQuinn, 1b	5	0	1	10	1	0
Judnich, cf	3	1	1	5	0	0
Cull'bine, lf	4	1	2	1	1	0
Clift, 3b	3	0	0	2	3	0
Laabs, rf	3	0	0	5	0	0
Ferrell, c	4	0	1	1	0	0
Strange, ss	4	0	1	1	4	0
Harris, p	2	0	0	1	2	0
ªEstalella	1	0	1	0	0	0
Kramer, p	0	0	0	0	0	0
Total	34	2	7	27	13	0

ªBatted for Harris in eighth.

New York	2 0 0	0 0 1	0 1 2	—	6
St. Louis	2 0 0	0 0 0	0 0 0	—	2

Runs batted in—Henrich 2, Cullenbine 2, Gordon, Dickey, DiMaggio 2. Two-base hits—Keller 2, Dickey. Home runs—Henrich, Cullenbine, Gordon, DiMaggio. Double plays—Rolfe, Gordon, and Sturm; Cullenbine, Clift, and McQuinn. Bases on balls—off Russo 7, off Harris 3. Struck out—by Harris 1. Hits—off Harris 11 in 8 innings. Losing pitcher—Harris. Umpires—McGowan, Quinn, and Grieve. Time of game—2:10. Attendance—1,625.

GAME 51: JULY 12

NEW YORK	ab	r	h	po	a	e
Sturm, 1b	5	0	1	6	0	0
Rolfe, 3b	5	0	0	1	1	0
Henrich, rf	3	1	1	1	0	0
DiMaggio, cf	5	1	2	2	0	0
Keller, lf	4	1	1	7	0	0
Dickey, c	4	1	1	5	0	0
Gordon, 2b	3	2	0	2	1	0
Rizzuto, ss	4	1	2	3	2	1
Bonham, p	4	0	0	0	0	0
Murphy, p	0	0	0	0	0	0
Total	37	7	8	27	4	1

ST. LOUIS	ab	r	h	po	a	e
Heffner, 2b	5	0	2	2	5	0
Clift, 3b	4	0	0	2	2	1
McQuinn, 1b	5	1	2	11	2	0
Judnich, cf	4	0	1	3	0	0
Cull'bine, lf	4	0	1	1	0	1
Grace, rf	4	1	1	3	0	0
Ferrell, c	4	0	0	4	1	0
Strange, ss	2	0	0	1	2	0
Lucadello, ss	2	2	2	0	0	0
Auker, p	1	0	0	0	0	0
Muncrief, p	1	0	0	0	0	0
Ost'mueller, p	0	0	0	0	0	0
aLaabs	1	1	1	0	0	0
bEstalella	1	0	0	0	0	0
Total	38	5	10	27	12	2

aBatted for Muncrief in seventh.
bBatted for Ostermueller in ninth.

New York	0	0	0	5	0	2	0	0	0	—	7
St. Louis	0	0	0	1	0	0	3	0	1	—	5

Runs batted in—DiMaggio, Keller, Dickey 2, Cullenbine, Rizzuto, Sturm, Laabs 3, McQuinn. Two-base hits—DiMaggio, Rizzuto, Henrich, Cullenbine. Home runs—Dickey, Laabs. Stolen base—Rizzuto. Bases on balls—off Auker 2, off Muncrief 1, off Bonham 2. Struck out—by Auker 1, by Murphy 2, by Muncrief 1, by Ostermueller 1, by Bonham 3. Hits—off Auker 5 in 3 innings (none out in the fourth), off Muncrief 3 in 4 innings, off Bonham 7 in 7⅓ innings. Winning pitcher—Bonham. Losing pitcher—Auker. Umpires—Quinn, Grieve, and McGowan. Time of game—2:11. Attendance—2,841.

GAME 52: JULY 13 (first game)

NEW YORK	ab	r	h	po	a	e
Sturm, 1b	5	0	1	9	0	0
Rolfe, 3b	4	1	1	1	2	1
Henrich, rf	5	1	1	3	1	0
DiMaggio, cf	4	2	3	4	1	0
Keller, lf	4	1	1	1	0	0
Dickey, c	3	1	0	2	0	0
Rosar, c	1	0	1	0	0	0
Gordon, 2b	5	1	1	5	4	0
Rizzuto, ss	5	1	2	2	3	1
Chandler, p	4	0	2	0	1	0
Total	40	8	13	27	12	2

CHICAGO	ab	r	h	po	a	e
Knick'ker, 2b	4	0	1	3	3	1
Kuhel, 1b	4	0	0	11	2	1
Kreevich, cf	4	0	0	0	0	0
Appling, ss	3	0	1	2	5	0
Wright, rf	3	0	0	2	0	0
Solters, lf	3	0	1	3	0	0
Kennedy, 3b	3	0	1	0	1	0
Tresh, c	3	0	1	4	0	1
Lyons, p	1	1	1	1	1	0
Hallett, p	2	0	0	0	2	0
Total	30	1	5	27	13	4

New York	0	0	0	6	0	0	0	0	2	—	8
Chicago	0	0	1	0	0	0	0	0	0	—	1

Runs batted in—Sturm, Henrich 2, Rosar 2, Gordon, Chandler 2, Knickerbocker. Two-base hit—Knickerbocker. Home run—Henrich. Double plays—Rizzuto, Gordon, and Sturm; Hallet, Appling, and Kuhel; Hallet, Knickerbocker, and Kuhel; Gordon and Sturm. Bases on balls—off Lyons 1, off Hallet 2. Struck out—by Chandler 1, by Lyons 1, by Hallet 2. Hits—off Lyons 8 in 3⅓ innings, off Hallet 5 in 5⅔ innings. Hit by pitcher—by Hallet. Losing pitcher—Lyons. Umpires—Ormsby, Pipgras, Passarella, and Hubbard. Time of game—1:54. Attendance—50,387.

STREAK

GAME 53: JULY 13 (second game)

NEW YORK	ab	r	h	po	a	e
Sturm, 1b	5	1	1	15	1	0
Rolfe, 3b	5	0	3	2	3	0
Henrich, rf	5	0	0	5	0	0
DiMaggio, cf	4	0	1	3	0	0
Gordon, 2b	4	0	1	2	5	0
Rosar, c	3	0	0	1	0	0
Keller, lf	4	0	0	3	0	0
Rizzuto, ss	4	0	0	1	5	0
Ruffing, p	4	0	0	1	2	0
Total	38	1	6	33	16	0

CHICAGO	ab	r	h	o	a	e
Knick'ker, 2b	5	0	0	2	4	0
Kuhel, 1b	4	0	0	16	0	0
Kreevich, cf	4	0	1	3	0	0
Appling, ss	3	0	1	0	6	0
Wright, rf	2	0	0	2	0	0
Solters, lf	4	0	0	4	1	0
Kennedy, 3b	2	0	0	1	3	0
aHoag	1	0	0	0	0	0
G. Dickey, c	4	0	1	4	1	0
bKolloway	0	0	0	0	0	0
Lee, p	2	0	0	1	3	0
cChapman	1	0	0	0	0	0
Total	32	0	3	33	18	0

aBatted for Kennedy in eleventh.
bBatted for Lee in eleventh.
cRan for G. Dickey in eleventh.

New York.. 0 0 0 0 0 0 0 0 0 0 1 — 1
Chicago .... 0 0 0 0 0 0 0 0 0 0 0 — 0

Run batted in—Henrich.
Two-base hits—Rolfe, Sturm. Double plays—Ruffing, Rizzuto, and Sturm; Rolfe, Gordon, and Sturm. Bases on balls—off Ruffing 3, off Lee 3. Struck out—by Lee 2, by Ruffing 1. Umpires—Ormsby, Pipgras, Passarella, and Hubbard. Time of game—1:59. Attendance—50,387.

GAME 54: JULY 14

NEW YORK	ab	r	h	po	a	e
Sturm, 1b	4	0	1	9	1	1
Rolfe, 3b	4	0	0	0	2	0
Henrich, rf	4	0	2	2	0	0
DiMaggio, cf	3	0	1	2	0	0
Keller, lf	4	0	1	2	0	0
Gordon, 2b	4	0	1	2	4	0
Rosar, c	3	1	1	5	1	0
Rizzuto, ss	3	0	1	2	2	0
Breuer, p	1	0	0	0	3	0
aSelkirk	1	0	0	0	0	0
Stanceu, p	0	0	0	0	0	0
Branch, p	0	0	0	0	0	0
Total	31	1	8	24	13	1

CHICAGO	ab	r	h	po	a	e
Knick'ker, 2b	3	1	0	3	5	1
Kuhel, 1b	4	1	2	13	0	0
Kreevich, cf	4	1	1	2	0	0
Appling, ss	3	2	1	1	2	0
Wright, rf	4	2	2	0	0	0
Solters, lf	4	0	1	2	1	0
Kennedy, 3b	4	0	2	1	2	0
Tresh, c	4	0	0	5	3	0
Rigney, p	2	0	0	0	1	0
Total	32	7	9	27	14	1

aBatted for Breuer in eighth.

New York.. 0 0 1 0 0 0 0 0 0 — 1
Chicago .... 0 2 0 1 0 0 0 4 X — 7

Runs batted in—Sturm, Kreevich 2, Appling, Wright, Solters, Kennedy 2.
Two-base hits—Kuhel, Appling, Wright. Three-base hit—Kennedy. Stolen base—Appling. Double plays—Rizzuto, Gordon, Sturm; Knickerbocker, Appling, and Kuhel; Tresh and Knickerbocker; Solters and Knickerbocker. Bases on balls—off Breuer 2, off Stanceu 1, off Rigney 2. Struck out—by Breuer 3, by Branch 2, by Rigney 5. Hits—off Breuer 5 in 7 innings, off Stanceu 3 in 0 inning. Passed ball—Tresh. Losing pitcher—Breuer. Umpires—Passarella, Hubbard, Ormsby, and Pipgras. Time of game—1:52. Attendance—8,025.

APPENDIX

GAME 55: JULY 15

NEW YORK	ab	r	h	po	a	e	CHICAGO	ab	r	h	po	a	e
Sturm, 1b	5	0	1	7	2	0	Knick'ker, 2b	4	0	0	1	3	0
Rolfe, 3b	3	2	1	0	2	0	Kuhel, 1b	5	1	1	9	0	0
Henrich, rf	3	1	2	1	0	0	Kreevich, cf	5	0	2	5	0	0
DiMaggio, cf	4	1	2	3	0	0	Appling, ss	4	1	3	2	3	1
Gordon, 2b	3	1	1	4	1	0	Wright, rf	3	1	1	1	0	0
Rosar, c	5	0	1	4	2	0	Solters, lf	4	1	3	0	0	0
Keller, lf	4	0	0	1	0	0	Kennedy, 3b	2	0	1	2	3	0
Rizzuto, ss	4	0	2	7	4	0	Tresh, c	3	0	0	7	0	0
Peek, p	2	0	0	0	1	0	Smith, p	4	0	1	0	0	0
Branch, p	2	0	0	0	2	0							
Total	35	5	10	27	14	0	Total	34	4	12	27	9	1

New York .... 1 0 4   0 0 0   0 0 0   — 5
Chicago .... 0 2 0   1 1 0   0 0 0   — 4

Runs batted in—DiMaggio 2, Rosar 3, Kuhel, Solters 2, Tresh.
Two-base hits—DiMaggio, Solters. Three-base hit—Rosar. Home runs—Solters, Kuhel. Stolen bases—Rizzuto, Kreevich, Appling. Double plays—Appling and Kennedy; Kennedy, Knickerbocker, and Kuhel; Sturm, Rizzuto, and Sturm. Bases on balls—off Peek 4, off Smith 6. Struck out—by Peek 1, by Branch 2, by Smith 6. Hits—off Peek 7 in 4⅔ innings. Passed ball—Tresh. Winning pitcher—Branch. Umpires—Ormsby, Hubbard, Pipgras, and Passarella. Time of game—1:57. Attendance—8,680.

GAME 56: JULY 16

NEW YORK	ab	r	h	po	a	e	CLEVELAND	ab	r	h	po	a	e
Sturm, 1b	5	0	0	8	1	0	Boudreau, ss	4	1	1	2	1	0
Rolfe, 3b	4	0	0	2	2	0	Keltner, 3b	4	0	1	0	3	0
Henrich, rf	4	1	0	2	1	0	Weatherly, cf	3	0	0	2	0	0
DiMaggio, cf	4	3	3	3	0	0	Heath, rf	4	1	2	5	0	0
Gordon, 2b	4	2	2	2	3	0	Trosky, 1b	3	0	1	7	1	1
Rosar, c	5	1	3	5	1	0	Campbell, lf	4	0	0	2	0	0
Keller, lf	3	3	2	4	0	0	Mack, 2b	3	1	1	3	3	0
Rizzuto, ss	5	0	1	0	2	0	[a]Bell	1	0	0	0	0	0
Donald, p	4	0	1	1	0	0	Desautels, c	3	0	0	6	0	0
							[b]Walker	1	0	1	0	0	0
Total	38	10	11	27	10	0	Milnar, p	2	0	1	0	1	0
							Krakauskas, p	1	0	0	0	0	0
							[c]Rosenthal	0	0	0	0	0	0
							Total	33	3	8	27	9	1

[a]Batted for Mack in ninth.
[b]Batted for Desautels in ninth.
[c]Batted for Krakauskas in ninth.

New York .... 2 0 0   1 4 0   0 1 2   — 10
Cleveland .... 1 1 0   0 0 1   0 0 0   — 3

Runs batted in—Gordon, Rosar 5, Rizzuto 2, Keller, Trosky, Milnar, Heath.
Two-base hits—Mack, Rosar 2, Rizzuto, DiMaggio, Walker. Three-base hit—Keller. Home runs—Keller, Heath. Double play—Rosar and Rolfe. Bases on balls—off Donald 4, off Milnar 4, off Krakauskas 3. Struck out—by Donald 5, by Milnar 3, by Krakauskas 3. Hits—off Milnar 8 in 5 innings. Losing pitcher—Milnar. Umpires—Stewart, Summers, and Rue. Time of game—2:17. Attendance—15,000.

STREAK

STREAK ENDS: JULY 17

NEW YORK	ab	r	h	po	a	e
Sturm, 1b	4	0	1	10	2	0
Rolfe, 3b	4	1	2	2	3	0
Henrich, rf	3	0	1	4	0	0
DiMaggio, cf	3	0	0	2	0	0
Gordon, 2b	4	1	2	0	1	0
Rosar, c	4	0	0	5	1	0
Keller, lf	3	1	1	0	0	0
Rizzuto, ss	4	0	0	2	1	0
Gomez, p	4	1	1	2	1	0
Murphy, p	0	0	0	0	1	0
Total	33	4	8	27	10	0

CLEVELAND	ab	r	h	po	a	e
Weatherly, cf	5	0	1	4	0	0
Keltner, 3b	3	0	1	1	4	0
Boudreau, ss	3	0	0	0	2	0
Heath, rf	4	0	0	0	0	0
Walker, lf	3	2	2	1	0	0
Grimes, 1b	3	1	1	12	0	0
Mack, 2b	3	0	0	4	7	0
[a]Rosenthal	1	0	1	0	0	0
Hemsley, c	3	0	1	5	1	0
[b]Trosky,	1	0	0	0	0	0
Smith, p	3	0	0	0	0	0
Bagby, p	0	0	0	0	0	0
[c]Campbell	1	0	0	0	0	0
Total	33	3	7	27	14	0

[a]Batted for Mack in ninth.
[b]Batted for Hemsley in ninth.
[c]Batted for Bagby in ninth.

New York	1	0	0	0	0	0	1	2	0	— 4
Cleveland	0	0	0	1	0	0	0	0	2	— 3

Night game.
Runs batted in—Henrich, Gomez, Walker, Gordon, Rolfe, Rosenthal 2.
Two-base hits—Henrich, Rolfe. Three-base hits—Keller, Rosenthal. Home runs—Walker, Gordon. Double play—Boudreau, Mack, and Grimes. Bases on balls—off Smith 2, off Bagby 1, off Gomez 3. Struck out—by Gomez 5, by Smith 4, by Bagby 1. Hits—off Smith 7 in 7⅓ innings, off Gomez 6 in 8 innings (none out in ninth). Passed ball—Hemsley. Winning pitcher—Gomez. Losing pitcher—Smith. Umpires—Summers, Rue, and Stewart. Time of game—2:03. Attendance—67,468.

NAME INDEX

SUBJECT INDEX